Mutual Funds in India

Mutual Funds in India

Structure, Performance and Undercurrents

Rakesh Kumar

PARTRIDGE

To order additional copies of this book, contact
Partridge India
000 800 10062 62
orders.india@partridgepublishing.com

www.partridgepublishing.com/india

Dedication

The Loving Memory of my Parents

Contents

Preface

The mutual fund industry has recorded a remarkable growth in India in recent two decades. Its size, in terms of assets under management, has increased to the level of 13 billion rupees in 2015. This growth appeared in response to the liberal policy towards mutual fund industry. Private and foreign sector are given enough space to try their fortunes in this asset management business. Almost every industrial conglomerate in India has entered in this business. However, they did not have much experience in the asset management; hence, started joint ventures with the established foreign firms. Besides, the SEBI has been provided additional teeth to act as regulator of mutual fund industry.

The investments in these instruments are dominated by better aware people concentrated in metropolitan cities; for, the levels of financial education standards are not up to the mark in India. Therefore, there is lot of scope for penetration of these instruments in smaller cities. Though, mutual fund industry provides service to its customers, even then it can be organised in the form of market structure similar to goods producing industries. There is, now, about 45 asset management companies operating in this industry. Besides, this industry has experienced entry and exit of firms' overtime along with mergers and takeovers. Thus, the levels of concentration and competition have experienced changes overtime.

The principal job of asset management companies is to perform in terms of generating returns for investors. Fund managers should have adequate prowess to beat the returns of benchmarks. They are expected to time the market, that is, when to enter, hold and quit the market. Besides, they should have stock picking capacity by identifying the undervalued and overvalued stocks to take positions and formulate the diversified portfolios. Economic environment or macroeconomic performance of the economy can also be factored in while estimating the performance of the mutual fund schemes.

Every investor is not capable enough to enter the stock market directly and generate adequate returns. They have, therefore, to depend on the services of the professionals that mutual fund companies can provide. Unlike the traditional investment areas, mutual funds' units are more liquid, provide adequate diversification and risks are hedged. So, the investors can invest according to their objectives and risk aptitude.

This book is organsied in seven chapters. Chapter one is devoted to the introductory knowledge about the mutual funds for the ease of reader to study the subsequent chapters. There are many undercurrents in the industry of mutual funds which may not be visible from the surface; hence, an attempt has been made in chapter two to figure out such intricacies. Organisation structure of the industry and regulations are discussed in detail in chapter three. India is a growing economy and its mutual fund industry is at initial stage of development. The potential of industry and its penetration in the un-served areas has been explored in chapter four. The structure of the industry determines its conduct and performance of firms present in the industry. Concentration and competition have their bearing on the monopoly power and strategies; hence, calculated in chapter five. The investor is very much concerned about the returns of his investments. The returns, in turn, depend on the performance of the mutual fund schemes. Performance of Indian mutual fund industry through standard statistical and econometric techniques has been estimated in chapter six. Since the risks involved in the mutual funds are not only unique to the firms concerned, but they emerge from the economic environment of the economy. Thus, performance conditioned with such factors has been analyzed in chapter seven.

This book is a combination of basic and advanced set up regarding mutual funds. Therefore, it may prove to be useful to the teachers and students involved in financial economics and financial management both at undergraduate and post graduate levels. Moreover, this book may be valuable for the researchers pursuing research in finance and investments. Investors may feel better informed after going through this book. People involved in the mutual fund industry can be benefited from this book in terms of distributing schemes of mutual funds. Policy makers and regulators may improve their maneuvering after getting insights provided in this book.

Rakesh Kumar

Abbreviations

ABS Asset Backed Securities
ADRS American Depository Receipts
AGNI AMFI Guidelines and Norms for Intermediaries
AMC Asset Management Company
AMFI Association of Mutual Funds of India
AUM Assets under Management
BGs Business Groups
BPs Basis Points
CBDT Central Board of Direct Taxes
CDs Certificate of Deposits
CPs Commercial Papers
CR Concentration Ratio
DTAA Double Taxation Avoidance Agreement
ELSS Equity Linked Saving Schemes
EMT Efficient Market Theory
EPF Employees' Provident Funds
ETFs Exchange Traded Funds
FIIs Foreign Institutional Investors
FIPB Foreign Investment Promotion Board
FIs Financial Institutions
FOF Fund of Funds
FPO Follow on Public Offer
GAAR General Anti-Avoidance Rule
GDRs Global Depository Receipts
HHI Harishman Herfindhal Index

HNIs High Net-Worth Individuals
IFAs Independent Financial Advisors
IMFI Indian Mutual Fund Industry
IPO Initial Public Offer
IRDA Insurance Regulatory Development Authority
ITA Income Tax Act
MBSs Mortgaged Backed Securities
MFs Mutual Funds
NAHS National Automated Clearing House System
NAV Net Asset Value
NBFCs Non-Banking Financial Companies
NFO New Fund Offer
NPAs Non-Performing Assets
PIN Personal Identification Number
PPF Public Provident Fund
PWCs Price Waterhouse Coopers
QFI Qualified Foreign Investor
RBI Reserve Bank of India
SAI Statement of Additional Information
SBI State Bank of India
SCP Structure-Conduct-Performance
SEBI Securities and Exchange Board of India
SEC Securities and Exchange Commission
SID Scheme Information Document
SIP Systematic Investment Plan
SROs Self Regulatory Organizations
STP Systematic Transfer Plan
SWP Systematic Withdrawal Plan
TER Total Expense Ratio
UTI Unit Trust of India

List of Tables

Chapter-1
Mutual Funds: An Introduction

1.1   Introduction

With the progress of financial markets, varieties of investment instruments[1] have also proliferated along with. Such instruments or systems have provided ample scope for the investors to invest in multiplicity of fields to earn reasonable returns with minimum risks. Mutual funds are such investment vehicles[2] which have reformed the investment world. Under this system, money is pooled from potential investors with common investment objectives. It, then, invests their money in multiple assets, in accordance with the stated objective of the scheme (USSEC, 2010). For instance, an equity fund would invest in stocks and equity related instruments, while a debt fund would invest in bonds, debentures etc. As an investor, one can put ones money in financial assets like stocks and bonds. Investor can do it by either buying them directly or using investment vehicle like mutual funds.

Every investor, who plans to invest in any instrument, is not efficient enough to decide over its investment portfolio for adequate returns. He may be lacking in financial education, time, decision making and confidence. And such features are very much prevalent among the developing countries. Therefore, it is considered that some relevant investment vehicle is required to overcome such flaws. Hence, mutual funds are regarded as the best answer due to many reasons (Pozen & Hamacher, 2014).

1.2 Why Mutual Funds?

Mutual funds hire the *services of professionals* who are well established in the investment world and have apt expertise. Moreover, they are competent, to large extent, to gauge the market for the use of best interests of the investors. Therefore, when funds are entrusted to mutual funds, they are managed by professional experts. Being full time, high-level investment professional, a good investment manager is more resourceful and capable of monitoring the companies in which mutual fund has invested in, as compared to individual investors. These mangers have access to real time access to crucial market information and are able to execute trades on the large and most-effective scale. Putting in other words, they possess the wisdom to trade in the markets that retail investors may not possess.

Mutual funds enable the investors to enjoy the benefits of diversified portfolio even at *minimum investment* (as little as Rs 500). Hence, every strata of society can participate in this form of institutionalized investment. This enhances the financial inclusion as well and they may, consequently, enter into the process of wealth creation. Nonetheless, financial education is a basic requirement in a developing country like India which should be strengthened through appropriate arrangements. Besides, it is convenient for the investors; for, investors are saved from additional paper-work that comes with every transaction, the amount of energy investor put in researching for the stocks, as well as actual market-monitoring and conduction of transactions. Mutual funds provide for simply go online or place an order with the broker to buy a mutual fund. In addition, investor can move funds easily from one fund to another, within a mutual fund family. This allows the investor to rebalance the portfolio in response to significant change in fund management or economic changes.

The mutual funds provide investment with a character of *highly liquid*; for, in open ended schemes[3], investment can be redeemed at any point of time at the prevailing net asset value (NAV)[4] from the fund itself. Therefore, investors can take the advantage of high returns as compared to fixed deposits as well as benefits of demand deposits. Liquidity of mutual fund schemes make the investors highly satisfied; as these can be encashed according to need and exigency.

The mutual funds invest funds in *variety of products* like stocks, debt instruments, derivative markets[5], gold and many other assets. Therefore, they provide variety to the investors to invest in according to their set objectives. Hence, varieties of schemes are there to choose from. There are funds that focus on blue-chip stocks, technology stocks, bonds or a mix of stocks and bonds. Infact, the greatest challenges can be sorting through the variety and picking the best. The SEBI regulations for mutual funds have made the industry very *transparent.* Investor can track the investments that have been made on the investors' behalf by mutual funds to know the sectors and stocks being invested in. In addition to this, they get regular information on the value of their investment. Mutual funds are mandated to publish the details of their portfolio regularly.

1.3 Choosing a Fund

Investors have hard earned money and it cannot be put in an investment vehicle without adequate research. Therefore, he should be deeply concerned while making a choice for the investment scheme. The fund schemes that perform better overtime are likely to be preferred to relatively less performing schemes. The previous periods' performance may or may not be sustained in future; even then such performance is taken into consideration while choosing a fund scheme. Past performance may help the investor to discover the investment strategies of the fund and the returns that have been generated by fund. The consistency in performance is more important than the erratic performance. The strength of a fund can also be gauged from the fact that whether the funds are able to sustain the performance during the bear market.

The mutual funds are supposed to diversify their investments in various unrelated (low correlation) assets. Investors should be careful enough that portfolio of the fund scheme is adequately diversified. Besides, investor should judge suitability of fund scheme to him given his risk appetite and time period for which he is ready to make investment. Here, the choice of fund depends on the risk taking capacity of the investors. If he is averse to risk, he may choose debt fund schemes. On the other hand, if he is an aggressive investor, he may go for equity based and sector specific fund schemes. Investor may desire for returns and safety of the assets; then he may choose the balanced fund scheme - a combination of debt and equity assets.

The capability of fund manager to perform and generate excess returns for the investors is an important element of mutual funds. Therefore, to enquire about the dependability of fund manager concerns the investors. Investor should adequately explore that the fund scheme in which he is investing is still managed by the same manager or somebody else. In addition, the investor should compare the expense ratios of various comparable fund schemes before investing. For, it has been established in the empirical literature that minor difference in fund costs can have big difference in the returns over a period of time.

Mutual funds are subject to market risks and all relevant documents should be scrutinized carefully while making investments. Every fund scheme has some investment strategy and is subject to some risk (even corporate and government bonds are not free from risk). Hence, investor should learn about them in advance and select the fund scheme according to his financial goals and risks involved.

Though movements of markets are, generally, not predictable; but it is very sure that they make cycles overtime. The investor should be able to understand, to some extent, such market moves. For, systemic risk is beyond the control of fund manager as well as investor. Any downward movement in the market due to economy related factors should not be exclusively considered as weak performance. Therefore, investor should observe patience while deciding to enter and exit the market. He should ensure that returns are consistent. If some investment scheme is not performing continuously, it is better to quit.

1.4   Terms and Concepts

Here are some terms and concepts which are frequently in use in the operations of mutual funds:

Net Asset Value: Net Asset Value (NAV) is the market value of all the securities held by the scheme. NAV is calculated by dividing the total net assets by the total number of units issued. The total net assets is the market value of all the assets a mutual fund holds (less any liability) as of a certain date. This term is similar to the book value of a company. Moreover, it helps an investor to determine if the fund is overvalued or undervalued. Since market value of securities changes every day, hence NAV changes accordingly. This is considered as most important term to know, as it provides the performance value of any mutual fund scheme. However, mutual funds pay out virtually all of their income and capital gains. As a result, changes in NAV are not the best measure of mutual fund performance. NAV is calculated once in a day, generally, at the closing price of the day of the portfolio of the fund. All mutual fund orders of buy and sell are executed on the NAV of the day. NAV is obligatory to be revealed by the fund on regular basis.

Assets under Management (AUM): These are market value of assets that an investment company manages on behalf of investors. Therefore, generally, seen as a measure of success against the competition and consists of growth or decline due to both capital appreciation or losses and new money inflow or outflow. Assets under management are also an indicator of size of the fund; hence, discussed in the context of economies of scale also. Larger size of the fund entrust more discretion to the fund manager to allocate the funds in the components of the portfolio. Developing countries are endeavoring to instill the habit of investing in mutual funds among the masses.

Automatic Re-investment: The returns of the mutual funds occur in two parts namely-dividends and appreciation in value of units. The latter can be encashed only when the units are redeemed. The dividends, however, are available as soon as they are distributed. An investor can choose for either dividend reinvest or payout. When latter option is opted, the dividend is credited in investor's bank account. In case of reinvestment, the dividend amount is utilized to buy more mutual fund units of the scheme. The automatic reinvestment option is a service the fund house provides to shareholders, giving them option to purchase additional shares using dividends automatically. Apart from dividends, mutual funds also distribute the profits it makes from selling some of the underlying assets at higher values. This is called capital gains distribution. This can also be used to buy more MF units (reinvestment).

Compounding: This is an ability of an asset to generate earnings which are then reinvested in order to generate their own earnings. Putting in other words, compounding refers to generate earnings from the previous earnings. 'The power of compounding was said to be deemed the eighth wonder of the world'[6]. When an investment is made in a financial asset, we earn on the amount invested. Over time, we can either reinvest this amount or put it in any other investment vehicle; hence, we earn earnings on the previous earnings. Thus, total returns increase overtime and compounding can produce significant growth in the value of an investment.

Diversification: Diversification is an important feature of mutual funds. It is the practice of investing in diverse types of securities or asset classes. This is basically done to trim down risk. The underlying principle is that every asset does not move in tandem. Some register rise; however, other record fall at the same time. So, when investor owns both the stocks in its portfolio, losses from one would be nullified by the gains in the other, thus reducing the investor's overall risk.

Depreciation: This is the decline in value of investor's investment in mutual fund. This means, he will register a capital loss when sell the mutual fund units. It is just the opposite of 'appreciation'.

Portfolio: This is a grouping of financial assets of divergent categories owned by mutual funds such as stocks, bonds and cash equivalents, exchange traded and closed funds. The experts handle all these assets. This specialist decides which assets to buy or sell and he is called the portfolio manager. The frequency of the trading activity-how often assets are sold and bought-in the portfolio is called the 'portfolio turnover'. Prudence suggests that investors should construct an investment portfolio in accordance with risk tolerance and investing objectives. So, conservative investor favours defensive portfolio whereas risk loving investor prefers aggressive portfolio. Such an arrangement reduces the overall risk of the portfolio; for, loss in one variety of assets can be recovered from other segments of the portfolio.

Ex-Dividend Date: The amount of dividend to be distributed among the unit holders is announced a few days before the actual distribution. The date of the distribution is called the dividend date. Once this happens, the fund's net asset value reduces as the dividends are deducted from the fund's assets. The day of this deduction is called the 'ex-dividend date'.

Load: This is the amount that a mutual fund charges from investors for various reasons. This may include management fees, entry or front-end loads and exit loads. The amount paid to the fund manager for his expertise and portfolio management skills is called management fees. Entry or front-end load is the amount a mutual fund charges when units are purchased by investors. Similarly, exit load is the amount a mutual fund charges for selling or redeeming of units. Though, the effectiveness of such loads also depends on the policy that the regulators follow.

Expense Ratio: There are some expenses that a company bear to operate a mutual fund. An expense ratio is calculated through dividing fund's operating expenses by the average rupee value of its assets under management. Operating expenses are taken out of a fund's assets and lower the return to fund's investors. The largest component of operating expenses is the fee paid to a fund's investment manager. Other costs include recordkeeping, custodial services, taxes, legal expenses, and accounting and auditing fees. The fund's trading activity, the buying and selling of portfolio securities, is not included in the calculation of the expense ratio.

Fund Switch: A firm that operates in the business of capital management, generally, runs with multiplicity of schemes. Fund houses provide investors an option to transfer their investments within the fund family from one scheme to another with or without cost. For instance, a family of funds may include an equity scheme, a debt scheme and a balanced scheme. An investor could then choose to move his/her money amongst the funds as and when needs and objectives change.

Investment Objective: Mutual funds offer variety of funds that may go well with the investors' requirements and termed as their 'investment objectives'. They may be willing to amass wealth, planning to buy something in future, or he may shield his money from general price rise. Likewise, the mutual fund too has goals, which it intends to realize on behalf of its investors.

Prospectus: Mutual Fund Company is required to give details about its business which, in turn, concerned about the financial security of the buyers. It commonly provides investors with material information about the mutual fund schemes, financial statements, risks it perceives, services offered, investment strategies, fees and so on. This official document is called 'the prospectus'. Investors are expected to read this offer document carefully before investing.

Exchange-Traded Fund (ETF): This is a form of mutual fund that can be traded on the stock exchanges. These funds derive their value from the performance of index (benchmark) on which it is based. The value of such funds keeps on changing like shares due to demand-supply forces. ETFs mostly follow certain index; hence, stock picking capacity of fund manager does not matter here. Therefore, ETFs, generally, charge lower fees and have better liquidity. Consequently, make ETFs instruments attractive amongst investors. As it trades like a stock, an ETF does not have its NAV calculated once at the end of every day like a mutual fund does. ETF shareholders are entitled to a proportion of the profits, such as earned interest or dividends paid, and they may get a residual value in case the fund is liquidated. The ownership of the fund can easily be bought, sold or transferred in the same way as shares of firms, since ETF shares are traded on public stock exchanges.

Fund of Funds (FOF): The mutual funds can invest across mutual funds, that is, an investment strategy to hold investment portfolio of other investment funds. A fund of funds allows investors to achieve a broad diversification and an appropriate asset allocation with investments in a variety of fund categories that are all wrapped up into one fund. However, if the fund of funds carries an operating expense, investors are essentially paying double for an expense that is already included in the expense figures of the underlying funds.

New Fund Offering (NFO): When a mutual fund starts a new scheme and invites investors to put in money in exchange for units, it is called a New Fund Offering or NFO. NFOs are offered for a stipulated period. This means that the investors opting to invest in these schemes at the offer price can do so in this stipulated period only. After the NFO period, investors can take exposure in these funds only at the prevailing NAV. New fund offers are often accompanied by aggressive marketing campaigns, created to entice investors to purchase units in the fund.

Redeem: When an investor exit from a mutual fund or we can say, sell the units back to the mutual funds company at the current NAV, this is termed as redeeming. Some mutual funds may have redemption fees attached. This charge is deducted from the NAV and the remaining is paid to the investors. This is called the redemption price.

Risk-Return Trade off: The principle of risk-return trade off states that an investment would potentially give higher returns with an increase in risk. Low levels of uncertainty (low-risk) are associated with low potential returns. According to risk return trade off, invested money can render higher profits only if it is subject to the possibility of being lost. Due to the risk-return trade off, investor must be aware of your personal risk tolerance when choosing investments of portfolio. Taking on some risk is the price of achieving returns, if we want to make money, we cannot cut all risks. The goal instead is to find an appropriate balance one that generates some profit, but still allows investor to sleep at night.

1.5 Mutual Funds: Various Types

There are multiplicities of mutual funds. They can also be grouped into different categories on varying factors. Here is a glance at the types of mutual funds.

1.5.1 Fund Scheme Based

These categories of mutual funds is divided into two categories namely close ended schemes and open ended schemes;

Close-Ended Schemes: These schemes are offered to investors for a fixed maturity period during a specified period of time and they are supposed to be subscribed during this particular time period. New units cannot be issued after this period; however, there is provision for bonus and right issues. After this specified period, units of the scheme are listed in stock exchanges. The investors can trade in these units on the market determined price. This price can be different from NAV of the scheme due to market forces.

Open-Ended Schemes: The investors can enter in or exit from such schemes as and when they wish on the ongoing NAV. There is no limit of maturity period in such schemes. The mutual fund companies may issue units to the investors without any restriction of number of units. Increased demand for units can be met through issue of additional units. There is no upper limit of investment. These units are not, generally, listed on any exchange and can be bought or redeemed on NAV of the day. Therefore, such schemes are liked for their liquidity. Even investment can be made either in lump sum or on regular intervals.

1.5.2 Nature of Investments Based

In this form of mutual funds investments are categorized on the basis of portfolios which the asset management companies select. They may invest in equity, debt and other related instruments. In this context, the mutual funds are classified as equity, hybrid and debt funds.

Equity Funds: Equity based funds generally invest in the securities of the companies based in domestic or foreign economies. Depending on the objective of the scheme, funds can be invested in large, medium and small cap firms, technically known as large cap funds, medium cap funds and small cap funds. And sometimes combination of different sizes can be chosen. Besides, there are equity funds that concentrate on particular business sector such as infrastructure, banking and pharmaceuticals. The basic objective of an equity fund is growth through capital gain along with generating dividends for investors. Since investment in equities are relatively more risky; hence, expected to generate more returns, given the risk return relationship.

Hybrid Funds: These funds invest in both equities as well as debt instruments. Since, conservative investors are concerned about the assured returns at lesser risk; therefore, some portion of capital is invested in debt along with equities. Such funds are likely to produce returns better than debt funds but less than equity funds. This type of fund is a mixture of aggressive and conservative portfolios. The ratio of equity and debt instruments in portfolios may change or stay constant overtime depending on the policy that fund follows. Risk avoiders, generally, prefer such funds.

Debt Funds: These funds are generally meant for risk averse investors. For, debt funds invest in the instruments that generate fixed income. Since the returns are fixed or certain, therefore, debt instruments are considered low-risk, low return financial assets. Such funds are further classified on the basis of maturity period of the underlying assets - long term and short period. The main investing objectives of a debt fund will usually be preservation of capital and generation of income.

1.5.3 Investment Objective Based

Investors have varied objectives to invest in mutual funds. Some may be concerned about profits and increasing wealth, while others may be interested in additional source of regular income. Investors may also be interested in combination of both. Keeping these requirements in mind, there are three key kinds of mutual funds based on the investment objective.

Growth Funds: These schemes are, generally, committed to capital appreciation in long period. These schemes, usually, invest in diversified stocks of the firms with high growth potential. The companies in the portfolio, generally, contain that with above average growth in earnings that reinvest their earning into expansion, acquisition and research and development. Such assets are volatile in returns; hence considered as risky schemes. In order to increase assets under management, such schemes barely declare dividends and such undistributed profits are reinvested. Investment in such funds needs patience and holding period should be sufficient.

Balanced Funds: The balance between risks and returns is generally created through these funds.

These funds are suitable for investors who are concerned for returns and security of their money invested. Therefore, they invest in equities and debt instruments and sometimes money market instruments in a particular portfolio. Consequently, their risk is lower than the equity funds and higher than debt or fixed income funds.

Fixed-Income Funds: These fund schemes guarantee recurring earnings for a specified period of times. So, it is obvious that they invest in debt funds and we can say they are usually a kind of debt fund. This makes fixed-income funds low –risk schemes, which are unlikely to give a large amount of returns in the long run.

1.5.4 Some Special funds

These are funds which invest in a specific kind of assets. They may be a kind of equity or debt fund.

Index Funds: Such funds are termed as passive funds; as, the fund managers do not need much research in asset allocation. The base of asset allocation is a particular stock index. The fund invests in the index stock participants in the same proportion as the index. For instance, if a stock has a weightage of 5 percent in an index, the schemes will also invest 5 percent of its funds in the stocks. Since, much effort is not needed on the part of fund manager; hence, expense ratio of such schemes is relatively less. Consequently, the fee charged is also very low. Index funds may be diversified or sector specific as both types of indices are available.

Real Estate Funds: These funds deploy their funds in real estate directly. Besides, they may be acquiring property or financing real estate developers. The shares of housing finance companies may be in their portfolio or their securitized assts. The risks in these schemes depend on the momentum in sector.

Gilt Funds: Investment in government securities is considered as risk free; for, no default risk is associated with these instruments. The mutual funds sometimes introduce schemes that exclusively invest in government securities. Hence, the investor usually does not have to worry about credit risk. Though, like any other debt fund interest rate risk is embedded in them. Such schemes are basically choice of investors who do not want to indulge in risk activities. These funds can have different maturity profiles. Some may be short term while others are medium term or long term.

Sector Funds: These fund schemes invest in equities of specific sector firms such as real estate, banking, infrastructure etc. Investors, who are aware and know the complexities of a particular sector, decide to invest in a particular sector. Since the entire funds are invested in a particular sector, therefore schemes prove to be more risky than general schemes. The success of the sector may generate handsome returns also. But, the investment should be very careful.

Tax Saving Schemes: Investors are now encouraged to invest in the equity markets through the Equity Linked Savings Scheme (ELSS) by offering them a tax rebate. When money is invested in such schemes, total taxable income decreases. But the units purchased through these schemes cannot be redeemed, sold or transferred for a period of three years (lock-in period) (India). However, in comparison with other tax-saving financial instruments like Public Provident Funds (PPF) and Employees' Provident Funds (EPF), ELSS funds have the lowest lock-in period.

Money Market Schemes: These schemes invest their funds in short term instruments such as commercial papers (CPs)[8], treasury bills (T-Bills), certificates of deposits (CDs)[9] and call money. These schemes are a kind of debt funds with least risk involved. These schemes have become popular with institutional investors and high-net worth individuals (HNIs) having short-term surplus funds.

1.6   Hedge Funds and Mutual Funds

Hedge funds and mutual funds are sort of investment vehicles. They have the similarity that both collect money from investors and then deploy such funds in various instruments on behalf of their clients. However, there are some differences between mutual funds and hedge funds.

- *According to size of investor:* Big and small investors can invest in mutual fund but hedge funds are available for high net worth investors.
- *According to investment portfolio:* The regular financial instruments like stocks and bonds are in the portfolios of mutual funds. However, hedge funds invest in complex and riskier financial assets.
- *According to borrowing for investments:* The mutual funds have limited borrowing capacity; they can play only with the assets under their management. Hedge funds can borrow additional amounts. Even they can also bet on twice of their total assets.
- *According to charges:* Hedge funds highly depend on the expertise of managers; hence, have very high charges as compare to mutual funds.
- *According to size of investment required:* The mutual funds allow investments of small amounts whereas such threshold is very high in case of hedge funds.
- *According to risk involved:* Mutual funds do not invest in complex assets, hence are less risky. Hedge funds, on the contrary, more risky given their complex investments.
- *According to objective:* Mutual funds protect the investors' money through diversification. The diversification is not compulsory in hedge funds; rather their investments are more concentrated.
- *According to regulations:* Retail investors avail the services of mutual funds and more regulated than hedge funds.

1.7   Periodic Plans for Investors

Systemic Investment Plan (SIP): Mutual funds provide an opportunity to investors to invest small fixed amounts periodically (monthly or quarterly) in a particular scheme at a particular date. The total investment planned for such scheme is spread over a period of time. SIP helps an investor to invest bigger amounts without managing funds at one time and gradually accumulate the units of fund scheme. This also helps to inject discipline in investment habit. Under SIP, monthly mutual fund investment activities are automated. SIP can be started with very small amount, say rupees 500, therefore very convenient for small investor.

The investment through SIP the investor can be benefited through 'rupee cost averaging'. For, NAV experiences changes every day and units are, thus, available at a different price every month. So, when investors invest a fixed amount every month, during different market cycles, they buy varying amount of MF units. So, on the whole, the average cost is expected to fall.

Continuing SIP for long period helps the investor to take advantage of compounding; for, investments earn returns annually and such reinvestments ended up with higher returns. That is why; it is always advised to start investing as early as possible and thus earns profit through continuous reinvestment. While investing in the equity market, timing the market is very crucial and complex. With an SIP, we invest across times, irrespective of the market timing. This increases the overall probability of getting the timing right.

Systematic Transfer Plan (STP): The investors can protect themselves from the harms of volatile market by using systematic transfer plan (STP). Under this plan, investment in one asset or asset type can be transferred into another asset or asset type periodically. There are, generally, two types; fixed STP, and capital appreciation STP. In fixed STP, investors transfer a fixed amount from one investment to another. In capital appreciation STP, investor transfers the appreciated part of money from one asset to another.

Thus, mutual fund portfolio is continuously readjusted. For instance, suppose investor has some money invested in an equity fund and now he wanted to generate an additional source of income. Besides, he is also interested to earn higher returns expected from the rise in equity markets. So, he can opt for an STP plan through which some money is shifted to a debt scheme on monthly basis. In this way, some returns can be earned through exposure in equity fund and also start building debt fund portfolio for his future income needs.

A Systematic Withdrawal Plan (SWP): This is a plan to withdraw money from a scheme in a systematic manner instead of in one go. By opting SWP plan, investor is permitted to withdraw a fixed amount from the fund portfolio at regular intervals. This plan is very much important for the investors who want to have regular source of income. But they should have sufficient funds in their portfolio. An SWP helps to meet liquidity needs of investor. It is, therefore, usually used by retired investors. Most of the times, investors are not intelligent enough to decide about the timing of exiting the market. So, withdrawing through SWP, he may take the advantage of up and low market by averaging. Besides, tax liability can be spread across time too. Investor will have to pay capital gains tax over a period of years, instead of paying it in lump sum in one year. In the meanwhile, he may also enjoy further appreciation in the value of his mutual funds.

1.8   Mutual Funds and Financial Planning

As already stated, money collected from investors with 'general financial objective' and invested in financial assets – stocks, bonds, government securities – with the aim of generating income and capital growth. While making financial planning with the aid of mutual funds, investor should be very clear about its investment objective and accordingly his planner pursue specific investment strategy and consider relative merits of each class of security. Besides, constantly examines the strengths in the context of financial indicators, government policy, and economic climate change and so on. Each investor can use a combination of funds to create a customized portfolio to reach his/her goals.

It should be taken care about a general myth that a fund with higher NAV is not necessarily worse than another with lower NAV. Comparing funds simply on the basis of NAV is not a practical idea. There are more than one specific ways of comparing funds in the same category.

The process of meeting financial goals considers many aspects to guide individual towards fulfillment of objectives. Such planning requires complete and accurate risk planning by a qualified financial planner. Each individual is unique; so, each financial plan is unique as well. Besides, financial planning assesses the risk taking capability, so a detailed examination of specific risks is needed; even large macro risks must be analyzed. Exact considerations include – the individual's age, investment horizon, present financial status, commitments, liabilities, income generation capabilities, projected changes in income and so on. A reliable plan leads to accurate asset allocation. A financial planner will recommend modification in a client's allocations when his life stage changes. New commitments, liabilities, windfall profits, inheritances, medial crises will generally imply fresh allocation strategy.

Generally, investment through mutual funds falls in two categories - equity and debt. Younger investors can generally focus more on equity, as this is more volatile. Debt is recommended for older investors, this is more predictable. However, there is no hard and fast rule. Even in the same asset class, allocations must be done sensibly; for instance, how much in diversified growth funds, sectoral funds, international feeder funds.

Mutual funds are apt for those who desire to build a corpus for their years in retirement. Mutual funds are suitable for those who are planning to meet long term goals, keeping specific needs in mind. SIP is done for long periods, as it can withstand the impact of a volatile market. In such ways, funds can help an individual realize aspirations like - purchase of property, children's education and marriage, commencement of a business enterprise, travel, and repayment of loans and so on. Therefore, the importance of understanding one's time horizon and backing each goal with the required financial commitment are two critical issues for fund investors.

Besides, financial planning should include put money aside in liquid and fixed income funds with near term maturity to meet exigencies like imminent loan payments. Hence, investments in conventional income funds and monthly income plan to derive regular income for meeting household expenses.

When an investor invests in equity diversified schemes, he should divide the investment funds in large, medium and small cap equities to build a corpus. Besides, the financial planner relooks at the portfolio in due course. When a planner has to recommend funds, he must know their scope, nature and purpose. A particular fund may be chosen for the reasons - investment objective, quality of the portfolio, past performance, track record of promoters and so on.

The investment planner should pay due consideration to appropriateness of the products recommended to investors. He should be exposed to new as well as traditional products. Besides, tax implications should also be taken care. Long period investment does not levy taxes on dividends. Besides, equity linked saving schemes that provide income tax benefit in India can also be recommended.

Two mantras are repeated constantly by planners who recommend funds are (a) the earlier the better through which chances of optimizing returns are stronger; (b) regularity of investment has no substitute. As the short-term volatility is here to stay; so remain in funds for long period.

An investor is exposed to variety of risks. While making a plan for investments such risks cannot be overlooked; otherwise, it would be a step towards failure. These risks may come under the categories of unique risks and systemic risks. Unique risks are specific to the fund scheme in which money is invested. The systemic risks are generated by the operation of economic system. An individual's risk-taking ability will determine what sort of funds will suit him. The higher the risk, the greater is the chance of being rewarded. Yet, nothing is assured or guaranteed.

As already stated that markets are unpredictable; hence, generate market risk, as prices may change in either direction in the times to come. So, market risk has bearing on the returns of mutual fund investments. Investors are also subject to the risk of the non performance of the fund managers. He may fail to accomplish his task and investor may suffer in terms of returns. A specific sector or industry may cease to perform due to certain developments at national or international levels. Large exposure to such sector may be a sheer loss to the investor. The developing economy like India is inflation prone due to supply and demand side factors. Therefore, the real return from mutual fund investments may be relatively less. The interest rates in our country are policy determined. The decision to change the interest rate may have impact on the returns. It may negatively affect the returns on mutual fund investments. Debt funds are more popular than equity funds in India. Investment portfolio of debt funds may face the risk of failure to repay interest and principal on the part of issuer of such instruments. The risk discussed here should be factored in while making an investment plan for investor.

There is an important caveat for mutual fund users for financial planning; a planning may fail if there is inadequate diversification, over or under allocation to a particular class and poor portfolio because of wrong choice. Putting in other words, this is a common drawback - under emphasized risks and over stated rewards.

A good financial planning builds up the affluence of investor. He can fulfill his financial pursuits as visualized in the plan.

1.9 Mutual Fund Myths

Due to low awareness levels there are some misconceptions that prevent investors from making the most that mutual funds have to offer. Here is an attempt to debunk some of the common myths that investors have. *Many investors feel that the NAV of a mutual fund is similar to market price of stocks and therefore buying funds at low NAV is better.* They believe that as the NAV is low and more units can be bought and hence, there is higher potential for appreciation, as compared to a fund with a higher NAV. However, in reality, a mutual fund's NAV represents the market value of all its investments. Hence, any appreciation in the NAV will depend on the price movement of its portfolio of companies.

It has been considered by the investors that *dividends are an extra income.* A scheme that pays dividends is better than a scheme that doesn't. But dividend income from stocks and mutual funds are different. When a mutual fund announces dividend, the NAV is adjusted accordingly. If a dividend option is opted, a part of the profits made by the scheme are distributed to investors. Then, the dividend is subtracted from NAV of the scheme on the record date and accordingly the NAV drops to the extent to dividend and dividend distribution tax paid. So, a fund which pays dividend is in no way better or worse than one that doesn't pay dividends.

Sometimes investors think that *need to open a demat account* to start investing in a mutual fund. The fact is that to invest in a mutual fund investor do not need any demat account. It needs to be KYC compliant. Then all that he needs to do is fill up the relevant application form, attach a cheque and submit the form at the mutual fund office, its registrar office directly or through advisor or distributor. Once investment is processed, investor will get a statement showing details of his investments.

Mutual Funds invest only in equities is a myth. Investors need to understand that there are various kinds of mutual funds. While some invest their corpus in equity, others invest the money into debt schemes, such as government bonds and bonds issued by companies and financial institutions. There are some funds that also invest in money market instruments such as treasury bills issued by the government, call money market used primarily by banks and short-term paper issued by companies. Mutual Funds, therefore, invest in all kinds of instruments and do not confine themselves to equity. The choice of a fund, in this context, needs to be based on the risk investors are willing to take and the time duration of their investment. Markets are at a peak, I should defer my investment, and research shows that any time is good to invest, provided we invest for the long term. We could also invest using the Systematic Investment Plans (SIP) method which helps investors to accumulate units in good bull and bear markets thereby optimizing their returns over a long period of time and creating wealth.

Mutual funds with good performance in last one year are best choice. This is a common misconception among the mutual fund investors that funds which have performed very well in the past one year are the best choice.

Past performance is one of the things to look at when investing; however it makes sense to look at performance across market cycles and for longer durations of 7 - 10 years or even more and not just recent past. In addition, investors should also consider the fund manager's experience, his track record and the fund house's track record.

1.10 Concluding Remarks

Mutual funds have emerged an important investment vehicle in the modern era. They have gained significance in the operation of financial markets; for, every segment of such markets is supposed to be affected by the operation of such funds. Mutual funds are preferred instruments of investments due to many reasons such as: services of experts in the capital market are used; very small amount is needed to enter into; such instruments are of very liquid nature; comfortable degree of diversification of portfolio. Moreover, regulatory bodies are very active to make the transactions in mutual funds very transparent. The investors is expected to take calculated risk while choosing a fund scheme and expected to choose appropriate combination of risk and returns, given the objective of the investor. Moreover, the capability and credentials of the fund manager are of wide importance. Besides, the fund schemes should not be chosen under the influence of heat of emotions. Developing countries are endeavouring to instill the habit of investing in mutual funds.

Mutual funds can be open-ended and close ended funds, depending on the time of permission to enter in the fund schemes, Moreover, such schemes fall in the category of equity, debt, and hybrid funds depending on the weight in the overall portfolio. And investors reveal their preference of such funds based on their risk appetite. Mutual funds are, now, considered as dominant section of investment planning of investors. Hence, there are multiple facets of mutual funds. There are some myths regarding the operation of mutual funds and the investors should educate themselves to avoid them and take full benefits of this investment vehicle.

Notes

1. This is a real or virtual document that represents a legal agreement involving some sort of monetary value. In modern days financial markets, financial instruments are classified, generally, as equity based, representing ownership of the asset, or debt based, representing a loan made by an investor to the owner of the asset. Similarly, foreign exchange instruments comprise a third, a unique type of instrument.
2. A product used by investors with the objective of generating positive returns.
3. Discussed in the ensuing section.
4. Discussed in detail in the title of terms and concepts in this chapter.
5. A derivative is a security with a price that is dependent upon or derived from one or more underlying assets.
6. This is a quote coined by Albert Einstein-who developed prowess in the world of investing.
7. A rights issue is an invitation to existing shareholders to purchase additional new shares/units in the company.
8. Commercial paper is a money-market security issued (sold) by large corporations to obtain funds to meet short-term debt obligations, and is backed only by an issuing bank or corporation's promise to pay the face amount on the maturity date specified on the note. Since it is not backed by collateral, only firms with excellent credit ratings from a recognized credit rating agency will be able to sell their commercial paper at a reasonable price. Commercial paper is usually sold at a discount from face value, and generally carries lower interest repayment rates than bonds due to the shorter maturities of commercial paper.
9. A savings certificate that entitles the bearer to receive interest. A CD bears a maturity date, a specified fixed interest rate and can be issued in any denomination. CDs are generally issued by commercial banks. The term of a CD generally ranges from one month to five years.
10. Sometimes very catchy names are given to the fund scheme that they seem to be lucrative investment; hence, one should go by performance instead of enticed by the name.

References

- Kotak Securities (2014), "Mutual Funds in India", available at: www.kotaksecurities.com.
- Kumar D. (2013), "Mutual Funds: A Selective Saving Grace", *Business Standard*, July 9.
- Matthew P. F. (2011), "The Rise of Mutual Funds: Insider's View (2nd ed.)". Oxford University Press.
- Pozen R. & Hamacher T. (2014), "*The Fund Industry: How Your Money is Managed (Second Edition)*", John Wiley & Sons.
- Pozen R. & Hamacher T. (2015), "The Fund Industry: How your Money is Managed", Hoboken, NJ: Wiley Finance.
- US Securities and Exchange Commission (2010): "*A Guide for Investors*", available at: www.sec.gov.
- www.economictimes.indiatimes.com/mutual funds
- www.mutualfundindia.com
- www.moneycontrol.com/mutualfundindia
- www.amfiindia.com

Chapter-2
Mutual Funds: Some Undercurrents

2.1 Introduction

Small investors[1] are, generally, short of the knowledge of the operation of financial markets; thus, they are unable to formulate their investment portfolios[2] as per their goals. Besides, investors are not well aware of the working of the economic systems[3], both at micro and macro level. They have limited resources to invest; therefore, cannot spend very high amount on acquiring professional advice. Consequently, putting money in equity market without comprehending the technicalities of such market, they may place high value at risk (VaR).[4] Under such circumstances, 'mutual funds' are considered as safe source of investments to earn steady returns as well as safety and liquidity of their investments. It is a special type of 'institutional device' or an 'investment vehicle' through which investors' savings are pooled and invested under the supervision of experts in wide variety of portfolios at minimum possible risk. Mutual funds have become significant part of capital market in nowadays, given their magnitude and dimensions in recent decades[5]. Hence, such institutions (mutual funds) may influence the supply and demand segments of capital markets. Consequently, MFs can generate several under-currents in the macroeconomic environment of an economy; nevertheless, such impacts may be different between developed and less developed countries.

Almost every emerging market, directly or indirectly, has introduced financial reforms in recent decades. The ultimate aim was augmenting the generation of domestic resources; so that, it may lessen its dependence on the outside funds. Therefore, to tap the vast potential of domestic savings and need for efficient deployment of such funds has emerged remarkably. Mutual funds are considered as best suited for this purpose and capable of meeting these challenges. Moreover, typical investors are concerned about the yield, liquidity and security of their capital. Mutual funds have the capacity, to large extent, of satisfying such issues. Such capability is assured due to the fact that funds are managed by professionals with diversity of knowledge and information about the financial markets. For, in due course, they develop prowess of stock selection and timing of the market[6].

Investors, who directly subscribe to corporates' IPOs or FPOs, are not sure of their allotment. However, such allotment is certain in case of mutual funds. Therefore, investors repose extreme faith in mutual funds. Besides, mutual funds make available the provision of automatic re-investment of dividends and capital gains[7]. Compounding effect of such investments is spectacular in long run. Dissemination of the knowledge about the benefits of such investments among the middle income groups, mutual funds are able to acquire surplus funds available with these people. The mutual funds also provide opportunity to benefit from the investment avenues emerged in the international capital market[8]. For, mutual funds can open off shore funds and attract foreign capital affecting the macroeconomic stability[9] as well.

Investors are not homogeneous in terms of information they hold concerning financial markets. Besides, they wish to share particular risks, basically, arising out of consumption and employment. Consequently, they seek heterogeneous fund strategies for idiosyncratic reasons. It has been established in the literature related to mutual funds that they are well informed agents (Allen and Gorton, 1993; Dow and Gorton, 1997; Das and Sundaram, 2000). Hence, investors are aspired to attain the services of best mutual funds to maximize their returns. Moreover, risk sharing characteristic of mutual funds make them more popular among investors, given the risk appetite of the investors. This background makes it clear that investors trade among themselves (heterogeneous knowledge and risk sharing). These institutions trade in a variety of instruments with divergent amount of risk. Therefore, they are able, to large extent, to hedge the risks involved. Investors differ in the type of risk they are willing to face, thus, differ in the investment strategies they prefer.

Financial markets are not perfect entities and even cannot be. Therefore, investors use dynamic trading strategies in an endeavor to make them near perfect. Basically, investors enter into financial markets, overtime, to share various risks as these emerge. Consequently, some of them may be interested in positive relation with the real variables concerned. However, others may be looking for negative relationship to hedge the risks. As already stated, investors lack financial market knowledge, career and other obligations discourage them to participate in such markets continuously. As a result, they create financial market intermediaries (such as mutual funds, banks and so on) to trade on their behalf. Funds and other financial firms cater to a populace with different desired dynamic strategies. Investors carry their preferred trading strategies by selectively buying shares in these different funds to match as closely as possible their preferred dynamic trading strategy. There is distinction between the trading strategies and selection of securities. Former refers to change in portfolio according to the market situations, whereas latter depends on the buy and hold some fixed portfolio of securities. That is why; mutual funds are getting popular day by day and generating several undercurrents with lots of ramifications.

2.2   Genesis of Mutual funds

The European companies in their pursuit to expand their imperial power in Asian and other countries had borrowed heavily during 16th and 17th century. The increased expenditure could not be financed through returns from the colonial expansions. The financial stress on these European firms appeared due to heavy leverage before the boom years to smooth the progress of colonial interests. The size of such firms was very large and any activity, positive as well as negative, could have repercussions around the world. The risk taken by such firms with the support of imperial powers led to financial crisis in Europe which can be compared to the banking crisis in 2008.

To come out of this crisis, a Dutch trader form an investment trust in 1774 to pool money from a number of subscribers, it can be described as the first mutual fund in the world. The risk involved in investing in the colonies was diversified[10] by spreading such investments in divergent colonies. Earlier this investment facility was available to big investors; gradually it had been made available to the small investors. Meaning thereby, the elements of modern day mutual funds were existing that time.

Mutual funds came into sight gradually, and widened the extent of investment opening to the general public during eighteenth century. Securitization[11] and stock substitution, two major innovations, came into existence during eighteenth century. These innovations came to light from the efforts of traders and brokers to broaden the range of investment opportunities to the general public.

Securitization and stock substitution are innovations that facilitate the trading of assets in the financial markets. Securitization converts the illiquid assets into the small sizes of equity shares which can, subsequently' be traded in the financial markets. In stock substitution, existing securities are repackaged individually or as part of a portfolio to make them easier to trade, either in smaller denominations or at a lower cost than the underlying claims. This broadening of the capital market ultimately led to the beginning of the today's close-ended mutual funds and depository receipts.

2.2.1 Predecessors of Mutual Funds

The elements of mutual funds in the form of pooling financial assets were present even before the eighteenth century. Though, these investment vehicles were not analogous to modern mutual funds, they had demonstrated many such characteristics. Their growth throws light on the investment trusts to create tradable ownership of financial securities portfolio. The 'contract of survival'- first major type of its kind, includes life 'annuities' and in particular we may call it 'tontines'. Life annuities refers to a form of contract in which borrower is liable to pay interest to the supplier for the rest of lender's life, or to third person nominated by the lender and included his name in the agreement. The evidences of life annuities are available in the before Christ era also. Therefore, it can be concluded here that mutual funds have their genesis in the ancient history. The tontines are also a format of agreement between borrower and lenders. Here, the lenders are generally more than one who pooled their money to fund the projects of borrower, like the modern consortiums'. A borrower agrees to pay to a group of individuals an annuity which will be divided among the surviving members. As members die, the payout to the survivors increases. Therefore, it can be concluded here that mutual funds have their genesis in the ancient history.

2.2.2 The Arrival of the Modern Fund

The modern form of mutual fund firms came into existence in 1924 when the Massachusetts Investors' created a trust and formalized in 1928. Besides, the services of a custodian were also taken, which is part and parcel of the modern day investment firm. A historic year in the evolution of the mutual fund, 1928 also saw the launch of the Wellington Fund, which was the first mutual fund to include stocks and bonds, as opposed to direct merchant bank style of investments in business and trade.

2.2.3 Regulation and Expansion

The business of mutual funds started expanding and by 1929, there were 19 open-ended mutual funds competing with nearly 700 close-ended funds in USA. With the stock market crash of 1929, the dynamics began to change as highly-leveraged[12] close-ended funds were wiped out and small open-ended funds continued to exist. The growth of mutual funds led the government to create the regulators. Consequently, the Securities and Exchange Commission (SEC) was created with the passage of the Securities Act of 1933 and the enactment of the Securities Exchange Act of 1934 put in place safeguards to protect investors. Mutual funds were required to register with the SEC and to provide disclosures in the form of a prospectus. The Investment Company Act of 1940 put in place added regulations that required more disclosures and sought to minimize conflicts of interest.

The mutual fund industry in USA and other developed economies continuously grew by leaps and bounds, however with some passive phases. Hundreds of new funds were launched throughout the 1960s until the bear market of 1969 cooled the public appetite for mutual funds. Money flowed out of mutual funds as quickly as investors could redeem their shares, but the industry's growth later resumed.

2.3 Mutual Fund Theorem

Risk appetite of every investor is different, he may either be risk averse (conservative investor) or risk taker (aggressive investor), given the investor's psychology and aspiration for superior returns. Accordingly, mutual funds are capable to launch schemes suitable to almost every segment of investor. Investors, generally, strive to undergo calculated risk[13] that makes the best combination of risks and returns. James Tobin (1958), a Nobel laureate, suggests that all investors should hold a portfolio that combine the risky assets and risk free assets or cash for better returns and security of the money invested. Usually, a conservative investor holds a higher percentage of cash or risk free assets; however, converse is true for the aggressive investor. Psychology of the investors is determined by the multiplicity of factors such as social pressure, liabilities, peer group, education level, and financial knowledge and so on.

The mutual fund theorem appeared as a consequence of the 'mean-variance framework' developed by Harry Markowitz (1952) and his theories on how diversification reduces portfolio risk. Since, mutual funds diversify the funds in various categories with different levels of risks; therefore, risks are hedged. Though, very useful theoretical proposition, but its viability has been questioned due to several important assumptions must be in place for the theorem to be proved. These assumptions include lack of transaction costs and perfectly transparent markets.

In portfolio theory, a mutual fund separation theorem or separation theorem states that, under certain conditions, investor's optimal portfolio can be constructed by holding each of certain mutual funds in appropriate ratios, where the number of mutual funds is smaller than the number of individual assets in the portfolio. Here, a mutual fund refers to any specified benchmark portfolio of the available assets. There are two advantages of having a mutual fund theorem. First, if the relevant conditions are met, it may be easier (or lower in transaction costs) for an investor to purchase a smaller number of mutual funds than to purchase a larger number of assets individually. Second, from a theoretical and empirical standpoint, if it can be assumed that the relevant conditions are indeed satisfied, and then implication for the functioning of asset markets can be derived and tested.

2.4   Market Structure of Mutual Fund Firms

Market structure of an industry is determined by the factors like sellers' concentration, buyers' concentration, product differentiations, barriers to entry for the potential firms and so on. Mutual fund industry is market for the services instead of the physical products. Moreover, it comes under the category of experienced good[14] instead of making advance judgment of the product before buying it. So far the sellers' concentration is concerned the most glaring fact about the mutual funds is the large number of fund families with various categories with degree of segmentation. This fact can hardly be explained in the realm of standard theory of finance; for, market segmentation does not assure to improve absolute performance. Indeed, segmentation reduces the scope and range of activity of manager and forces him to invest only in the assets specific to fund category, potentially hampering his market timing skills. Market segmentation and fund proliferation can also be seen as marketing tactics used by the families to take advantage of investors' heterogeneity (Massa, 1998).

Funds are considered as heterogeneous products, differentiated in terms not only of fund-specific characteristics but also of family specific ones. The investor may consider fund families heterogeneous even when they are similar in performance and fees. There are number of fund schemes that are offered by a particular fund family. The fund families provide an opportunity to investors to move funds from one scheme to another in the same family at negligible cost. This opportunity is more useful in the fund families where number of schemes is large. This option will be more valuable for investors who intend to rotate their portfolio regularly. Investors consider funds as heterogeneous goods and affiliation to a family perform a key role in segmenting the market (Massa, 2003). Hence, funds having similar investment profile and generating similar yield may be appropriate to diverse investors.

The conduct of fund families depends on the market structure, that is, number of fund families operating in the industry and product differentiation. The families compete in terms performance and non performance characteristics. If non-performance characteristics are strength (less fees, for instance) of families, they may compete better.

Studying concentration and competition in the mutual fund industry is of paramount importance for several reasons. Like other industries, the degree of competition is important for the quality, variety and costs of products. In other words, the lack of competition can create inefficiencies in fund diversity, performance, and fees. For instance, studies have documented about economies of scale not passing to investors or that on general the performance of funds is too poor for the level of fees charged (Gruber, 1996; Korkeamaki and Smythe, 2004; Gil-Bazo and Ruiz-Verdú, 2007).

Second, there are evidences of 'distortions' caused by competition inside categories and families. Since mutual funds inflows are sensible to past performance, portfolio managers have incentives to manipulate their position in the category ranking by changing the fund volatility (Brown, Harlow and Starks, 1996; Chevalier and Ellison, 1997). Moreover, fund families are tempted to coordinate actions across funds in the family complex in order to enhance performance of the funds that are most valuable to the family, even if that comes at expenses of other funds. Gaspar, Massa and Matos (2006) conclude that 'favouritism' generates distortions in delegated asset management. Therefore, competition in the mutual fund industry can exacerbate conflicts of interest between investors and fund families.

Third, this is an issue relevant for financial regulators. Fee disclosure is considered crucial for 'investor-driven competition' as investors can only exert fee pressure if they are fully aware of their level. The results indicate that countries with common law and higher stock market turnover are associated with low levels of industry concentration. Industry contestability is higher, i.e. more firms competing and more entry of new firms, in countries with better quality of institutions and where regulations are more open. All the indicators related with regulation like economic freedom, fund regulation and the level of restrictions faced by financial institutions are related with industry contestability. Bank concentration with simultaneous restrictions to engage new activities in the financial industry tends to decrease firm entry in the industry. Also, more developed financial systems have less entry of new firms. In the same line, the launch of new funds is also associated with regulation (Ferreira & Ramos, 2009). Moreover, the financial regulations in the industry determine the barriers to entry of the new firms. Established firms (considered as brands) in the mutual funds industries that have high reputation among investors act as a deterrent to the new firms.

The basic economic contention is that concentration intensifies market power and thereby limits competition. Basically, large fund families have some potential advantages that can make them strengthen their market share increasing industry concentration. Some factors are discussed here:

Economies of scale and scope: Early evidence reported economies of scale for mutual funds and families funds (Baumol, Goldfeld, Gordon, and Koehn, 1990; Collins and Mack, 1997; Latzko, 1999). Chen, Huang, Hong and Kubik (2004) argue that large fund families benefit from economies of scale from trading commissions and lending fees. Also, by using the same economic data and experts to interpret data across many funds, fund families benefit from the scope economies (Ang and Lin, 2001). Therefore, being part of large family or being a large fund can economize some fixed costs which can be reflected in lower fees or enhance net performance. Both actions are likely to be effective strategies in increasing market share. Nevertheless, a competitive environment is important for passing these economies to investors.

Distortions caused by performance spillover. "Star performance" generates a substantial amount of inflows not only for the fund but also for the family (Nanda, Zheng and Wang, 2004). Fund families have high incentives to launch new funds and to transfer means to create "high value" funds. Larger fund firms are the ones more likely to do it as they have more means and experience to generate funds, reinforcing market share in that way.

Though, very few fund managers could outperform consistently once risk loading has been accounted for. Even then funds which have done well in the past tend to attract investors in futures. And fund families which charge lower fees and offer a wide range of products tend to have a higher market share.

The rise in number of funds has increased the public desire for more information, more information has also made more difficult for mutual fund companies to differentiate themselves. This has led to rely on increasingly on market strategies in order to raise the market heterogeneity and to make the inter-fund comparison harder, so as to affect the way investors "perceive" funds. From this perspective, market segmentation and fund proliferation become optimal strategies.

Market segmentation increases product differentiation, limiting competition to the funds belonging to the same category, while fund proliferation increases market coverage. It relies either on the creation of many funds in order to hide the poor performers and merging them into the best ones. Mutual fund industry is considered as service industry and firms are competing (price and non-price) for more buyers with other firms. Here are mentioned some competitions among the mutual fund firms.

Price competition: One could argue that mutual funds are very much like standard commodities. Hence, investors try to work out the optimum price of the fund unit (NAV) prevailing in the market. Moreover, in these days, number of websites provides the facility to make the comparison of peer group funds for the convenience of the investor.

Product differentiation: Performance may well be the most important approach for fund managers to differentiate themselves. Managers that can earn excess returns than benchmark index are likely to attract more funds and are, therefore, able to increase the family's market share. Funds with relatively improved performance draw more funds in the subsequent periods, while poor performance do not see fund outflow in the identical magnitude (Ippolito,1992; Sirri and Tufano,1998). This asymmetric response suggests that families can experience an increase in their market share; even they are average performers as a whole, as long as they have one or more top performers in their portfolio of product offerings.

Product Innovation: There are three reasons why families may want to open new funds. First, a family may offer a new fund with a variation on an existing product line that may appeal to new investors. The characteristics of new funds should differ as much as possible from those of existing funds, both across families and within families (Mamaysky and Spiegel, 2002). Innovations does not necessarily increase market share. New funds may simply cannibalize existing funds in the family; either because of new funds appears to be a better investment option or because marketing efforts and allocations of shares with expected superior performance is directed to the new funds (Gaspar, Massa and Matos, 2006). Differentiating the new product offering from existing offerings is, therefore, an important consideration (Tirole, 2004). It is also possible that the introduction of additional funds create confusion in the minds of the potential customers, who may prefer to invest with a more focused family. The second reason why families may open new funds is not to be innovative per se but to increase the likelihood of having a top performing fund. Thirdly, marketing and distribution can reduce the search costs for potential investors and hence create an opportunity to increase market share.

Forms of Segmentation in Mutual Fund Industry

The concept of segmentation has already been discussed in this part can take many forms depending on desires of the mutual fund managers and various categories of investor:

Market Segmentation: Different segments of markets have different equations of their risk return parity, on the basis of which they take investment decisions. This parity depends on the differential preference for various investment attributes of financial products. Different attributes, an investor expect in a financial product are: liquidity, capital appreciation, safety of principal tax treatment, dividend or interest income, regulatory restrictions, time period for treatment, hedge against inflation etc.

Retail Segment: This segment portrays large number of participants but little individual volumes. It consists of Hindu Undivided Families and firms. It may be further sub divided into: (i) salaried class, (ii) retired people, (iii) businessmen and firms having occasional surpluses, (iv) HUFs for long term investment purpose. Similarly, the investment preference for urban and rural prospects would differ and, therefore, the strategies for taping this segment would differ on the basis of differential life style, value and ethics, social environment, media habits and nature of work. Broadly, this class requires security of the principal, liquidity and regular income more than capital appreciation. It lacks specialized investment skills in financial markets and highly susceptible to mob behavior. The marketing strategy involving indirect selling through agency network and creating awareness through appropriate media would be more effective in this segment.

Institutional Segment: This segment has less number of participants and large individual volumes. It consists of banks, public sector units, financial institutions, foreign institutional investors, insurance corporations, provident and pension funds. This class normally looks for more professional investment skills of the fund managers and expects a structured product than a readymade product. The tax features and regulatory restrictions are the vital considerations of their investment decisions. Each class of participants provides a niche to the managers in this segment.

Corporates: The investment needs of this segment are to park their occasional surplus that earns more return than what they have to pay on account of holding them. Alternatively, they also get surplus funds due to seasonality of business, which are getting due for payment within a year or a quarter or even a month. It offers a vast potential to specialized money market managers. Given the relaxation in regulatory guidelines, the fund's managers are expected to design the product suitable to this segment, at least to compete with bank deposits with more than 46 days. Thus, each segment and sub-segment having their own risk-return preferences forms niches in the market. The Indian fund managers are required to analyze in detail the intrinsic needs of the prospectus and design variety of suitable products for them.

2.5 Issues in Marketing of Mutual Funds

Financial products especially whose performance depends on the behavior of the market are quite different than any ordinary consumer product and, therefore, the marketing of them are also subtly different. A marketing manager of a typical consumer product may convince the prospective consumer by stating identifiable and measurable consistency of the performance in respect of attributes of the product like mutual funds, however professional and expert one is, can't make promises about future performance. The fund managers have to persuade the investor only by way of their past performance and assurances about their professional expertise. It is quite a complex activity than a marketing manager of a consumer product has to perform. What then the prospective investor expect when they hand over substantial amount of their hard earned money to the faceless fund managers[15]? What then these fund managers sell? They offer the hope of achieving desired returns on their investment. They offer professional investment services, which otherwise, investors would have to invest on their own. They are in the business of creating the conviction in the mind of the investors that they are better equipped with the specialized skills to invest their money. And the last but not the least, they offer good quality of services-this includes simple procedural formalities, timely and appropriately reporting of performance and timely remittance of returns on their investment. Thus, it is the reputation of integrity and good quality of services, the fund managers have to sell along with the investment characteristics of their products.

Funds' marketing strategies rely on investors' heterogeneity and limited information of investors. Fund category proliferation is one such tool to market the products of the fund management company. Basically, three externalities effect category proliferation namely – signaling[16], risk hedging and learning by doing. Moreover, price competition and product differentiation are both effective strategies for obtaining market share. Families that pass economies of scale to investors and those that charges lower fees than the competitor's gains market share. Families that perform better, offer a wide range of products and start more funds relative to competitors (a measure of innovation) also expect higher market share. Innovation is rewarded more if the new fund is more differentiated from existing offerings. Market share is the culmination of all the decisions made by fund families and the investors' response to that decision. It is the ultimate reflection of the choices made by investors, that is, revealed preferences of investors. Market share is an important variable, as the revenues of the fund family are function of assets under management. Hence, economies of scale and economies of scope matter, that is family size has an important implication for profitability.

Fund proliferation becomes an additional tool that can be used to limit competition and increase market coverage. If the fund family realizes that the level of performance it offers is much lower than that of its competitors and that it would be very costly to compete on the performance dimension alone, it will focus on other ways of attracting investors, such as reducing fees or increasing the number of funds within the family. It follows that performance-maximization is not necessarily the optimal strategy. In fact, the profit-maximizing mix of fees, performance, and number of funds could even involve a level of performance that would otherwise be defined as 'inferior' in a standard performance evaluation analysis.

Besides, larger firms have more means to spend on advertising. Huij and Verbeek (2007) find that funds with high marketing expenses generate spillovers and enhance cash inflows to family members with low marketing expenses.

2.6 Financial Firms as Corporations

Financial firms (Asset Management Firms here) are like modern corporations. As, with any corporation, agency problems may result in some exposition from the objectives set by investors, and such objectives will have a substantial impact on final outcome. Agency issues influence the observed outcomes. Given the continuous rating by various agencies, principal-agent issues are important as investors clearly wish to have the best managers handle their money. Investors have preferences over mutual fund types and how the industry will form to satisfy those preferences. The organization of such firms is like joint stock companies and most of the times they are also listed in the stock exchanges. Their existence is permanent irrespective of the movement of the managers. Moreover, there is separation between managers and owners. They have to seek the legal permissions before starting the business. And, varieties of disclosures are essential for such corporates.

Besides, there are concerns on the ability of mutual fund managers to outperform some benchmarks, and on the effects that such performance has on future fund flows. Portfolio managers follow a wide variety of approaches and adopt different criteria for stock selection –identifying under appreciating or cheap securities, seeking growth potential, or following past price trends. These corporations continue with almost all the strategies which are inherent to product producing firms. Hence, they are not less than modern corporations. Managerial and behavioral theories are equally relevant here.

2.7. Strategies of Fund Families

Since, fund families are supposed to play with multiplicity of risks; so, they collect variety of macro and micro information to formulate their strategies in order to reduce such risks. Fund families strive to spread their funds across a range of categories. This comes under the components of their strategies to generate comfortable returns for their investors. Sometimes they are able to generate excess returns and at others they may fumble on this account. So, fund families have important role to play in providing platform to their principals.

Here, an inquisitive question also arises about the existence of the fund families? Besides, why people frequently invest in several funds both within and across fund families? For, fund families, in equilibrium, offer to trade portfolios which are useful to investors who are concerned 'especially' with the economic information to which the fund families have access. The newly created fund families should provide trading strategies which are chiefly different from those of existing funds. At the fund family level, new funds should be created which allows investors to take advantage of the firm's research in new approaches. Another set of theory, in this regard, emerges from the fact of asset allocation decision made by funds. Also, investors should value funds that help them to time their entry into and out of particular parts of the market. Hence, we investors value a range of dynamic trading strategies offered by funds. One situation to look for this effect is in a fund's dynamic loading (or time varying betas) on economic risk factors (such as market portfolio). If a fund is engaged in market timing strategies, we should expect to find time variation in its loading on the market factors. It can be interpreted as time varying beta series for a given fund as a proxy for its dynamic trading strategies. The time varying betas are expected to be highly correlated for funds within the family; for, intra-family funds share a common signal from the family's research department. Across the families such correlation is, obviously, expected to be lower. As a fund family sets off, it should follow relatively a unique strategy. This means time varying betas of early funds within a given family should display particularly low correlation with the betas of funds offered by other families. Funds introduced early in the family exhibit lower time varying beta correlations with other funds than funds which are introduced later. It justifies the novelty of dynamics strategies of the newly created funds in the family.

The correlation of fund returns increases with fund age. That is, while funds' time varying beta correlations decrease with fund age, return correlation increases. If fund families simply seek to diversify their offerings, then we can expect decreasing return correlation between pairs of newer funds, but not increasing with beta correlations.

Degree of Family Focus: Some fund families focus on particular investment category along with some investment in other categories. This may be due to the fact that more focused families may have expertise in particular category/style or /and they may be able to enjoy economies of scale; hence, improve their market share in due course.

Active versus Passive Management: The active fund management involves fund manager's ability in terms of stock picking and correctly times the market. The level of 'portfolio turnover' is considered as a measure of actively managed fund. On the other hand, passive fund management does not involve the efficiency of the fund manager. These fund schemes follow a particular market index. The fund allocation to various stocks is according to the weight of that particular stock in the index. High portfolio turnover can be taken as positive; for, investors may consider it as better quality of fund management. The empirical research has established that high turnover equity funds have better selectivity and beat the performance of their respective benchmarks (Wermers, 2000; Cremers and Petajisto, 2009; Petajisto, 2010). However, others have favoured the passive fund management and rejected the fund managers' ability.

2.8 Business Groups (BGs) and Mutual Funds

There is sufficient evidence that large business houses with substantial market capital are also active as asset management companies (AMCs). Such characteristics of business firms have implications for the performance of mutual funds. The manager of such a BG fund is likely to have access to private information about firms that are owned by that BG as well as superior information of the industries in which these BG firms operate (Ghosh et.al., 2014).This information may emanate from the manager's personal knowledge or experience interacting with these BG firms and their industries; or the manager may be part of a social or professional network that includes managers from these BG firms and industries. If the manager, indeed, has this informational advantage, then she can use it to improve the wealth of her fund investors by generating superior returns to the BG fund it manages. She can either invest a larger portion of her assets under management (AUM), or a smaller portion, depending on whether she anticipates good or bad information on her group firms. Similarly, she can exploit informational advantage on industry prospects by over weighting or underweighting other firms that operate in the same industry as the BG firms. This informational advantage would imply that the fund would generate superior (appropriately risk-adjusted) returns by deviating from the investment levels of a typical fund.

On the other hand, the BG fund manager may also use the fund's assets to trade in her BG firms' stocks for selfish motives that may not essentially do well to the investors in her fund but rather help the management of the BG firm. The BG fund manager's opportunistic motives can arise for a variety of reasons including loyalty to her BG family or her own career concerns. The fund manager can take numerous actions that can benefit the management of the BG firm. For instance, the fund manager may overweight BG firms' stocks in her fund portfolio when the BG firm is to release adverse information in order to sustain the BG firm's stock price. If opportunistic motives exist, then overinvestment in BG firms (as compared to a typical mutual fund) by BG funds should result in inferior risk-adjusted performance to the disadvantage of the BG fund's investors.

It is possible that the BG fund manager may have societal rapport with the BG firm managers, or may have been recruited by the BG owner/managers, or her job may depend on stay in their good books. As an outcome of these associations, the BG fund manager may have the encouragement to carry out actions that are more in the interest of the BG firms than fund investors.

Given their repute, recognition and financial strength, business groups are probable owners of asset management companies. To the extent that new equity investors seek "names they trust", regulations allowing a strong business group presence in the asset management industry could quicken financial development and economic growth in emerging markets. One important potential risk, however, of business groups in the asset management industry is that business group mutual fund managers have access to a large amount of proprietary information emanating from other divisions within the group. If there is a perception that business-group fund managers use non-public information in their trading decisions, the presence of business groups in the asset management industry could potentially slow the development of financial markets.

Such diversified conglomerates (BGs), can demonstrate spillovers across the various business segments (Sialm & Tham, 2012). Also, studying the spillovers in mutual fund management companies may help to better understand the industrial organization of diversified conglomerates.

Offering mutual funds as part of a financial conglomerate has advantages because the mutual fund segment can benefit from synergies, information spillovers, diversification, economies of scope, and easier access to capital markets.

However, conglomerates have more complicated and less transparent structures and might aggravate agency problems. In addition, the corporate financial literature has indicated that financially distressed firms might lose their customers and employees. Therefore, such segments in the business conglomerates are protected and spillover effects are oblivious here.

2.9 Mutual Funds and Stock Market

Is there any relationship between the inflow and outflow of fund from mutual funds with the stock market prices movements? For, large part of their funds is invested in equity market and some consequences are obvious. However, in an efficient market, changes in stock prices should be compatible to the macroeconomic fundamentals of the economy. Therefore, stock market prices may drift away from fundamental equilibrium[17] value for a short period of time, but such digression can be expected to be random and short-lived. Thus, flows into or out of mutual funds, no matter how large, should arguably have no effect on equilibrium asset prices. Hence, in the absence of changes in economic fundamentals, it is logical to consider that buying or selling by mutual fund investors will not affect stock prices (Edward & Zhang, 1998); as, such demands will quickly be met by selling or buying on the part of other more knowledgeable investors.

Others have diametrically opposite view on markets and states that 'equity mutual funds' flow can affect stock prices (Wyatt, 1996; McGough, 1997). Finance theory makes available two possibilities. The first may be described as the 'informed traders' theory. In particular, if mutual fund investors can be viewed as being especially smart or well informed investors, their purchases and sales might be seen as revealing information about economic fundamentals to less informed investors, who in turn then trade in the same direction as the mutual fund investors. Thus, increased purchases (sales) by equity mutual funds may signal that current stock prices are below (above) fundamental values, resulting in all investors trading in the same direction as equity mutual fund investors and causing stock prices to rise (fall). This behaviour would also result in a positive correlation between net equity fund flows and stock returns.

Another theory of why mutual fund flows might affect stock prices is the 'noise traders' theory of De Long, et.al. (1990). The central point of the theory is existence of the significant body of 'noise' traders (or investors) who are largely uninformed and behave "irrationally". Noise traders are epitomized as investors who erroneously believe that they have the special information about the future stock prices and as a consequence buy and sell stocks in erratic ways. They may, for example, overestimate expected stock returns and demand more stocks, or under-estimate expected stock returns and demand fewer stocks, causing stock prices to rise or fall in a random or unpredictable way. The contribution of noise trader theory is to provide a framework to explain why, in the face of such irrational buying or selling, arbitrage by informed investors may fail to keep asset prices from being affected by the actions of noise traders. Why do not the actions of noise traders create profitable trade opportunities for informed traders to trade against the irrational noise traders, thereby preventing prices staying very far from fundamental values? An essential element of noise traders' theory is that the unpredictability of noise traders' beliefs and actions creates another price risk that deters rational investors from betting too heavily against them.

The investment behavior of mutual fund shareholders could, in theory, influence equity market prices. Mutual fund investors could also distort equity prices if their enthusiasm for investing in mutual funds were to go beyond general market assessments of fundamentals and tolerance for risk, pushing equity prices temporarily above the level that other equity market participants would tend to settle on. If fund shareholders were to request large redemptions from their accounts when faced with a sharp decline in equity prices, mutual fund managers might be forced to sell some of the funds' equity holdings in the slumping market, aggravate the decline.

2.10 Mutual Funds' Investment Styles

Many vital investment decisions are usually delegated to professional investment managers by investors. Portfolio managers, however, follow range of approaches and adopt different criteria for stock selection-identifying underappreciated or cheap securities, seeking growth potential, or following past price trends.

The variety of styles followed by fund managers raises two broad questions. The first concern is the 'nature of the product' that professionally managed funds delivers. A fund's stated objective, such as growth, income or balanced, historically served as a limited form of product differentiation. These descriptions are generally too vague to be very informative. The second question related to managers' personal career considerations may lead them to alter their behaviour and adopt approaches that are more in favour with investors and financial consultants, with possibly adverse consequences for fund performance.

The style categories are based on two dimensions - market capitalization (size) and value growth orientation (value). Given the large amount of money that is allocated on the basis of the size-value style classification, it is important to evaluate whether it provides a meaning to fund managers' behaviour.

Fund's preference for one investment style over another (due to behaviour or agency reasons) may affect the structure of asset prices. 'Size of the fund' (stocks' equity market capitalization and 'value' (book to market value of equity) are considered as two important style dimensions. Investment managers, generally, break the domestic investment universe into classes based on large capitalization value stocks and small capitalization value stocks. The distribution of net fund assets by firm size, book to market, past performance in recent years and most recent years are the basic characteristics of mutual fund portfolios.

2.11 Does the Mutual Fund firm's Size Matters?

Optimum size of the firm is an important component of theoretical business organization. It has considerable bearing on the performance of the firm. Mutual fund firms are expected to be performing in a similar manner so far as the size of the firm is concerned. Better performing firms are expected to get more clients in future and justify the common thinking that past performance determines the future outcomes. Expense ratios and management fees decline with size and success, with the top-performing funds decrease fees and the poor-performing funds increase fees. This makes sense, since management fee schedules normally decline with size and administrative costs have a large fixed component. However, Berk and Green (2004) have made a strong theoretical argument for why past performance should not predict future performance. There are two possible economic explanations that are consistent with their model: increasing expenses or increase in size following good performance along with diseconomies of scale. The other possible way that predictability might disappear is for funds to grow with good performance and for diseconomies of scale to erode performance (Chen et.al. 2004). If this is true, then we should see no predictability when funds get larger. Hence, it can be concluded here that economies and diseconomies of scale are equally relevant here.

2.12 Incentives to Generate Alpha[18]

The mutual fund literature characteristically assumes that retail funds compete for homogenous investors within a single market. However, in reality, market for retail funds is segmented, catering to distinct clienteles. It has been recognized that different funds compete for different types of investors and it also sheds light on the underperformance of actively managed funds. It has been established in the literature (Christoffersen, Evans, and Musto, 2012) that retail mutual funds sold through intermediaries, or brokers face a weaker incentive to generate alpha than mutual funds sold directly to retail investors, and that this disincentive helps to explain the underperformance of the average actively managed fund. The mutual fund families will spend resources to generate alpha only to the level that they expect the investments to increase investors' flow. The lower the expected benefits associated with investing in active management-investors flows are less responsive to alpha-the weaker the incentive to do so.

The retail mutual funds can be classified as providing unbundled[19] portfolio management services, or packaged bundle[20] of portfolio management and investment advice. These two types of funds target at different types of investors. Investors use the services of advisers as they need help with asset allocation decisions and want a financial professional to explain various investment options and because it gives them peace of mind about their investments. Differences in investor preferences and experiences across the direct-sold and broker-sold market segments have important implications for the nature of competition within each segment. Specifically, we expect competition in the broker-sold segment to focus much less on risk adjusted returns, thereby reducing the incentives for broker-sold funds to expend resources to generate alpha (Guercio & Reuter, 2013).

2.13   The Behaviour of Mutual Fund Investors

The mutual fund investors behave differently in different circumstances. They give considerable weight to the past performance of the mutual fund schemes. They consider that recent performance is representative of a fund's future prospects. It has been established in the performance of mutual fund literature that past performance is important in determining the future performance (Goetzmann and Peles, 1997; Capon, Fitzsimons, and Prince, 1996). In contrast, it has also been established that when the investor redeem the mutual fund units, they have the tendency to hold the low performing units for longer period and redeem the better performing scheme units (Shefrin and Statman, 1985) and the role of past performance as an indicator of future performance takes the back seat (Odean, 1998; Grinblatt and Keloharju, 2000). The investors hold the losers in the hope that such funds would improve their performance in due course and units can be redeemed accordingly.

A particular investor may benefit from chasing past performance, but investors in aggregate do not. If investors overestimate their ability to identify superior funds based on past performance, this will lead to over-investment in active management. Performance chasing pours more money into funds with high expense ratios and high turnover. Expense ratios are a drain on investors' returns; in addition to accelerating capital gains taxes, high turnover increases trading costs.

2.14 Efficiency of Mutual Funds

The specifications of efficiency conditions in mutual fund industry have changed overtime and more importantly over past two and half decades. During the period of first generation mutual fund papers, the efficient market theory (EMT) was in its infancy and it was generally stressed that EMT meant that stock prices reflect all available information (Fama, 1970). Within this framework, mutual funds through research, innovations and trading cannot improve on this information and are destined to lose money as they expend resources with no possibility of beating a 'fully efficient' market.

If information is expensive to attain and difficult to put into operation, full information equilibrium makes it impossible for the market to compensate information gathering activity. Infact, equilibrium cannot be characterized by prices that reflect all available information. In some sense, a 'fewness' condition on the number of informed traders is required to generate a wedge between trade prices and full information prices. This wedge must be sufficient to compensate the market arbitrage function (Grossman, 1976). Hence, passive investors essentially pay informed traders a sufficient amount to pay for information gathering activity. Informed traders 'beat the market' before expenses but make no excess returns after netting out the expense of gathering information. Thus, in equilibrium, there is no incentive to favour either an actively managed fund or a passive index fund.

2.15 Optimal Attention Allocation of Investment Managers

Do investment managers add value for their clients? The answer to this query matters for issues ranging from the discussion of market efficiency to practical portfolio advice for households. The large amount of randomness in financial asset returns makes it a difficult question to answer. The multi-billion investment management business is first and foremost an information-processing business. The investment managers not only as agents making optimal portfolio decisions, but also as human beings with finite mental capacity (attention), who optimally allocate that scarce capacity to process information at each point in time. Since the optimal attention allocation varies with the state of the economy, so do investment strategies and fund returns. As long as a subset of skilled investment managers can process information about future asset payoffs, a higher covariance of portfolio holdings with aggregate asset payoff shocks, more cross-sectional dispersion in portfolio investment strategies and returns across funds, and a higher average outperformance in recessions (Kacperczyk et.al., 2014) . Beyond the mutual fund industry, a sizeable fraction of GDP currently comes from industries that produce and process information (consulting, business management, product design, marketing analysis, accounting, rating agencies, equity analysts, etc.). Ever increasing access to information has made the problem of how to best allocate a limited amount of information-processing capacity ever more relevant. While information choices have consequences for real outcomes, they are often poorly understood because they are difficult to measure. By predicting how information choices are linked to observable variables (such as the state of the economy) and by tying information choices to real outcomes (such as portfolio investment), we show how models of information choices can be brought to the data. This information-choice-based approach could be useful in examining other information-processing sectors of the economy.

Fund managers due to their information processing skill; choose to what information to process in different states of business cycle. They optimally choose to process information about aggregate shocks in recessions and idiosyncratic shocks in booms.

A fraction of investment managers have skill. These skilled managers can observe a fixed number of signals about asset payoffs and choose what fraction of those signals will contain aggregate versus stock-specific information. The aggregate signals as macroeconomic data that affect future cash flows of all firms and of stock-specific signals as firm-level data that forecast the part of firms' future cash flows that is independent of the aggregate shocks. Based on their signals, skilled managers form portfolios, choosing larger portfolio weights for assets that are more likely to have high returns.

Optimal allocation based on the business cycle macro perspectives can be represented as - in recessions, more volatile aggregate shocks should draw more attention, because it is more valuable to pay attention to more uncertain outcomes. The elevated price of risk amplifies this re-allocation; for, aggregate shocks affect a large fraction of the portfolio's value, paying attention to aggregate shocks resolves more portfolio risk than learning about stock-specific risks. When the price of risk is high, such risk-minimizing attention choices become more valuable. While the idea that it is more valuable to shift attention to more volatile shocks is straightforward, whether changes in the price of risk would amplify or counteract this effect is not obvious.

Since recessions are times when large aggregate shocks to asset payoffs create more co-movement in asset payoffs, passive portfolios would have returns that also co-move more in recessions, which would imply less dispersion. In contrast, when investment managers learn about asset payoffs and manage their portfolios according to what they learn, fund returns co-move less and dispersion increases in recessions. One reason is that when aggregate shocks become more volatile, managers who learn about aggregate shocks put less weight on their common prior beliefs, which have less predictive power, and more weight on their heterogeneous signals. This generates more heterogeneous beliefs in recessions and therefore more heterogeneous investment strategies and fund returns. The other reason is that a higher price of risk induces managers to take less risk, which makes prices less informative. Like prior beliefs, information in prices is common information. When prices contain less information, this common information is weighted less and heterogeneous signals are weighted more, resulting in more heterogeneous portfolio returns.

Since the average fund can only outperform the market if there are other, non-fund investors who underperform along with taking into consideration the skilled and non skilled managers. Both the heightened uncertainty about asset payoffs and the elevated price of bearing risk in recessions make information more valuable. Therefore, the informational advantage of the skilled over the unskilled increases and generates higher returns for informed managers. The average fund's outperformance rises.

2.16   Risk Shifting

A rational investor who faces the classic trade-off between risk and expected return would seek to maximize return relative to his or her level of risk aversion. Among funds and fund managers there exist many investment strategies that over time have led to different returns through taking positions on different risk levels. The level of risk in mutual funds are of importance to investors as they want to know what return they can expect and for how large losses they have to be prepared for.

In the mutual fund industry, a fund manager is in a position to manipulate the performance, the characteristics or other factors related to the fund, in order to gain benefits or to prevent job loss. An agency conflict exists between investors and managers. This creates incentives for the fund company to adjust risk levels to increase inflow of new capital. Chevalier and Ellison (1997), Khorana (2001) and Khorana (1996) find evidence of strategic risk shifting in fund portfolios prior to manager replacement, and also that returns improve when underperforming managers are replaced. Kempf, Ruenzia and Thielea (2009) use bull / bear market as a proxy for when manager employment risk is more important than incentives and show that low (high) employment risk make underperforming fund managers increase (decrease) risk to catch up with outperformers and prevent job loss.

Compared to funds that keep stable risk levels over time, the funds that shift risk significantly are, generally, smaller in terms of managed assets, younger and they charge higher expense rates. These tangible characteristics are observable to a private investor, but the degree of risk shifting is not, implying that there a problem for individual investors who cannot draw conclusions on performance without making an assessment of the fund managers risk shifting preferences (Gustavsson & Riben, 2012). Thus, there exists a principal-agent problem since the fund manager knows if the fund increases or decreases risk while the principal investor does not. Increasing risk is always hazardous as it is associated with both lower and higher realized returns.

2.17   Corporate Governance in Mutual Funds

Corporate ethics, corporate transparency as well as corporate accountability are considered as major components of corporate governance. Mutual Fund Company is also, as already stated, a corporate entity and the fundamental objective of corporate governance is the enhancement of shareholders' wealth, the approach and instruments are quite different in different regions. The US, the country with the utmost degree of social respect for corporate governance and the responsibilities it involves, embraces a soft approach to minimize the conflict between the owners (investors) and the manager. This includes giving financial incentives (stock options) to the investors. Stock exchanges (through listing conditions) play an important role in imparting transparency and accountability to the activities of the corporate managers. In order to inculcate transparency, insider-trading illegally prohibited and disclosure norms have been made an essential part of corporate governance in the US. The approach is, thus, basically market oriented.

On the other hand, in Germany, corporate governance is implemented through interactions and consensus between the management and supervisory boards. Banks play an important role in the market because of their role as holders of company stocks and providers of long term finance. The banks are run by supervisory and management boards. While the supervisory board is responsible for the company's accounts, major capital expenditure, strategic acquisitions and closures, dividends and most importantly, appointments of the management board, the management board is responsible for the company. In Japan, the basic approach centers on the concept of obligation to the company, country and family. It is implemented through cross-holding and networking among group companies, and there is less focus on the boards. Corporate governance in Japan is more concerned about all out appreciation of the value of the Yen, the promotion of the entrepreneurial and innovative talents of the people for the development of the society, and the best means of making them accountable. Financial institutions play a pivotal role in promoting and sustaining the growth and development of the economy. We have already mentioned the recent trends towards disintermediation and the fact that the leading role of the banks is being overtaken by other financial institutions, like mutual funds, pension funds, insurance and investment banking, broking houses. The focus is on financing led by the capital market instead of bank finance. The shareholders of financial institutions are large in number than those of manufacturing companies. Financial institutions, in addition to enhancing the shareholders value to increase the wealth of the depositor investors, who are the core of their business activities. Moreover, the activities of a financial institution are having a wider spread and a failure of any kind of institutions is a collapse in the entire economy. Therefore, corporate governance is more important for such institutions, not only in the interest of the shareholders, investors/ depositors and other stock holders, but also in the greater interest of the national economy. The economic influence of Mutual Funds can be seen from the fact that about 30 percent of the investors fall within the low income group. The existence of large number of unit holders, with a very high percentage belonging to the low and medium income groups, speaks of efficiency, transparency and accountability in fund management.

Indian Mutual Funds are regulated by SEBI whose regulations are quite comprehensive and qualitatively better than many other countries. Thus, they have an implicit bias towards the SEC Regulations. Many of the recommendations of the Kumar Mangalam Committee (1999) for establishing the practice of corporate governance in India are already incorporated in the SEBI's Regulations, i.e. the responsibility of the trustee/ board of directors of AMC, norms for disclosure, formation of an audit committee and so on. Apart from these the guidelines on accounting policy, advertisement, investment restrictions, frequency of disclosure, formation of a valuation committee, etc., are aimed at protecting the investors and providing checks and balances for managers. These measures have an explicit as well as implicit bearing on corporate governance. Mutual funds are expected to enhance the wealth of the investors by investing the money they have mobilized. It is the prudence and appropriateness of the investment and asset allocation strategies which influence the returns from the money invested in mutual funds. Therefore, the AMC and trustees must see to it that appropriate investment strategies are developed and implemented to ensure safety and growth of investments.

Corporate governance plays a key role in keeping the fund manager alert and industrious about protecting the interests of the investors. Responsible corporate governance in a mutual fund ensures that the right type of strategy or a combination of strategies are developed before the funds of any schemes are invested, keeping in view the declared objectives of the fund (short term, medium term and long term). The basic pre-requisite for responsible corporate governance in the context of mutual funds is ability, responsibility, accountability and transparency. The various regulatory measures initiated by SEBI have undoubtedly put in place a well-defined corporate governance mechanism for Indian Mutual Funds. Many, of course, term it as 'policing by the regulator'. However, the basic thrust of Indian regulation is regulation through control, similar to the model adopted by the US and unlike the UK model of regulation through SROs. Apart from the nature of regulation, it must be admitted that SEBI has laid the foundation of a well-conceived corporate governance mechanism, which needs to be implemented in the true spirit by the entities involved in the management and supervision of the funds. The mutual funds are the managers while the investors are the true owners, who have placed their faith in the management of the funds. Therefore, the managers must be sensitive to the considerations and vulnerability of the investors. It is true that SEBI is there to monitor the regulations, but their real implementations also require the active participation of the investors, owners and the other stake- holders like registrars, bankers and brokers. The active involvement of these entities would not only eliminate the scope of diversion of the fund managers' objectives and functions as per the goal of the funds, but would also help the managers/supervisors achieve the fund's objective and create value for it.

2.18   Career Concerns of Mutual Fund Managers

Since, mutual fund management firms are like corporates, and there is separation between the owners and managers. Hence, it is obvious, that managers are concerned about their career progress and security of job.

Therefore, he might be striving to make a balance between performance and his own job security. In this context, he may take decisions that are in favour of his career and may distort the portfolio holding. Job security is more concern of the younger managers as compared to seniors. Hence, they are not inclined to take risky decisions which may put their job in danger. It is considered that 'termination' is more performance-sensitive for younger managers. There are possible implicit incentives created by the termination-performance relationship. The shape of the termination-performance relationship may give younger managers an incentive to avoid unsystematic risk (Chevalier, 1999). Direct effects of portfolio composition may also give younger managers an incentive to "herd" into popular sectors. Hence, younger managers are expected to hold less unsystematic risk and have more conventional portfolios.

In the theory literature, the idea that manager's behavior might be influenced by career concerns was introduced by Fama (1980) and Lazear and Rosen (1981) who focused on how career concerns might solve agency problems. Holmstrom (1982) analyzed the nature of career concerns which arise when a competitive labor market is trying to learn about managers' abilities. He noted that, while career concerns can overcome agency problems in particular cases, a number of distortions typically remain. For instance, managers may exert excessive effort when young and slack off when old. A number of more recent papers have followed Holmstrom in looking at the types of distortions which career concerns may induce when managers make investment decisions, select between projects, etc. Of late, particular interest has centered on whether career concerns may lead to herd behavior (Scharfstein and Stein, 1990; Zwiebel, 1995; Prendergast and Stole, 1996).

Examining the determinants of termination in some more detail, for young managers, the probability of termination is a convex function of performance. Specially, the probability of termination decreases steeply with performance when managers have negative excess returns, but it is fairly insensitive to differences at positive excess return levels. As a result, young managers may have an incentive to avoid unsystematic risk when selecting their portfolios. Young manager is more likely to be terminated if his fund's sector weightings or unsystematic risk[21] level

54

deviates considerably from the mean of the fund's objective group. Young managers may, thus, have an incentive to herd, as has been suggested in the theoretical literature. Desire to avoid termination is one of the incentives a manager faces. Managers may also have explicit incentive contracts and may be concerned about possible promotions.

2.19 Management Structure and Risk

Investors select their mutual fund objectives based on specific risk tolerances and time horizons. But how can ingenuous investors be familiar with whether they are exposed to the appropriate level of risks for a given level of expected return. A portfolio manager's selection of securities should be consistent with the mutual fund's investment objective, which is stated in the fund's prospectus. In the mutual fund literature, several studies documented that mutual funds tend to be misclassified. This misclassification[22] has resulted in increased risk exposure for fund shareholders without the appropriate risk adjusted returns. Kim et al. (2000) shows that, on average, about half of the mutual funds land on the same groups as the stated objectives. That is, misclassification of portfolio is very common in contravention to objectives of the fund schemes.

Various points of view can be made for such misclassification. Since investors are attracted to funds with high historical performance and the actual investing activities are not observable by investors, fund managers tend to increase their performance by investing in high return securities. Besides, misclassification can be a marketing tactic. Chan et al. (2002) studied mutual fund style consistency. They propose that mutual fund style drift can be caused by non-performance distortions caused by behavioral and agent reasons. A fund manager might attempt to time the performance benchmark, recover from previous loss, or follow the herd to imitate funds with successful strategies. They find that style shifting is related to poor performance, especially for the value funds. Walter and Weber (2006) find the herding behavior of mutual fund managers in Germany. Besides, it is expected, fund's risk can be spilled over to other funds managed under the same fund manager which makes a mutual fund's actual objective deviate from the stated one. When fund managers manage multiple funds simultaneously, the risk of one of the managed funds is significantly increased, minimizing the inherit benefits of mutual fund stock diversification. Thus, all else equal, the more time that a manager devotes to an individual fund the more likely the fund will reduce its risk exposure (Bryant & Chen Liu, 2009). This increased risk exposure of the multiple management structure results in fund misclassification.

Depending on the fund manager's risk appetite, if the manager is more risk-oriented, the conservative fund would tend to behave more like an aggressive fund. On the other hand, if the manager is more risk averse, the aggressive fund would behave more like a conservative one. At any rate, this management style deviates from the investors risk preference as requested by the selected mutual fund objective.

Mutual fund complexes employ a simultaneous fund management structure to (a) utilize the management skills across multiple funds and (b) to minimize fund expenses. This management structure has mixed implications regarding whether managers of multiple funds will provide superior service to investors and, therefore adds to shareholder value. Besides, the multiple fund management system reduces costs due to economies of scale (Kwan and Laderman, 1999).

2.20   How Funds Add Value?

A section of investment managers have skill. These skilled managers can monitor a fixed number of signals about asset pay offs and choose what fraction of those signals will contain aggregate versus stock specific information. We think of aggregate signals as macroeconomic data that affect future cash flows of all firms, and of stock-specific signals as firm-level data that forecast the part of firms' future cash flows that is independent of aggregate shocks. Based on their signals, skilled managers form portfolios, choosing larger portfolio weights for assets that are more likely to have high returns.

The volatility and risk affect attention allocation, portfolio dispersion, and portfolio returns. Attention should be reallocated over the business cycle. In the recession, more volatile aggregate shocks should draw more attention, because it is more valuable to pay attention to more uncertain outcomes. The increased price risk strengthens this reallocation.

The higher price risk induces managers to take less risk, which makes prices less informative. When prices contain less information, this common information is less and heterogeneous signals are weighted more, resulting in more heterogeneous portfolio returns. Since the average fund can only outperform the market if there are other, non-fund investors who under-perform it may also include unskilled non-fund investors. In recessions, funds hold portfolios that differ more from one another. As a result, their cross-sectional return dispersion increases, consistent with the theory. How do funds go about adding value for investors? One strand of the literature focuses on changes in fund performance that arise when fund managers change. Risk factors, portfolio choice and dispersion, information updating, skill of investors, and general economic environment are the factors that determine the level of value that mutual funds add.

2.21 Mutual Funds as a Source of Finance Capitalism

Finance capital in any economy has considerable implications for the real sector of the economy. Sometimes, it may be able to distort the important macroeconomic variables in the economy. For example, in USA, mutual funds, as a group, hold about 30 percent of corporate ownership. Moreover, the industry's assets are highly concentrated in a few institutions. Mutual funds have discretion over buying, selling, and voting corporate equities, giving some of them the potential to exercise influence over large network of corporate USA. This is a concentration of corporate ownership in a few hands not seen since the early days of finance capitalism. Consequently, some reflections in the other markets of the economy are obvious consequences.

Level of participation in the stock market from the household has increased dramatically in almost all developing and less developing economies. Several reasons can be cited for such trends. Bank savings accounts lost their attraction as the interest rates fall short to keep pace with inflation. Financial innovations such as money market accounts and mutual funds, typically invested in corporate and government bonds, provided a more appealing outlet for savings and introduced savers to mutual funds. In addition, the transaction costs for equity mutual funds declined substantially. Duca (2001) documents a strong correlation between declining transaction costs and levels of household investment in mutual funds. The tax laws favoured the creation of private retirement accounts and corporate employees increasingly replaced defined benefit plans with defined contribution plans. These plans are ultimately owned by the employees, not employer, making them transferable when workers change jobs. The most common plans offer employees a set of five to ten mutual funds as options, and well known funds are particularly popular choices.

2.22 The Sum Up

Mutual Funds are special type of 'institutional device' or 'investment vehicle' through which investors' savings are pooled and invested under the supervision of experts in wide variety of portfolios at minimum possible risk. Such institutions can generate several under-currents in the macroeconomic environment of an economy; nevertheless, such impacts likely to be different for developed and less developed countries. Typical investors are concerned about the yield, liquidity and security of their capital. These asset management firms are capable, to large extent, satisfy such issues.

To tap the vast potential of domestic savings and need to deploy efficiently of such funds has emerged remarkably. Mutual funds are deemed as best suited for this purpose and also capable of meeting this challenge. Risk sharing characteristic of mutual funds make them more popular among investors. These institutions trade in a variety of instruments with divergent amount of risk. Therefore, they are able, to large extent, to hedge the risks involved. Investors differ in the type of risk they are willing to face, thus, hold opposing views in the investment strategies they prefer.

Risk appetite of every investor is different, he may either be risk averse (conservative investor) or risk taker (aggressive investor), given the psychology of investor and aspiration for superior returns. Accordingly, mutual funds are capable to launch schemes appropriate to almost every segment of investor. Investors, generally, strive to undergo calculated risk that makes the best combination of risks and returns.

Mutual fund industry is market for the services instead of the physical products. Moreover, it comes under the category of experienced good instead of making advance judgment of the product before buying it. Funds are considered as heterogeneous products, differentiated in terms not only of fund-specific characteristics but also of family specific ones.

The choice among alternative strategies depends on both the structure of the market and its degree of competitiveness. In particular, the level of performance of a fund will be negatively related to the degree of product differentiation in the category the fund is in, measured as the dispersion in the 'services' (fees, performance) that the competing funds offer. If families are able to differentiate themselves in terms of non-performance-related characteristics (e.g., a higher degree of fee differentiation), they have less need to compete in terms of performance.

The organization of such firms is like joint stock companies and most of the times they are also listed in the stock exchanges. Their existence is permanent irrespective of the movement of the managers. Moreover, there is separation between managers and owners. There exists a significant degree of heterogeneity in both the total number of funds and the types of funds offered by fund families. Some families are extremely focused in terms of the types of funds offered whereas other families compete by offering plethora of funds in different investment goals. Fund families diversify across investment styles to enhance investors' welfare.

Large business houses with substantial market capital are also active as asset management companies (AMCs). Such characteristics of business firms have implications for the performance of mutual funds. The manager of such a BG fund is likely to have access to private information about firms that are owned by that BG as well as superior information of the industries in which these BG firms operate. She can either invest a larger portion of her assets under management (AUM), or a smaller portion, depending on whether she anticipates good or bad information on her group firms.

Similarly, she can exploit informational advantage on industry prospects by over weighting or under weighting other firms that operate in the same industry as the BG firms. This informational advantage would imply that the fund would generate superior (appropriately risk-adjusted) returns by deviating from the investment levels of a typical fund.

In an efficient market, changes in stock prices should be compatible to the macroeconomic fundamentals of the economy. Therefore, stock market prices may drift away from fundamental equilibrium value for a short period of time, but such digression can be expected to be random and short-lived. Thus, flows into or out of mutual funds, no matter how large, should arguably have no effect on equilibrium asset prices. However, if mutual fund investors can be viewed as being especially smart or well informed investors, their purchases and sales might be seen as revealing information about economic fundamentals to less informed investors, who in turn then trade in the same direction as the mutual fund investors. Thus, increased purchases (sales) by equity mutual funds may signal that current stock prices are below (above) fundamental values, resulting in all investors trading in the same direction as equity mutual fund investors and causing stock prices to rise (fall). This behaviour would also result in a positive correlation between net equity fund flows and stock returns.

The perplexing variety of styles followed by fund managers raises two broad questions. The first concern is the 'nature of the product' that professionally managed funds delivers. A fund's stated objective, such as growth, income or balanced, historically served as a limited form of product differentiation. The style categories are based on two dimensions - market capitalization (size) and value growth orientation (value).

Investors consider it as right that recent performance is markedly representative of a fund's future prospects. Thus, investors largely chase past performance. In contrast, when redeeming mutual funds, the disposition effect - the tendency to hold losers too long and sell winners too soon - dominates investors' decisions. When redeeming mutual funds, investors do not behave as though past returns predict the future. Hence, mutual fund investors hold their losers and sell their winners.

The multi-billion investment management business is first and foremost an information-processing business. The investment managers not only as agents making optimal portfolio decisions, but also as human beings with finite mental capacity (attention), who optimally allocate that scarce capacity to process information at each point in time.

Since the optimal attention allocation varies with the state of the economy, so do investment strategies and fund returns. As long as a subset of skilled investment managers can process information about future asset payoffs, a higher co-variance of portfolio holdings with aggregate asset payoff shocks, more cross-sectional dispersion in portfolio investment strategies and returns across funds, and a higher average outperformance in recessions. Fund managers due to their information processing skill; choose to that information to process in different states of business cycle. They optimally choose to process information about aggregate shocks in recessions and idiosyncratic shocks in booms.

A rational investor who faces the classic trade-off between risk and expected return would seek to maximize return relative to his or her level of risk aversion. Among funds and fund managers there exists many investment strategies that over time have led to different returns through taking positions on different risk levels. The level of risk in mutual funds are of importance to investors as they want to know what return they can expect and for how large losses they have to be prepared for.

Besides, managers are concerned about their career progress and security of job. Therefore, he might be striving to make a balance between performance and his own job security. In this context, he may take decisions that are in favour of his career and may distort the portfolio holding. Job security is more concern of the younger managers as compared to seniors. Hence, they are not inclined to take risky decisions which may put their job in danger.

The emergence of mutual fund industry has given a scope for the development of new form of finance capital. The industry's assets are highly concentrated in a few institutions. Mutual funds have discretion over buying, selling, and voting corporate equities, giving some of them the potential to exercise influence over large network of corporate. This is a concentration of corporate ownership in a few hands. Consequently, some reflections in the other markets of the economy are obvious consequences.

Notes

1. A 'small investor' is an individual who invests in small quantities of securities and bonds, also known as retail investors. The group of investors makes up a minimal fraction of total stock ownership. They are, unlike institutional investors, are not much influential to change the operation of the market.

2. 'Investment portfolio' is a pool of different investments where an investor invests to make profit or income while protecting the principal (invested) amount. These investments are, generally chosen, on the basis of risk reward combinations and the risk appetite of the investors. It may range from 'low risk, low yield' to high risk high yield' ones; or on the basis of different types of income streams: steady but fixed or variable with potential for growth. The monetary value of each asset may influence the risk-reward ratio of the portfolio and is referred to as the asset allocation of the portfolio.

3. An economic system is a system of production and exchange of goods and services as well as the allocation of resources in a society. It comprises the arrangement of the various institutions, agencies and consumers that consists of the economic structure of a given community. Besides, how these agencies and institutions are interconnected and way information flow among them. In addition, type of social relations establishes between them. The major formats of economic systems present are capitalism, redundant socialism and mixed - the most prevalent. Alternatively, they are distinguished on the basis of production forces and production relations.

4. This is basically quantification of level of financial risk that an investor is exposed to over a specific time frame. The amount of potential loss, the probability of loss and the time frame are three components used to measure the 'value at risk'. By using this measure, risk manager endeavours to ensure that risks are not taken beyond the level at which the firm can absorb the losses of a probable worst outcome.

5. The mutual funds are now available in multiplicity of categories depending on the risk exposures and risk bearing capacity of the investors. Moreover, in recent decades fund flows in such investment vehicles have increased by leaps and bounds in all over the world.

6. This is the capability of the fund manager to select the portfolio in such a manner that it can beat the returns of the relevant benchmark. Besides, he is able to time the market movement, that is, the time to enter into the market and quit from the market to take full advantage of the volatility and movement of the markets.

7. Earnings of investors from mutual funds in the form of dividends or/and capital gains are automatically reinvested, as directed by the investor. It helps the investor to build large corpus. In the globalised world, asset management companies can now explore and exploit the best investment opportunities emerge in the international market in the category of portfolio investment. In such a way, returns of the investors, who are willing to diversify their investments in the international market' can maximize their returns.

8. This is a situation, when macro economic variables are in sync with one another. And possibility of deflationary and inflationary impulses is bleak and economy move steadily.

9. The diversification of portfolio is a risk management technique that combines a wide variety of investments. It strives to smooth out unsystematic risk events in a portfolio so that the positive performance of some investments will neutralize the negative performance of others. Such benefit can be captured if different investments are not perfectly correlated.

10. Securitization is a process through which the illiquid assets are transformed into securities. That is, financial benefits of illiquid assets can be taken as liquid assets. Asset Backed Securities are important examples of such process.

11. This is high content of debt in total assets of the business concern. Sometimes, may be unsustainable when the earning from the borrowed funds is less than the interest payment. The business concern may go into bankruptcy.

12. Risk taken is calculated if the probability of the failure of the project undertaken has been estimated in advance and factored in the final

decision. Many business operators need to take a calculated risk to expand their business activities into a new competitive arena.

13. Quality of the product cannot be judged without using it.
14. Investor is not in direct contact with fund manager.
15. The agent (mutual fund here) credibly conveys some information about its credentionals to the principal (investor here).
16. Macro economic variables are in sync with one another and provide the stability in the economy.
17. The excess return of the fund relative to the return of the benchmark index is a fund's alpha, especially in the CAPM.
18. Unbundled portfolio management services are provided according to the objective of the investors. Unbundling is done for a variety of reason, but the goal is always to create a better performing company or companies.
19. Several funds are managed simultaneously for the investor.
20. Such risk is fund specific.
21. When some or large portion of investments are not according to the targeted objectives.

References

- Allen F. and Gorton G. (1993), "Churning Bubbles", *Review of Economic Studies*, 60 (4), 813-836.
- Ang J. and Lin W. (2001), "A Fundamental Approach to Estimating Economies of Scale and Scope of Financial Products: The Case of Mutual Funds", *Review of Quantitative Finance and Accounting*, 16 (3), 205-222.
- Barber B.M., Odean T., Zheng L. (2000), "The Behaviour of Mutual Fund Investors", Graduate School of Management, University of California-Davis, working Paper.
- Baumol W. J., Goldfeld S. M., Gordon L. A., & Koehn M. F. (1990), *"The Economics of the Mutual Fund Markets: Competition versus Regulation"*, Boston Kluwer.
- Berk J. and Green R. (2004), "Mutual Fund Flows and Performance in Rational Markets", *Journal of Political Economy*, 112 (6), 1269–1295.

- Brown K. C., Harlow W. V., and Starks L. T. (1996), "Of Tournaments and Temptations: An Analysis of Managerial Incentives in the Mutual Fund Industry", *Journal of Finance*, 51 (1), 85–110.
- Bryant L.L. and Chen Liu H. (2009), "Management Structure and the Risk of Mutual Fund Managers, *Journal of Finance and Accountancy*, 1 (1), 1-17.
- Capon N., Fitzsimons G., and Prince R., (1996), "An Individual Level Analysis of the Mutual Fund Investment Decision", *Journal of Financial Services Research*, 10 (1), 59-82.
- Carhart M. M. (1997), "On Persistence in Mutual Fund Performance", *Journal of Finance*, 52 (1), 57–82.
- Chan L. K. C., Chen H. L. and Josef L (2002), "On Mutual Funds Investments Styles", *The Review of Financial Studies*, 15 (5), 1407-1437.
- Chen J., Hong H, Huang M., Kubik J. D. (2004), "Does Fund Size Erode Mutual Fund Performance? The Role of Liquidity and Organization", The American Economic Review, 94 (5), 1276-1302.
- Chevalier J. and Ellison G. (1997), "Risk Taking by Mutual Funds as a Response to Incentives", *Journal of Political Economy*, 105 (6), 1167–1200.
- Chevalier J. and Ellison G. (1999), "Career Concerns of Mutual Fund Managers", *Quarterly Journal of Economics*, 114 (2), 389-432.
- Christoffersen S., Evans R. and Musto D. (2012), "What do Consumers' Fund Flows Maximize? Evidence from their Brokers' Incentives", *Journal of Finance*, 59 (6), 1979-2012.
- Cremer M. and Petajisto A. (2009), "How Active is your Fund Manager? A New Measure that Predicts Performance", *Review of Financial Studies*, 22 (9), 3329-3365.
- Das S.R. and Sundaram S. R. (2000), "Fee Speech: Signaling, Risk-Sharing, and the Impact of Fee Structures on Investor Welfare", *Working Paper*. AEI Brookings Joint Center for Regulatory Studies.
- De Long, Bradford J., Summers L. and Waldmann (1990), "Noise Traders Risk in Financial Markets", *The Journal of Political Economy*, 98 (2), 703-738.
- Dow J. and Gorton G. (1997), "Noise Trading, Delegated Portfolio Management, and Economic Welfare", *Journal of Political Economy*, 105, 1024-1050.

- Duca, J. V. (2001), "The Democratization of America's Capital Markets", *Economic and Financial Review*, (second quarter), 10–19. Federal Reserve Bank of Dallas.

- Edwards F. R. and Zhang X. (1998), "Mutual Funds and Stock and Bond Market Stability", *Journal of Financial Service Research*, 13 (3), 257-282.

- Fama E. (1970), "Efficient Capital Markets: A Review of Theory and Empirical Work", *Journal of Finance*, 25 (2), 383-417.

- Fama E.F. (1980), "Agency Problems and the Theory of the Firm", *Journal of Political Economy*, 88 (2), 288-307.

- Ferreira M. A. and Ramos S. B. (2009), "Mutual Fund Industry Competition and Concentration: International Evidence", Social Science Research Network, Working paper.

- Gaspar J., Massa M. and Matos P. (2006), "Favoritism in Mutual Fund Families? Evidence on Strategic Cross-Fund Subsidization", *Journal of Finance*, 61 (1), 73-104.

- Ghosh P., Kale J. R. and Panchapagesan V. (2014), "Do Indian Business Group Owned Mutual Funds Maximize Value for Their Investors?" *IIM Bangalore Research Paper*, (463).

- Goetzmann W. N. and Peles N. (1997), "Cognitive Dissonance and Mutual Fund Investors", *The Journal of Financial Research*, 20 (2), 145-158.

- Grinblatt M. and Keloharju M. (2000), "What Makes Investors Trade", *Journal of Finance*, 56 (2), 589-616.

- Grossman S. (1976), "On the Efficiency of Competitive Stock Markets Where Trades have Diverse Information", *Journal of Finance*, 31(2), 573-585.

- Gruber M. J. (1996), "Another Puzzle: The Growth in Actively Managed Mutual Funds", *Journal of Finance*, 51(3), 783–810.

- Guercio D.D., and Reuter J. (2013), "Mutual Fund Performance and the Incentive to Generate Alpha", *Journal of Finance*, 69 (4), 1673-1704.

- Gustavsson M. & Riben J. (2012), "Risk Shifting and Mutual Fund Performance: A Swedish Perspective", Bachelor's Thesis Department of Finance, Stockholm School of Economics.

- Holmstrom B. (2000), "Managerial Incentive Problems-A Dynamic Perspective," *Essays in Economics and Management*, in Honor of Lars Wahlbeck, (Helsinki: Swedish School of Economics, 1982), available at: www.investopedia.com.
- Huij J. and Verbeek M. (2007), "Spillover Effects of Marketing in Mutual Fund Families" available at: ssrn.com/abstract.
- Ippolito R. A. (1992), "Consumer Reaction to Measures of Poor Quality: Evidence from the Mutual Fund Industry", *The Journal of Law and Economics*, 35 (1), 45-70.
- Kacperczyk M., Nieuwerburgh S. V., Veldkamp L. (2014), "A Rational Theory of Mutual Funds' Attention Allocation", NYU Working Paper.
- Kempf A., Ruenzi, S., and Thiele, T. (2009), "Employment Risk, Compensation Incentives, and Managerial Risk Taking: Evidence from the Mutual Fund Industry", *Journal of Financial Economics*, 92 (1), 92–108.
- Khorana A. (1996), "Top Management Turnover: An Empirical Investigation of Mutual Fund Managers", *Journal of Financial Economics*, 40 (3), 403-427.
- Khorana A. (2001), "Performance Changes following Top Management Turnover: Evidence from Open-End Mutual Funds", *Journal of Financial and Quantitative Analysis*, 36 (3), 371-393.
- Kim M., Shukla R., and Tomas M. (2000), "Mutual Fund Objective Misclassification", *Journal of Economics and Business*, 52(4), 309-323.
- Korkeamaki T. and Smythe T. (2004), "An Empirical Analysis of Finnish Mutual Fund Expenses and Returns", *European Financial Management*, 10 (3), 413-438.
- Kwan S. and Laderman E. (1999), "On the Portfolio Effects of Financial Convergence- A Review of the Literature", *Federal Reserve Bank of San Francisco Economic Review*, No. 2, 18-31.
- Lazear E., and Rosen S. (1981), "Rank-Order Tournaments as Optimum Labor Contracts" *Journal of Political Economy*, 89 (5), 841–864.
- Mamaysky H., and Spiegel M. (2002), "A Theory of Mutual Funds: Optimal Fund Objectives and Industry Organization", Working Paper, Yale University.

- Markowitz H. M. (1952), "Portfolio Selection", *The Journal of Finance*, **7** (1), 77–91.
- Massa M. (1998), "Are there too many Mutual Funds? Mutual Fund Families, Market Segmentation and Financial Performance", Working Paper, INSEAD.
- Massa M. (2003), "How do Family Strategies affect Fund Performance? When Performance Maximization is not the only Game in Town", Journal of Financial Economics, 67 (2), 249-304.
- McGough R. (1997), "Money Pours into Mutual Funds at Frantic Pace so far in January", *The Wall Street Journal*, PC1.
- Nanda V., Wang Z. J. and Zheng L. (2004), "Family Values and the Star Phenomenon", Review of Financial Studies, 17 (3), 667-698.
- Odean T., (1998), "Are Investors Reluctant to Realize their Losses?" *Journal of Finance*, 53 (5), 1775-1798.
- Petajisto A. (2010), "Active Share and Mutual Fund Performance", Working Paper, New York University.
- Prendergast C. and Stole L. (1996), "Impetuous Youngsters and Jaded Old-Timers: Acquiring a Reputation for Learning", *Journal of Political Economy*, 104 (6), 1105-1134.
- Scharfstein D. S. and Stein J. C. (1990), "Herd Behavior and Investment", *American Economic Review*, 80 (3), 465-489.
- Shefrin H. and Statman M. (1985), "The Disposition to Sell Winners too Early and Ride Losers too Long: Theory and Evidence", *Journal of Finance*, 40 (4), 777-790.
- Sialm C. and Tham T. M. (2012), "Spillover Effects in Mutual Fund Companies", *Management Science*, available at: http://ssrn.com/abstract.
- Sirri E. R. and Tufano P. (1998), "Costly Search and Mutual Fund Flows", *Journal of Finance*, 53 (5) 1589-1622.
- Tirole J, (2004), "*The Theory of Industrial Organisation*", MIT Press, Cambridge M.
- Tobin J. (1958). "Liquidity Preference as Behavior towards Risk". *Review of Economic Studies*, 25 (1), 65-86.
- Walter A. and Weber F. M. (2006), "Herding in the German Mutual Fund Industry", *European Financial Management*, 12 (3), 375-406.

- Wermers R. (2000), "Mutual Fund Performance: An Empirical Decomposition into Stock Picking Talent, Style, Transaction Costs and Expenses", *Journal of Finance*, 55 (4), 1655-1695.
- Wyatt E. (1996), "Some Worries about the Rush into Mutual Funds", *New York Times*, P A1.
- Zwiebel L. (1995), "Corporate Conservatism and Relative Compensation", *Journal of Political Economy*, 103 (1), 1-25.

Chapter-3
Evolution, Structure and Organisation

3.1 Evolution of Mutual Funds in India

Though, the smooth evolution of Indian capital market can be traced for over a century; however, it experiences unprecedented developments during recent decades[1]. This phase is considered as most radical in the growth of Indian capital market. Apart from the growth in various segments of capital market, we have witnessed the increased role of mutual fund industry that it played in financial intermediation.[2]

Mutual fund, as an institutional device, pools investors' funds in the capital market under the control of an investment manager. Hence, the gaps between the supply and demand for funds in the financial markets are bridged by the mutual funds. Though, the need of the establishment of mutual funds in India was felt in 1931; however, the concept of mutual fund was coined in 1964, by the shrewd vision of T.T. Krishnamachari, then finance minister. Responding to the recommendations of Shroff Committee and Central Banking Enquiry Committee, the Central Government established Unit Trust of India (UTI) in 1964 through an Act of Parliament. It provided the UTI to operate as a financial institution as well as an investment trust by way of launching 'UTI Unit Scheme-64'. The success and popularity of 'UTI Unit Scheme-64' and the 'Master Share Scheme' in 1986, subsequently, attracted the attention and interest of banks and other financial institutions to this industry. Since then, the mutual fund proved to be an investment avenue and an essential element of the Indian financial system.[3]

Consequently, in 1987, the public sector banks and insurance companies were permitted to set up mutual funds. Accordingly, the LIC and the GIC and six public sector banks kicked off the setting up of mutual funds, bringing out a 'new era' in the mutual fund industry. Besides, the financial sector reforms including the mutual fund industry were introduced in India as an integral part of the economic reforms in 1990s, with the principal objective of removing structural deficiencies and improving the working of financial markets.

The mutual fund reforms, introduced in 1990s, endeavored to create a competitive environment by permitting the participation of private sector. During this period, several mutual funds were set up by private and joint sectors. Besides, to improve their expertise, many private mutual funds opted for foreign collaboration of their counterparts.

Based on the recommendations of the Dave panel report in 1991, the Government of India issued new guidelines for setting up mutual funds in public, private as well as in joint sectors on February 14, 1992. On February 19, 1993, the first batch of 12 private sector mutual funds was given 'in-principle approval' by the Securities Exchange Board of India (SEBI). The erstwhile Kothari Pioneer Mutual fund (now merged with Franklin Templeton) was the first fund established in July 1993 in the private sector.

The SEBI prepared the Mutual Fund Regulations in 1993, set up a wide-ranging regulatory structure for the first time, while the Indian Mutual Fund Industry (IMFI) had already passed through two phases of developments. The first phase was between 1964 and 1987 when the UTI was the only player, managing total assets of Rs.4564 crores by the end of March 1987. In 1986, the first growth scheme[4], Mastershare was launched by UTI and was the first to be listed on stock exchange.

The second phase was between 1987 and 1993 during which period eight funds were established (six by banks and one each by LIC and GIC). SBI Mutual Fund was the first non UTI mutual fund established in June 1987, followed by Canbank Mutual Fund in December 1987. SBI Mutual Fund launched its first scheme namely, 'Regular Income Scheme' (RIS) 1987 with 5½ years of duration assuring 12 percent return. Canbank Mutual Fund launched its first scheme, 'Canshare' in December 1987 mopping up Rs.4 crores. The total assets managed by the industry shot up to Rs.47004 crores by the end of March 1993.

The third phase commenced with the entry of private and foreign sector mutual funds in 1993, as a result, adding to the share of private players. In addition, the industry developed a self-regulation mechanism to raise confidence among investors under the auspices of the Association of Mutual Funds of India (AMFI) incorporated on August 22, 1995 as a non-profit organisation. With the purpose of ensuring vigorous growth of mutual funds, the SEBI (Mutual Funds) Regulations 1993 were substituted by a more comprehensive and revised regulations in 1996 bringing out standards in Net Assets Value (NAV) calculation, accounting practices, exemption from listing of schemes, remuneration to Asset Management Companies (AMCs), fixation of a band of seven percent between purchase and repurchase prices. Since October 1999, Money Market Mutual Funds (MMMF) was brought under the supervisory control of SEBI at par with liquid funds. The acquisition of Pioneer ITI by Templeton in August 2000 was one of the biggest in the IMFI. At the end of January 2003, there were 33 mutual funds managing total assets of Rs. 1,21,805 crores after witnessing several mergers and acquisitions. The total Assets under Management of the mutual fund houses in the country crossed Rupees One trillion in June 2003, a decade after the entry of private sector in mutual fund business.[5]

The fourth had its beginning from February 2003, following the repeal of the Unit Trust of India Act 1964, bifurcating UTI into two separate entities, namely UTI Specified Undertaking regulated by Government of India and UTI Mutual Fund Ltd regulated by SEBI. With mergers taking place among mutual funds, the mutual industry entered its fourth phase of consolidation and growth. By the end of September 2004, there were 29 funds, managing assets of more than one and half lakh crores under 421 schemes. The industry touched Rs. 2 trillion in September 2005. The growth rate of the industry scaled up to three trillion in august. Now this amount surpassed 10 trillion with more than 45 mutual funds firms are in operation with more than 1000 schemes.[6]

3.2 Structure of a Mutual Fund

There is a procedure to establish a Mutual Fund that should be in compliance with the SEBI guidelines. A mutual fund is set up in the form of a trust consists of a sponsor, trustees, asset management company (AMC) and a custodian. The trust is established by a sponsor or more than one sponsor (as the case may be) who is akin to promoter of a company. The trustees of the mutual fund hold its property, which is for the ultimate benefits of the unit-holders. The AMC, endorsed by SEBI, deal with the funds by making investments in a range of securities. The custodian, who is registered with SEBI, holds the securities of various schemes of the fund in its custody. The trustees are vested with the general power of supervision and direction over AMC. They monitor the performance and compliance of SEBI regulations by the mutual fund.

3.3 Organisation of Mutual a Fund

The set up of a mutual fund involves three important players, namely-sponsor, mutual fund trust and Asset Management Company (AMC). Further, their operations are supported by other independent administrative bodies like banks, registrars, transfer agents and custodians (depository participants).

3.3.1 Sponsor

The fund is established with the backing of a sponsor. The sponsor of a fund is analogous to the 'promoter' of a company, as he gets the fund registered with SEBI. SEBI registers the mutual fund, provided; (a) it should have a good reputation and track record of honesty, reliability and integrity in all its business dealings; (b) The sponsor should be involved in the business of finances for not fewer than five years with positive net-worth (difference between assets and liabilities) in all the five years in recent past. The net-worth of the immediate preceding year should be more than capital contribution of the sponsor in AMC and the sponsor should show profits after providing for depreciation, interest, and tax for three out of the immediate preceding five years; (c) The sponsor and any of the director or principal officers to be employed by the mutual fund should not have been proved guilty of fraud or convicted of an offence involving moral turpitude or guilty of any economic offence; (d) The sponsor forms a trust and appoints a Board of Trustees; (e) He also appoints an Asset Management Company as fund managers; (f) The sponsor, either directly or acting through the Trustees, also appoints a custodian to hold the fund assets; (g) The sponsor is required to contribute at least 40 percent of the minimum net worth of the asset management company.

3.3.2 Mutual Funds as Trust

The sponsor of a mutual fund is legally required to create a 'Trust' and acts as the originator of the trust. This trust is then registered with securities and exchange board of India. The fund sponsor, as required by law, contributes its initial capital and trustees are appointed who hold the assets of the trust. Subsequently, investors can subscribe to units issued by the trust (mutual fund). Unit holders' interests are protected by board of trustees, as trustees also act as custodian of funds of respective schemes. Under the SEBI guidelines, at least fifty percent of the trustees should be independent.

3.3.3 Asset Management Company

The trustees appoint an asset management company with the prior sanction of SEBI. The Asset management company runs the business of mutual fund. For this purpose, it charges the fees for the services it provides. Net worth of an AMC should not be less than ten crore rupees in any circumstance. AMC maintains and discloses the details of business of the company including the NAVs and method of its calculation. The services of non-compliance and non-performing AMC can be terminated and new AMC can be appointed under the due legal process.

3.3.4 Obligations of AMC

An AMC basically performs the following functions;

- The AMC makes certain that all transactions are according to the contents of trust deed.
- In case of mistake, advertently or inadvertently, committed by the employees of the AMC, the AMC shall be held responsible.
- An AMC is liable to submit quarterly reports to appropriate authorities.
- An AMC is not permitted to hire the services of broker who is anyway connected with sponsor.
- An AMC cannot deal in more than five percent of its daily business of mutual fund in a firm associated with sponsor.
- An AMC is not allowed to put in the services of sponsor or any other person who is directly or indirectly associated with the sponsor for the purpose of transactions and distribution of units.
- The services of a person who is guilty of any economic and financial offence[7] cannot be hired by AMC.
- The persons who are appointed as the registrars and share transfer agents required to be enrolled with SEBI.

All the AMCs under SEBI regulations (2001)[8] are required to maintain transparency in their investment decisions. They are required to keep records of all investments and transactions. The AMCs are required to convey its compliance to the trustees which in turn report it to SEBI.

The AMCs may have some funds that are not claimed by investors due to several reasons. SEBI allows these funds to be deployed in short period instruments. If the investors ask for such funds in a time of three years from the due date, payment will be made on the current price of NAV. Such funds can be claimed even after three years, but the investor can take the NAV prevailing at the end of third year. Income earned after third year from investments of these unclaimed funds can be used for the purpose of investors' education. The details of such unclaimed funds and their use thereof will be reported in the annual report of the AMC. Besides, periodic reminders will be given to investors to take their due amount.

AMCs are required to upload their annual report under SEBI guidelines. The unit holders can ask for the copy of the annual report and AMC concerned is responsible to supply the same to the investor.

The AMCs are now permitted to invest in un-rated debt instruments provided the parameters are complied with. The prior approval of board of trustees is not required. This provision provides AMCs some flexibility in their working.

The employees of the AMCs at key positions are required to submit the details of their investments and trading to the trustees on quarterly basis. The purpose of this direction from SEBI is that inside information of the AMC should not be used for personal gain.

The mutual fund investment schemes select a benchmark index for the purpose of performance comparison. Under the SEBI guidelines, AMCs are required to disclose the performance of benchmark indices along with the performance of fund scheme on half yearly basis.

In 2002-03 union budget proposals, the mutual fund companies allowed to invest in foreign debt securities of AAA rating. They were also permitted to invest in government securities of AAA rated countries. These ratings should be assigned by well established rating agencies. SEBI had issued relevant guidelines in this context.

The illiquid or non performing assets of mutual funds at the time of the maturity of the scheme, if realized within two years of the closure of the scheme, should be disbursed among the stakeholders (investors) if the amount is considerable. However, if the amount is very small or it is realized after two years it may be shifted to investor's education fund maintained by each AMC.

3.3.5 SEBI (Mutual Funds) Regulations, 1996

The mutual funds investments involve sponsor, custodian, trustees, and AMC. It was recognized that mutual fund firms would play with the hard earned money of the commoners. If the strict regulations could not be imposed, it may prove to be detrimental to the interests of investors. Hence, SEBI had been provided additional powers to act as a regulator of mutual funds in India. SEBI came forward with regulations regarding mutual funds in 1996. The provisions of these regulations are highlighted here;

- No mutual fund scheme can be launched by AMC without the express approval from the trustees and copy of details of the scheme is required to be submitted with SEBI.
- The investors are deserved to make investment decisions based on adequate information. Hence, the AMCs are required by law that offers document of the scheme offered to investors should have sufficient disclosures.
- The announcements and advertisement code should be strictly followed as prescribed by SEBI.
- It is mandatory for the AMCs that 'close ended' schemes are listed on stock exchanges within 6 months of the closure of the scheme.
- There is a provision in the SEBI guidelines that units of a close-ended scheme can be changed into an open-ended scheme provided majority of the unit holders agree. This provision is required to be included in the offer document of the scheme.
- When a scheme is offered to investors, its subscription period, in no case, can be more than 45 days.
- The offer document of the scheme must disclose minimum amount of subscription. In case this level of subscription is not attained in specified period of time, the entire money will be refunded to the subscribers within 6 weeks. In case of over subscription, excess money will be returned to the investors within the six weeks of the closure of the scheme.
- If guaranteed returns are promised in a scheme, the investors cannot be kept in dark. The AMC will disclose the provision and sources of guaranteed returns. Moreover, the offer document will mention the name of the person responsible for guaranteed returns.
- In normal circumstances, a close ended scheme shall be wound up on redemption date. The scheme can be rolled over if 75 percent of the unit holders endorse.

3.3.6 Custodian

A mutual fund company is required to appoint mandatorily a custodian to carry out the custodial services for the schemes of the fund. A trust company, bank or similar financial institution responsible for holding and safeguarding the securities owned within a mutual fund. A mutual fund's custodian may also act as the mutual funds transfer agent, maintaining records of shareholder transactions and balances. The custodian's role is to safeguard and protect the assets of the mutual fund. Institutions with sufficient organizational strength, service ability in terms of computerization, and other infrastructure facilities are approved to act as custodians. The custodians typically deal with investor redemption, purchase and sales of mutual fund shares.

Investors buying and selling mutual fund shares do not perform so through fund managers. Transfer agents handle the direct responsibility for shareholders' purchases and sales of mutual fund shares. The custodian then records these transactions without fund manager's involvement. The custodians report these transactions to fund managers so they can continue to keep fund assets and fund cash positions healthy.

The custodian must be completely delinked from the AMC and required to be registered with SEBI separately. Under the Securities and Exchange Board of India (Custodian of Securities) Guidelines, 1996, any person proposing to carry on the business as a custodian of securities must register with the SEBI and is required to fulfill specified eligibility criteria. Additionally, a custodian in which the sponsor or its associates holds 50 percent or more of the voting rights of the share capital of the custodian or where 50 percent or more of the directors of the custodian represent the interest of the sponsor or its associates cannot act as custodian for a mutual fund constituted by the same sponsor or any of its associate or subsidiary company.

The custodian, by official recording of mutual fund transactions, safeguarding fund assets and tracking shareholder value provide a 'checks and balances' function. While both the custodian and fund manager have a fiduciary responsibility to the mutual fund and its shareholders, separating these requirements between the two entities minimizes perceived improprieties.

3.3.7 Schemes

As already stated, mutual funds can issue variety of schemes that may focus on the different investors depending on their risk aptitude and objectives. A scheme that has been decided to be launched by a particular asset management company, under the SEBI guidelines, it should be duly approved by the trustees of the AMC. Moreover, the offer document should be submitted to the SEBI for scrutiny. The disclosures in the document should be adequate enough that investors can make decisions on the basis of information provided by this document. AMC is also liable to reveal the proposal to allocate investments in the group companies of the sponsor. SEBI is required to register the objections, if any, within the 21 days of submitting this offer document to SEBI. If no issue arises in the stipulated period, AMC would be free, without any restriction, to offer this scheme to general public. Besides, unit holders are also provided with the nomination facility.

Once the scheme is launched, AMCs can advertise it for better subscription through several mediums. SEBI has laid down an 'advertising code' and the advertising should be within the provisions of such code. It should be ensured that investors were not betrayed in any way through these advertisements.

Close-ended schemes[11] are closed for subscription after the recommended period of subscription is over. Subsequently, within six months, these schemes are listed, as required by law, on a recognized stock exchange. However, some exceptions are there when listing is not mandatory, such as, in case of repurchase facility, compulsory monthly income provision, catering to special class and so on. The close ended schemes can be converted into open ended schemes, provided all SEBI rules are strictly followed (for more details reader may refer to SEBI website).

Under the SEBI guidelines, guaranteed returns can be promised to investors only if AMC provides name of a person in offer document responsible for returns. In addition, offer document is required to disclose the sources from which such returns can be guaranteed.

3.3.8 General Obligations

- AMC is required by law to maintain the proper records of each scheme separately. The transactions and financial position of the scheme will be explained to the SEBI and Trustees time to time.
- Every AMC is required to prepare an annual report and annual statement of accounts of the schemes in operation for each financial year.
- Annual statement of accounts is, as required by law, to be audited by an auditor. It should ensured auditor should be independent and in no way associated with asset management company

3.3.9 Investment Criteria

The Mutual Fund Regulations lays down specified investment criteria that the mutual funds need to conform to. There are certain restrictions on the investments made by a mutual fund.

The moneys collected under any scheme of a mutual fund shall be invested only in transferable securities in the money market or in the capital market or in privately placed debentures or securitized debts. However, in the case of securitized debts, such fund may invest in asset backed securities (ABS)[12] and mortgaged backed securities (MBS)[13]. Furthermore, the mutual fund having an aggregate of securities which are worth Rs.100 million (approximately USD 2.15 million) or more shall be required to settle their transactions through dematerialized securities.

In addition to the above, mutual funds are not permitted to borrow money from the market except to meet temporary liquidity needs of the mutual funds for the purpose of repurchase, redemption of units or payment of interest or dividend to the unit holders. Even such borrowing cannot exceed 20 percent of the net asset of a scheme and the duration of such a borrowing cannot exceed a period of six months. Similarly, a mutual fund is not permitted to advance any loans for any purpose. A mutual fund is permitted to lend securities in accordance with the Stock Lending Scheme of SEBI. The funds of a scheme are prohibited from being used in option trading or in short selling or carry forward transactions. However, SEBI has permitted mutual funds to enter into derivative transactions on a recognized stock exchange for the purpose of hedging and portfolio balancing and such investments in derivative instruments have to be made in accordance with SEBI Guidelines issued in this regard[14].

3.4   Fees and Expenses

The Mutual Fund Regulations lay down certain limits on the fees that can be charged by the AMC and also ceiling the expenses that can be loaded on to the Fund.

The AMC can charge the mutual fund with investment and advisory fees subject to the following restrictions:

- One and a quarter of one per cent of the weekly average net assets outstanding in each accounting year for the scheme concerned, as long as the net assets do not exceed Rs. 1 billion.
- One per cent of the excess amount over Rs. 1 billion, where net assets so calculated exceed Rs. 1 billion.

For schemes launched on a no load basis, the AMC is authorized to collect an additional management fee not exceeding 1 percent of the weekly average net assets outstanding in each financial year. In addition to the aforementioned fees, the AMC may charge the mutual fund with the initial expenses of launching the schemes and recurring expenses such as marketing and selling expenses including agents' commission, if any, brokerage and transaction cost, fees and expenses of trustees, audit fees, custodian fees etc.

3.5   Procedure in Case of Default

On and from the date of the suspension of the certificate or the approval, as the case may be, the mutual fund, trustees or asset management company, shall cease to carry on any activity as a mutual fund, trustee or asset management company, during the period of suspension, and shall be subject to the directions of the Board with regard to any records, documents, or securities that may be in its custody or control, relating to its activities as mutual fund, trustees, or asset management company.

3.6   SEBI Guidelines (2001-02) Relating to Mutual Funds

- A common format is set down for all mutual fund schemes to disclose their entire portfolios on half-yearly basis so that the investors can get meaningful information on the deployment of funds. Mutual funds are also required to disclose the investment in various types of instruments and percentage in each scrip to the total assets, illiquid and non-performing assets, investment in derivatives and in ADRs and GDRs.
- To enable the investors to make informed investment decisions, mutual funds have been directed to fully revise and update offer document and memorandum at least once in two years.
- Mutual funds are also required to;

  I. Bring uniformity in disclosures of various categories of advertisements, with a view to ensure consistency and comparability across schemes and mutual funds.
  II. Reduce initial offer period from a maximum of 45 days to 30 days.
  III. Dispatch statements of account once the minimum subscription amount specified in the offer document is received even before the closure of the issue.
  IV. Invest in mortgaged backed securities of investment for which grade given by credit rating agency or agencies.
  V. Identify and make provisions for the non-performing assets (NPAs) according to criteria for classification of NPAs and treatment of income accrued on NPAs and to disclose NPAs in half-yearly portfolio reports.
  VI. Disclose information in a revised format on unit capital, reserves, performance in terms of dividend and rise/fall in NAV during the half-year period, annualized yields over the last 1, 3, 5 years in addition to percentage of management fees,

percentage of recurring expenses to net assets, investment made in associate companies, payment made to associate companies for their services, and details of large holdings, since their operation.

VII. Declare their NAVs and sale/repurchase prices of all schemes updated daily on regular basis on the AMFI website by 8.00 p.m. and declare NAVs of their close-ended schemes on every Wednesday.

- The format for un-audited half-yearly results for the mutual funds has been revised by SEBI. These results are to be published before the expiry of one month from the close of each half-year as against two months period provided earlier. These results shall also be put in their websites by mutual funds.
- All the schemes by mutual funds shall be launched within six months from the date of the letter containing observations from SEBI on the scheme offer document. Otherwise, a fresh offer document along with filing fees shall be filed with SEBI.
- Mutual funds are required to disclose large unit-holdings in the scheme, which are over 25 percent of the NAV.

3.7 Association of Mutual Funds in India (AMFI)

The Association of Mutual Funds in India (AMFI) was set up in 1993 when all the mutual funds, except the UTI, came together and conceded the need for a common platform for addressing the concerns that have effect on the mutual fund industry as a whole. The AMFI is devoted to develop the Indian mutual fund industry on professional, healthy, and ethical lines and to improve and uphold standards in all areas with a vision to protect and promote the interests of mutual funds and their unit-holders.

Objectives of AMFI

- To suggest and promote best business practices and code of conduct to be followed by members and others involved in the activities of mutual fund and asset management, including agencies connected in the field of capital markets and financial services.

- To interact with the SEBI and to represent to SEBI on all matters related to the mutual fund industry.
- To represent to the government, Reserve Bank of India (RBI) and other bodies on all matters concerning the mutual fund industry.
- To develop a cadre of well trained agent distributors and to implement a programme of training and certification for all intermediaries and others engaged in the industry.
- To undertake countrywide investors' awareness programme so as to promote proper understanding of the concept and working of mutual funds.
- To spread information on mutual fund industry and to carry out studies and research directly and or in association with other bodies.

3.8 Tax Provisions

Indian tax system levy taxes on mutual funds and investors as per the provisions Income tax Act, 1961 and any amendment thereafter.

(a) Provisions regarding Mutual Fund

The mutual funds are exempted from deduction at source for the income they receive from their operations. Besides, they are not liable to pay any tax on earnings of schemes, which are sponsored by public sector banks / institutions and approved by the government or RBI as the case may be.

(b) Provisions regarding Resident Investors

Investment in mutual funds is considered as long term capital investment if it has been held for more than one year. The earnings from such assets come under the category of long term capital gains. These gains are subject to be taxed according to income tax laws of capital gains and are adjusted for inflation index as notified by Central Government of India.

There is a separate tax provision regarding resident Hindu Undivided Family (HUF). If the aggregate earning as reduced by the long term capital gains is less than the upper limit not subject to taxation, the long term capital gains shall be reduced to the extent of shortfall and only the remaining long term capital gains will be subject to flat rate of taxation of 10%. Besides, they are liable to pay surcharge at the rate of 5%.

Capital loss suffered by investor from the transaction of units of the mutual funds can be adjusted from the capital gains earned from other transactions. Only net capital gains are subject to capital gain taxes.

The mutual fund firms are required to deduct tax at source at the rate of 10.5% from any income paid to the investors provided it is not less than Rs. 1000 during a financial year. However, if a unit holder gives a declaration that his income will remain less than minimum income limit required to impose income tax, then deduction of tax at source is not mandatory.

(c) Provisions regarding Non-resident Individual Investors

The long term capital gains earned by non-resident individuals are subject to taxation under the provisions of long term capital gains of income tax act. That is they liable to pay at the rate of 10.5% of the capital gain earned. So far the tax provisions regarding short term capital gains are concerned, tax is deducted at source at the rate of 31.5%.

In case of non-resident investors, any income earned by them and credited to their accounts then tax is required to be deducted at source at the rate of 21 percent. If there is Double Taxation Avoidance Agreement (DTAA) between the governments and more beneficial to investors, then the provisions of DTAA will be applicable to deduct tax at source.

(c) Provisions regarding Non-Resident Investors (Company)

If it is a company that invests in Indian mutual fund units and earns long term capital gains, they are subject to be taxed at the rate of 10.5 percent as per Indian income tax laws. However, if the capital gains are in respect to short period, tax is required to be deducted at source at the rate of 42 percent.

Similar to the individual non-resident unit holders, non-resident investor companies if earn returns and amount is credited to their accounts are subject to tax deducted at source at the rate of 21 percent. If the provisions of DTAA are applicable and beneficial to investors, then taxes will be deducted according to such provisions.

(d) Provisions regarding FIIs

The FIIs that invest in Indian mutual funds are subject to tax provisions as per Indian tax laws. They are subject to be taxed at the rate of 10.5 percent for the long term capital gains earned. However, in respect to short term capital gains, tax is required to be deducted at source at the rate of 31.5 percent. If any dividend is credited to their accounts, such amount is required to be taxed at the rate of 21 percent and deducted at source.

3.9 Provisions regarding Foreign Investments in Domestic Mutual Funds

Foreign investors can enter in domestic mutual fund industry in two ways; (a) to start its own mutual fund operations and invite domestic investors to subscribe to its units; (b) to deploy its funds in Indian capital markets.

(a) Setting up own Operations

Indian asset management business has witnessed considerable exposure to rest of the world in recent years. For, various well established asset management companies of the western world have entered in Indian market either individually or with collaboration with Indian companies. Those who entered individually have set up their own asset management companies here. The regulations regarding mutual fund industry in India permit the foreign players to enter in India without any restriction. The complete list of foreign players active in Indian mutual fund industry is presented in next chapter.

The foreign asset management company in India comes in the category of non-banking finance activity; therefore, certain minimum capitalization norms are laid down by Foreign Investment Promotion Board (FIPB) for foreign investment. These capitalization norms are as follows;

Table-3.1: Foreign Holding as a Percentage of Equity Minimum Capital

Percentage of Foreign Holding	Equity Minimum Capital (US $)
51	500,000
51-75	5 Million
> 75	50 Million

Table 3.1 reveals that capital required to enter in Indian asset management business is very high. Thus, many international players decided to enter through joint ventures with domestic players. The Indian foreign investment regulations have put such investments under the automatic route and no prior approval is required from foreign investment promotion board. However, such investments are to be complied with the RBI regulations regarding foreign exchange and appropriate documents required to be submitted with RBI within a specified period of time.

(b) Foreign Firms Investing through a Domestic Mutual Fund

Foreign mutual funds that have developed interest in Indian mutual fund industry but are not willing to set up their own AMC in India can invest through schemes of existing domestic mutual funds. The overseas investment funds set up their operations in nations where tax structure is favorable to them. Subsequently, fund so collected are deployed in Indian mutual fund scheme. Such scheme is exclusively for the overseas fund that is all the units of the schemes are issued to the Overseas Fund. This scheme is generally managed by domestic AMC. The overseas investment manger can be allowed to participate in the management of scheme if he wishes to play a part. The scheme and the overseas fund are required to be registered with SEBI.

An overseas fund that invests in domestic scheme, as per SEBI guidelines, should be a broad based. That is the overseas firm should be involved in multiplicity of schemes abroad. Apart from the approval of SEBI, additional approval is required from Ministry of Finance and RBI. The agreement between the domestic investment company and overseas fund should be in public domain and put on records of SEBI. The scheme strictly follows the norms to calculate the NAV and to be reported on monthly basis.

Such combination of domestic and foreign firms in mutual funds has registered a remarkable success in India. Many asset management companies in India have floated offshore funds with considerable success.

(c) FII in the Indian Mutual Fund Industry

While pursuing financial sector reforms in early 90s, the Government of India recognized the role of foreign institutional investments. Therefore, relevant guidelines were issued in 1992. These guidelines enabled FIIs to make investment in listed and unlisted securities in India including the units of mutual funds. Apart from the registration with SEBI, FIIs take general permission from RBI under Foreign Exchange Management Act, 1999. FIIs are entitled for single window clearance from SEBI.

The FIIs are entitled to the following provisions of SEBI;

- FII may buy and sell stocks issued by any Indian companies.
- It is entitled to realize capital gains on investments made in India.
- It can subscribe to or give up rights offerings for shares.
- FII may appoint a domestic custodian.
- It can repatriate capital, capital gains and dividends etc.

FIIs including non resident Indians and foreign corporate bodies are subject to some restrictions imposed by SEBI and RBI;

- It may buy equity shares of each company in which it has invested on its own account not exceeding 5 percent of the total issued capital of that company.
- If FII invests on behalf of its sub accounts, the investment on behalf of each such sub-account shall not exceed 5 percent of the total issued capital of that company.
- In case of foreign corporates or individuals, each of such sub-account shall not invest more than 5 percent of the total issued capital of the company in which such investment is made.

(d) Investment in Indian Mutual Fund Market through Mauritius

India came into an agreement with Mauritius in 1982 labeled as Double Taxation Avoidance Agreement (DTAA). Under the provisions of this agreement, companies organised in Mauritius are not to be taxed on the capital gains earned by investing in Indian companies provided Mauritius' company does not have permanent existence in India. Hence, Mauritius firms consider such provisions as favorable to them in terms of tax provisions. Consequently, Mauritius is the largest investor in India. However, other nations that make direct investment in India are subject to tax laws and have to register with appropriate authority in India.

Mauritius is considered as relatively economical source of investment into the South East Asian region. Apart from India to which it has signed DTAA, about twenty other countries are in such agreement with Mauritius. Mauritius is making negotiations with many other countries for similar type agreement. Hence, Mauritius is a favorable area for international tax planning. Mauritius has appeared as a route for other nations to enter into India without tax obligations. Therefore, India-Mauritius DTAA has been under criticism from the Indian tax authorities. The Indian tax authorities have challenged the residence status of many companies and denied benefits under DTAA.

As tax accords are a component of international law and required to be honored by the concerned parties, India's Ministry of Finance issued a circular confirming the availability of the benefits under the India-Mauritius

DTAA to residents of Mauritius who hold the requisite tax residency certificate issued by the Income-tax authorities in Mauritius.

In response to repercussions of this agreement, Indian government has come into more favorable agreements with UAE and Cyprus in recent years. That may put the Mauritius into a less favorable position. It is not likely that the India-Mauritius tax agreement can be renegotiated. It would be essential to give due consideration to structuring of investment through Mauritius in order to reduce the risk of denial of India-Mauritius DTAA benefits.

3.10 Upcoming Trends in Mutual Fund Industry

Geographical Spread

The operations of Mutual funds are, until now, concentrated in the tier-1 cities and restrict its geographical spread. Mutual fund regulators are very much concerned about the spread of MFs in the two and three tier cities. For, lack of financial education and awareness, limited distribution network, cultural bias towards physical assets are some of the key impediments to growth in the smaller cities. Even the SEBI has allowed the fund houses to charge an extra load of 30 basis points from existing schemes subject to meeting certain conditions. The regulation has given incentive to fund houses to push mutual fund products in cities beyond the top 15.

The industry has adopted multi-pronged approach to reach out to investors in B-15 cities which includes investor awareness, training and enrolling new cadre of distributors. In addition, fund houses are paying additional commission to source applications from these areas.

Despite constant endeavor of the SEBI to increase penetration of mutual fund products beyond top 15 cities, the AUM composition has only marginally changed since SEBI directive on additional TER on inflows from smaller cities was implemented in October 1st, 2012. Contribution from the B-15 cities has remained at around 13 per cent for the last two years. Drivers like lack of financial education and awareness, limited distribution network, cultural bias towards physical assets are some of the key impediments to growth in B-15 cities.

Financial literacy is one of the most vital factors hampering the growth of penetration of any financial products in the smaller cities and towns. Investors are needed to be made aware of their financial goals and the means to accomplish the same. AMFI and SEBI along with the Industry are making efforts for investors' awareness campaign. Fund houses are also mandated by regulation to invest 2 BPs from scheme expenses towards investors' education and awareness campaigns but India has a long way to go.

The second critical issue for fund houses to distribute their products in smaller cities is the availability of quality distribution infrastructure. Fund houses need infrastructure like branches, adequate number of relationship managers and sales service staff in these locations to be able to increase their sales volume coming from these areas. Cost of establishing a distribution network in smaller cities is relatively high. It is the cost per transaction or the low sales volume that makes the pursuit economically unviable or at the least challenging.

Such unique problems of smaller cities call for unique solutions. Therefore, the fund houses could look at some innovative sale strategies for the smaller cites.

(a) A trusted Sales agent

Even today, in India, the financial investments are mostly driven by relationship and trust. In such cases, investors would prefer to buy from a known face rather than from unknown one. Independent Financial Advisers (IFAs) serves as an important link between the sellers and buyers of the financial products. They have a good hold and influence over their clients and their purchasing decisions. Therefore, it is important to tap the IFAs that have a client base in smaller cities. To increase the base of mutual fund distributors, the regulator has permitted a new cadre of distributors which includes postal agents, retired government and semi-government officials, retired teachers, retired bank officers and other persons (such as bank correspondents) to sell units of simple and performing mutual fund schemes.

(b) Partnering with a Bank

Fund houses could leverage from large network of bank branches covering the surrounding areas as well. Bank sponsored AMCs such as HDFC MF, SBI MF have a greater advantage over the other asset management players. Fund houses could leverage from a bank's network in multiple ways—the bank branches, employees, ATM network, banking correspondents'— could be used as point of sales at various levels. Partnering or forming a strategic alliance with a public sector bank with vast presence in non metro areas would help fund houses in amassing assets.

(c) Technology

Technology can play an important role towards this pursuit in the near future. For, the cost of set up a distribution network is relatively high in smaller cities; technology can play a crucial role in mobilizing new AUM through internet and mobile banking channels. Online channel for mutual funds is increasingly becoming popular amongst investors. Almost all fund houses in India provide service to transact online. India has very high tele-density and can be tapped through mobile phones. Using mobile phones to purchase mutual funds could have a huge potential to increase investments. Many mutual funds have already enabled purchase of mutual fund units through immediate payment services (IMPS) and more recent National Automated Clearing House system (NACH) platform, which have made the buying mutual funds for investors' paper less. The transactions can be done either by using sms or through an application. The technology is further developing to make it more user friendly and hassle free. For example, now investors can invest in SIPs of various schemes at once. A new investor needs to fill up the common application form, along with 'know-your-investor' documents and a registration form. After the folio is created and the investor receives personal identification number (PIN), he can download the mobile application to buy and sell fund units. The existing investors can also avail of this facility.

3.11   Looking Ahead

Increase the Distribution Strength

The strength of the mutual fund network is very weak. The network of insurance agents is relatively very strong. Quoting an industry CEO, "there are over 0.3 million insurance agents in India, while only 16,000 distributors for mutual funds." This data implies that investors are likely to meet insurance agents much more frequently than mutual fund distributors and consequently likely to park their surplus funds in insurance policies rather than mutual fund products. Therefore, there is dire need to reinforce the distribution strength in mutual funds for better performance in near future.

Alternative distribution model

The mutual fund industry needs to explore an alternative mode of distribution, for expansion and growth. The option of a tied distribution model could be explored, where the agent is tied to a particular institution. Although this model has worked in some countries it leans towards a closed architecture model, restricting the choice of the investor. The viability of its success in India needs to be measured. Fund houses can also look at the possibility of investing in an active sales force. The online channel of distribution also exists, although its full potential has not been exploited as yet.

Need to upgrade distribution networks

In the current scenario, the industry needs willingness from asset management companies to invest more in the distributor community. The smaller asset management companies due to lack of funds, find it more challenging to invest in the distribution channel. Training and educating the distributors are integral to increasing penetration of mutual fund products.

New cadre of distributors to take the industry forward

The new cadre of distributors, such as - postal agents, retired officials and school teachers etc. will likely to collect in inflows from smaller towns and cities. This cadre of distributors will be crucial in mobilizing the savings of the smaller towns and directing these savings towards mutual fund investments.

Product Design

Mutual fund products need to be simplified if they have be sold to the masses through a public sector bank channels. The product needs to be look like a fixed deposit, and provide a predictable income. Also, these products need to be solution oriented. In the past, some fund houses launched similar schemes with minor differences. The SEBI has directed a move towards a consolidation of schemes to make the process simpler for investors. If the right product or solution is not available to be sold to customers, it will be difficult to create a 'pull' factor.

Technology mix

To overcome operational challenges, measures need to be taken to improve the existing infrastructure and to bring in more efficiency while increasing the scale of operations. This is not possible without the back-up of a good technology mix. It is also a key facilitator to break down underpenetrated markets. Besides, the Indian mutual fund industry faces a lot of limitations with respect to product design and construction as compared to other markets.

Continuation of investor awareness initiatives

National awareness campaigns for mutual funds continue to remain a focus area for fund houses and distributors. Distributors and IFAs are taking it upon themselves to educate the investor and make them aware of the benefits of investing in mutual funds. The AMCs are trying to think of innovative ways of reaching the investors in smaller towns and cities and mobilize their savings.

Investors should be aware of the sectors in which they are investing and should have a clear outlook on the performance of their investments, with all the risks explained. Servicing the customers and guiding them to achieve their financial goals over a period of time will lead the industry towards sustainability and asset retention.

Growth of systematic investment plans

Fund managers need to enhance the growth of their systematic investment plan books. These plans have the capacity to deal with volatility over a long-time horizon and generate steady returns.

Focus on service initiatives

Fund houses can create a differentiator for themselves by offering a premium service proposition. The initiative to increase distribution needs to be matched with service quality to investors and distributors alike or else increased penetration will not attain its full value.

Tax as an Enabler

The past period has witnessed adverse impacts arising out of uncertainty created on the tax front. While some of these have been rationalized by the authorities, such as the deferral of GAAR and the amendment on taxability of securitization trusts, there are other areas which have created anxiety in the industry. The role of tax can be enhanced to be a growth enabler on various fronts - some examples include enabling the management of offshore funds from India, tax breaks on pension products and simplification of processes around the QFI regime.

Multiple share class structure

Some industry CEOs believes that a multiple share class structure can possibly be a viable model for the domestic mutual fund industry. In this kind of a structure, each share class can have its own expense ratio.

Pension products

Lastly, by allowing the fund houses to sell pension products will act as a huge catalyst for growth of the industry. This move will energize AMCs, distributors and investors alike, while contributing to the deepening of capital markets in India.

3.12 Investment in foreign Securities

(a) Investment in Foreign Debt

SEBI has allowed the Indian Mutual Funds to make investments in foreign debt securities. As per the circular (2012) issued by SEBI, Mutual Funds have been permitted to invest in foreign debt securities with highest credit rating (such as A-1/AAA by Standard and Poor, P1/AAA by Moody's, F1/AAA by Fitch IBCA, etc.) in the countries with fully convertible currencies provided the guidelines laid down in the circular are complied with. Similarly, the Indian Mutual Funds have also been permitted to make investments in non-Indian government securities where the countries are AAA rated. However, such investment is permitted subject to an overall cap of 10 percent of the net assets of a Mutual Fund, subject to the maximum of USD 50 million, per Mutual Fund for making investments in the Foreign Debt Securities and American Depository Receipts/Global Depository Receipts issued by Indian companies (ADRs/GDRs).

This has opened up newer opportunities for domestic mutual funds for investing in foreign securities. This also enables mutual funds to hedge their country risk by spreading their investments amongst different countries. Several funds have announced schemes for such overseas investments.

(b) *Investment by resident in Foreign Securities*

The Reserve Bank of India, as a part of its ongoing liberalization and with a view to usher in full convertibility of Rupee, has recently permitted Indian residents, including mutual funds, subject to an overall cap of USD 1 billion. Such investment will have to be made in foreign companies whose shares are listed on an overseas exchange and which has at least 10 percent holdings in an Indian company which is also listed on the Indian stock exchange. While these conditions may seem restrictive, it is only a matter of time when the RBI will look at further relaxations. This has opened up an opportunity for Indian investors to invest in the overseas market and this also throws up an opportunity for mutual funds to tap into these investments since individual investors would be more comfortable to invest through a mutual fund as compared to a direct exposure to foreign securities.

3.13 Concluding Remarks

The Indian mutual fund industry has evolved over a long period and passed through many stages of its progress. It has registered tremendous growth so far as the assets under management, number of mutual fund firms and diversity of schemes is concerned. To make this industry transparent and adequately regulated, comprehensive rules and regulations have been implemented to best interest of investors. In addition, broad guidelines have been issued towards the foreign firms investing in the Indian mutual fund industry. Indian firms have also been permitted to invest in the overseas mutual funds. Taxation policy towards mutual fund companies and investors has been sufficiently simplified. People are showing great interest in this industry given its returns, liquidity and security. New schemes are being offered everyday taking into consideration the investors' need. Moreover, efforts have also been made to penetrate this industry to the unexploited areas and classes. It is hoped that this industry will show tremendous growth in coming years.

Notes

1. In response to financial sector reforms, every segment of the capital market in India witnessed considerable effect and consequently it grew by leaps and bounds. Capital market reforms were introduced in terms of regulations, liberalization and removing the structural deficiencies.

2. An entity that play a role as a middleman between two parties in a financial transaction. A commercial bank is a typical financial intermediary; this category also includes other financial institutions such as investment banks, insurance companies, 'mutual funds' and pension funds. Financial intermediaries offer a number of benefits to the average consumer including safety, liquidity and economies of scale.

3. www.amfiindia.com/mfindustry, "History of the Indian Mutual Fund Industry".

4. A mutual fund whose primary investment objective is long term growth of capital (capital appreciation) with little or no dividend payout. Rather such capital is reinvested into expansion, acquisition and R&D.

5. www.amfiindia.com/mfindustry

6. www.livemint.com/money (2014), September 8.

7. Economic and financial offences cover fraud, forgery and counterfeiting, offences against the legislation governing cheques, forgery or use of credit cards, offences against companies.

8. SEBI (Mutual Funds) (Amendment) Regulations, 2011 vide notification dated August 30, 2011

9. Debt instruments which are not rated by any accredited/ registered credit rating agency.

10. The illegal practice of buying and selling of a security by someone who has access to confidential information about the security.

11. Regulation 2(f), Securities and Exchange Board of India (Mutual Funds) Regulations, 1996: "close-ended scheme" means any scheme of a mutual fund in which the period of maturity of the scheme is specified.

12. A financial security backed by a loan or receivables against assets other than real estate.

13. A MBS is a type of asset backed security that is secured by a mortgage or collection of mortgages. The mortgages are sold to a group of individuals that securitizes, or packages, the loans together into a security that investors can buy.
14. Guidelines for Participation by Mutual Funds in Trading in Derivative Products; February 1, 2001

References

- CII & PWC (2010), "Indian Mutual Fund Industry-Towards 2015, Sustaining Inclusive Growth-Evolving Business Models", available at: www.pwc.in.
- Dave S. A. (1992), "Mutual Funds: Growth and Development", *The Journal of the Indian Institute of Bankers*, 63 (1), 41-53.
- Khan M. Y. (2001), *"Indian Financial System"*, Tata Mc Graw-Hill, New Delhi.
- KPMG (2014), "Indian Mutual Fund Industry Distribution Continuum: Key to Success", available at: www.kpmg.com.
- Machiraju H. R. (2009), *"Indian Financial System"*, Vikas Publishing House Pvt. Ltd.
- Nishith Desai Associates (2003), "Mutual Funds in India: An Overview" A Report, available at: www.nishithdesai.com.
- Pandian P. (2008), "Security Analysis and Portfolio Management", Vikas Publication, New Delhi.
- PWC (2013), "Indian Mutual Fund Industry, Unearthing the Growth Potential in Untapped Markets", available at: www.pwc.in/assets.
- www.amfiindia.com
- www.camsonlime.com
- www.cic.com
- www.icraindia.com
- www.indiainfoline.com
- www.moneycontrol.com
- www.mutualfundindia.com
- www.prudentialchannel.com
- www.rbi.com
- www.sebi.com

Chapter-4
Market Penetration and Investment Pattern

4.1 Introduction

Firms engaged in production of goods and services are concerned about the strategic management[1] of its marketing. For, they may be able to attract additional buyers and bigger market share. In this pursuit, they endeavor to look at the potential of their products in the existing and new markets. These strategies are technically labeled as 'market penetration' (Armstrong and Kotler, 2009). This strategy (market penetration) increases the product sales through an aggressive marketing mix. Such approach is, usually, introduced to increase the rate of the product/service usage, encourage repeat purchases, attract consumers away from competitors and attract current non-users. In addition, such strategies include cutting prices, increasing advertising and promotional activities, and introducing innovative distributive tactics (Kotler and Keller, 2008). Marketing penetration is essential for the long term survival of firms.

The fundamental measures of a product's popularity are penetration rate and penetration share. The penetration rate is the percentage of the relevant population that has purchased a given brand or category at least once in the time period under consideration. A brand's penetration share, in contrast to penetration rate, is determined by comparing that brand's customer population to the number of customers for its category in the relevant market as a whole.

Market penetration can be materialized through existing markets and existing products (market penetration), new products and existing markets (product development), existing products and new markets (market development), new products and new markets (diversification) strategies. The targets of market penetration can be achieved through adequate information about the potential markets such as to identify the size of national markets, size of regional markets, and strategy to reach out such target groups at minimum cost. Market penetration is often very useful for the firms; as it may cause quick diffusion and adoption of product in the market along with creating goodwill among customers. Market penetration may generate efficiency for the firm; as, thinner profit margins due to aggressive pricing encourage the firm to perform better and it may discourage competitors to enter into the market. However, market penetration may always not be paying due to the fact that additional orders may be beyond the capacity of the firm.

An investment refers to the deployment of funds at present in anticipation of some positive returns in future. Funds can be invested in variety of assets, in the hope of maximizing the returns with minimum risk. Mutual funds are meant to invest in various categories of investment to maximize the returns for investors. Here, investment pattern of mutual fund firms refers to the share of different assets in total investment of the mutual fund firms. To understand the pattern of mutual fund investments have considerable bearing on the performance of the capital markets and subsequently on the entire macroeconomic environment. Therefore, it is interesting to study the investment pattern which has consequences for the individual in particular and economy in general.

The investment process is generally described in four stages namely - investment policy, investment analysis, valuation of securities and portfolio construction. Investment policy involves personal financial affairs and objectives before making investment. This stage may be considered appropriate for identifying investment assets and considering various features of investment. Further, the investors are supposed to make the analysis of available assets among the chosen class regarding their future behaviors and expected returns and associated risk. Besides, investor has to keep in mind the value of these investments. Each asset must be valued on its individual merit. Finally, a portfolio is constructed. A portfolio construction requires the knowledge of different aspects of assets, consisting of safety and growth of principal, liquidity of assets, selection of assets and allocations.

Investment pattern has its ramifications on the various sectors of the economy, especially when the mutual funds make their portfolio. Sometimes certain sectors are over weighted and others are under weighted. Therefore, in the developed economies, asset management companies have strength to influence the channelization of funds. In a country like India, where this industry is growing rapidly, investment pattern may affect the sectoral composition and structure of the economy to large extent. Besides, capital market may be affected by such decisions.

In wake of the foregoing discussion, present chapter is devoted to study the market penetration and pattern of investment of mutual funds in India. This chapter will endeavor to fathom out the potential of mutual funds to penetrate into un-served areas. This will help this industry to grow in future. Besides, the reader will become aware of the fact that how the investment of mutual funds are distributed that may help the people to make their guesstimates regarding their returns, safety and liquidity.

4.2 Market Penetration

This section is devoted to study the levels of market penetration of mutual funds over time and space. This has been established in the literature of financial theory that development and financial market developments are concomitant. Since, India is less developed country and large chunk of population resides in rural areas, therefore, less penetration is obvious consequence.

Mutual fund industry sells its products in the form of mutual fund schemes to the investors. Therefore, the concept of penetration is relevant here also. Indian mutual fund industry, though, grew at tremendous rate in recent decade and the assets under management are more than 13 trillion rupees and around 45 fund houses are in operation. The population served by such firms is meager and concentrated. And it is considered that there is large scope for such firms to penetrate. The lack of participation is due to two reasons namely; (1) low demand for the mutual funds outside the major (T-15) cities. This low demand is due to the fact that low level of financial literacy, cultural attitudes towards savings and investments; (2) there is low supply of mutual funds from AMCs outside these major cities. The low supply may be due to lack demand from the general retail investors or due to lack of manpower in these areas.

Gross domestic saving is around 30 percent of the GDP in 2015 (World Bank, 2015) which is one of the highest in the world and expected to be parked in mutual funds. However, a recent report (PWC, 2013) points out that the distribution of assets under management (AUM) across cities is highly skewed in favor of the top fifteen (T-15) cities of India. The T-15 cities contribute to 87% of the entire AUM in the country. Even within the T-15 cities, the top five cities (Mumbai, Delhi, Chennai, Kolkata and Bangalore) contribute 85% of the entire AUM at the T- 15 level i.e. 74% of the entire AUM in the country (PWC, 2013). These results have further been vindicated by the following table-4.1 generated from the information provided by AMFI.

Table-4.1: Market Penetration (Rs Crores)

Category of Investor	Dec-2015		Mar-2014	
	T-15*	B-15**	T-15*	B-15**
Retail	167256.51	96953.1	102557.19	60014.79
Corporates	569236.71	65834.41	403046.59	46073.6
Banks/FI	74197.56	9806.3	41556.12	4211.51
FIIs/FPIs	14316.75	107.42	7938.82	254.33
HNIs	309451.55	45863.49	202082.99	28616.19
Total	1134459.08	218564.72	757217.71	139169.82
(Percentage)	(83.85)	(16.15)	(84.47)	(15.53)

T-15: Top 15 Cities as identified by AMFI

B-15: Other than T15

Besides, the share of B-15 has shown decreasing trend in 2015 as compared to 2014. That is, the investable resources of mutual funds are further concentrated overtime. In addition, among the class of investors, large share is cornered by corporates and high net worth individuals. The dismal feature of penetration of Indian mutual funds is that retail investors share is very small. Hence, it can be concluded here that there is very large scope for the penetration of mutual funds both geographically and investors classes.

Out of the total net assets under management by all Mutual funds the percentage of Corporate/institutions is as big as 54.75%, whereas its percentage to total investor's accounts is just 0.95%. It clearly shows that the corporate sector which has a strong urban base is the real player in Mutual Funds industry. Whereas, out of the total net assets under management by all Mutual funds the percentage of individuals is only 39.77%, where as its percentage to total investor's accounts is 97.07%. This analysis clearly suggests a timely action to be taken by mutual Fund Industry regarding market penetration.

The structural deficiencies of Indian financial sector are very obvious. About half the population does not have access to formal banking system. Indian household are basically risk averse and do not like to put their hard earned money in risky assets. Therefore, they are more inclined towards physical assets such as real estate, precious metals, and fixed deposits and so on. They are very scared of the equity market, any investment in equity based assets is considered as gambling. This is evident from the fact that proportion of savings of Indian households in financial markets is very low. RBI in its annual report of 2015 has highlighted that the gross domestic savings by households and investments was 24.8 percent of GDP of 2015-16. The household investment in physical and financial assets was 14.3 percent and 8.0 percent respectively. The investment in shares and debentures as a percentage of gross financial savings by households was 3.6 percent in 2011-12. The gross financial savings by household in mutual funds is estimated at 2.5 percent out of total 3.1 percent in shares/debentures.

There is large scope for market penetration in case of mutual funds. For, mutual funds have variety of schemes to offer. Such schemes may fit in the risk appetite and objectives of everyone. Investors can choose schemes according to structure (open ended and close ended) or objective (growth, balanced, income etc.). The general public is needed to be adequately educated for making mutual funds as their favorite choice.

The same scheme is offered to investors in various formats such as growth, dividend, dividend reinvest etc. Besides, AMCs also offer several investment plans to their customers as systematic investments plan, systematic withdrawal plan and so on. All such formats are for the convenience of investors in terms of flexibility and some degree of control. However, these schemes, plans have proved to be puzzling for the less informed investors. Confused by all these complications, the investors channelize their savings to lesser complicated fixed deposits and/or physical assets (Halan, 2013). Lack of standardization in the processes and customer service standards create unnecessary hassles in investing (Adajania, 2013).

The foregoing discussion highlights that unawareness, risk-aversion and mutual fund complications are massive barriers that AMCs will have to overcome to improve retail participation in mutual funds. Investors need to be made to look beyond the conventional routes of investment through education. In addition to this, campaigns should be modified to increase the visibility of debt funds which usually tend to be secured than equity funds.

4.3   Guidelines for Mutual Funds regarding Investments

Investment by Index Funds

The investment pattern in index funds is in accordance with the weightage of scrips in the particular index as disclosed by information document of the scheme. If the scheme is sector specific, the highest limit on fund deployment in scheme will be in accordance with the weightage of the scrips in the relevant sector index (as disclosed in the information document of scheme).

Investment by Liquid Fund Schemes

This type of fund scheme can deploy funds in only debt and money market securities. In any circumstance, maturity period cannot exceed 91 days. This condition will remain valid in case securities are transferred to another scheme. The asset management companies cannot deviate from this criterion; otherwise it will be considered as violation of investment rules in liquid fund schemes.

Investment by Close - Ended Debt Scheme

These schemes are required to invest in debt securities. The securities in which funds are deployed should mature on or before the date of the maturity of the scheme. This condition is employed to make sure that funds should be disbursed among investors on time.

Approval for Investment in Unrated Debt Instruments

The AMCs can invest in unrated debt instruments, provided conditions set by SEBI are complied with. To invest in such instruments, prior approval of Board of AMC and trustees is required. Subsequently, such investments will be communicated to trustees in its periodical reports. The AMC has to make it clear to the trustees that parameters set for investments are complied with.

Investments in Units of Venture Capital Funds

Mutual fund schemes are permitted to invest in securities or units of venture capital funds. These securities may be listed or unlisted. The upper limit of investment should be within prescribed limits as specified by SEBI.

Investments in Short Term Deposits of Scheduled Commercial Banks

The mutual funds can deploy not more than 15 percent of their net assets in short term deposits of all scheduled commercial banks. In special circumstances, with the prior approval of trustees, this ceiling may be increased to 20 percent. Of the total funds invested in short term deposits of scheduled commercial banks, the share of one commercial bank including its subsidiaries cannot exceed 10 percent. The funds of a particular scheme cannot be deployed in the short term deposit schemes of a bank in which that particular bank is investor.

Overseas Investment by Mutual Funds

The mutual funds in India are permitted to deploy funds overseas provided restrictions imposed by SEBI are complied with. Aggregate upper limit for overseas fund deployment is US $ 7 billion and upper limit per mutual fund is US $ 300. The mutual funds can also invest in overseas ETFs that invest in securities. The upper limit for ETFs is US $ 1 billion and US $ 50 million per mutual fund. The instruments in which overseas investment is allowed include American Depository Receipts, Global Depository Receipts, securities of foreign companies listed in stock exchanges abroad. In addition, Indian mutual funds can also subscribe to IPOs and FPOs of foreign companies, foreign debt securities with convertible currencies, short term as well as long term debt instruments, money market instruments with rating not below investment grade by rating agencies and government securities where the countries are rated not below investment grade.

Investment by Mutual Funds in Derivatives

Every mutual fund would like to hedge the risks involved in investments; hence, they are permitted to have some exposure in derivatives. The total exposure via equity, debt and derivative positions should not exceed 100 percent of the net assets of the scheme. Exposure due to derivative positions taken for hedging purposes in excess of the underlying position against which the hedging position has been taken, shall be treated under the limits. Exposure is the maximum possible loss that may occur on a position.

4.4 Investment Pattern

Asset management companies are supposed to invest the funds mobilized from the investors in various schemes designed according to the requirements of the investments. The fund manager manages the funds in such a way that he is able to generate maximum returns. Besides, investment pattern also comprises the nature of investors who contributes to the assets under management of asset management companies. Such knowledge helps to understand the general trends of investments; consequently, suitable policies can be framed to direct them towards particular direction.

Instruments of Investment

There are various financial instruments for mutual fund organizations to investment reap returns, in turn distribute the same in the form of dividend or interest to their unit holders (investor). Such instruments are as under;

- Equity shares
- Convertible debentures
- Fixed Income Securities include - debt instruments (non-convertible debentures), bonds of public sector and government securities (Gilt)
- Money Market Instruments include - certificates of deposits, treasury bills, commercial paper, bill discounting, call money

The following table-4.2 highlights the investment pattern of mutual funds according to aforementioned instruments.

Table-4.2: Investment Pattern of Mutual Funds-Security Wise (in Rs Crores)

Instrument	2008-09	Dec 2015
Equity Shares	196893.49 (33.72)	427077.11 (32.65)
Debentures/Bonds	101598.19 (17.40)	324270.46 (24.79)
Govt. Securities	52692.96 (11.65)	128871.05 (9.9)
Bank FDs	19234.11 (3.29)	25436.28 (1.9)
Certificates of Deposits	141122.77 (24)	140750.70 (10.77)
CDs/CPs	22.132.89 (3.79)	195592.03 (14.96)
Others	50123.98 (8.6)	65751.75 (5)

The table reveals that there is considerable jump in investments in debentures/bonds category from 17.40 percent in 2008-09 to 24.79 percent in December 2015. Besides, remarkable increase has also been witnessed in CDs/CPs category from 3.79 percent in 2008-09 to about 15 percent in December 2015. However, a decline has been recorded in bank FDs. It can be concluded here that mutual fund companies' investments are trending towards debt instruments along with away from bank fixed deposits. Contrary to the established belief that equity investments increase overtime could not be proved in India as investments in equity instruments are more or less same during last 8 years. Therefore, we can say that aggressiveness in investments did not increase over time and mutual fund companies are also risk averse instead of being risk taking firms. This may be due the nature of demand for such instruments by investors.

Classification of Investments by AMFI

AMFI classifies the funds into the following eight categories:

1. Liquid/Money Market Funds
2. Gilt Funds
3. Debt Oriented Funds
4. Equity Oriented Funds
5. Balanced Funds
6. Gold Exchange Traded Funds
7. Exchange Traded Funds (Other than Gold)
8. Fund of Funds (Investing Overseas)

The ensuing discussion is devoted to investment pattern of mutual funds according to the AMFI classification of funds. In this context, table-4.3 through light on insights regarding such pattern overtime.

Table-4.3: Category-Wise Assets under Management

Fund Category	Dec 2004		Dec 2008		Dec 2015	
	No. of Schemes	Amount (Rs. Crore)	No. of Schemes	Amount (Rs. Crore)	No. of Schemes	Amount (Rs. Crore)
Income	136	47451 (32)	539	197132 (48)	1517	555364 (44)
Equity	141	31551 (21)	290	99081 (24)	416	364562 (29)
Balanced	37	5472 (04)	35	11348 (03)	27	42193 (04)
Liquid/ Money Market	38	59447 (39)	57	82776 (20)	54	232970 (18)
Gilt	30	4876 (03)	32	6368 (02)	41	17463 (01)
ELSS-Equity	37	1740 (01)	44	11577 (3)	58	41100 (03)
Gold ETF	-	-	5	734 (0.002)	13	5773 (0.004)
Other ETF	-	-	11	1761 (0.004)	44	11887 (01)
Fund of Funds (Overseas)	-	-	10	2588 (0.006)	31	2023 (0.002)
Total	419	150537 (100)	1023	413365 (100)	2201	1274835 (100)

Note: Figures in Parentheses are percentages

So far the number of schemes offered to the investors is concerned; these have recorded considerable growth overtime. For instance 2201 schemes were available to investors in December 2015 compared to 1023 in December 2008 and 419 in December 2004. This information indicates that scope of mutual fund industry in India has expanded overtime and better space has been provided to investors. So far the distribution of such schemes in various categories is concerned large chunk of increase in schemes is cornered by income category funds and followed by equity oriented funds. More than 80 percent of schemes fall in these two categories (income and equity). However, other categories did not witness much change except ETFs and FoFs. ETFs were non existents in December 2004, and now there are 13 schemes related to Gold ETFs and 44 other ETFs. Fund of funds is one more category which emerged on the scene in recent years.

So far category wise assets under management are concerned, major share (more than 70 percent) is dominated by income and equity categories. The share of income funds which was 32 percent in December 2004, has increased to 48 percent in 2008; however, declined to 44 percent in December 2015. The equity segment increased to 29 percent in December from 21 percent in December 2004. The liquid/money market category has lost its sheen overtime from 39 percent in December 2004 to 18 percent in December 2015. Therefore, it can be concluded here that Indian mutual fund companies invest in three main categories namely - income, equity and liquid/money market. The table also reveals that efforts to popularize the other categories could not be succeeded. The earlier result of risk avoiding society has further been corroborated.

The Indian mutual fund industry is almost Rs. 13 trillion strong with fixed income or debt having a two third share about Rs 9 trillion, the rest being largely equity. The share of debt funds has not changed much from a decade ago when the industry size was less than Rs 2 lakh crore.

Unit Holding Pattern

Mutual funds unit holders are generally classified into four major categories namely- individuals, NRIs, FIIs and Corporates/Institutions. Such classification helps to understand the distribution of mutual fund services and benefits of mutual fund schemes to the different segments of the society. In this regard, table-4.4 is presented below.

Table-4.4: Unit Holding Pattern of Mutual Fund Industry

Category	March 31, 2002				March 31, 2009				March 31, 2010			
	Number of Investors Account	%age of total Investors Accounts	Net Assets (Rs. Crore)	%age of total net assets	Number of Investors Account	%age of total Investors Accounts	Net Assets (Rs. Crore)	%age of total net assets	Number of Investors Account	%age of total Investors Accounts	Net Assets (Rs. Crore)	%age of total net assets
Individuals	30238065	98.04	55487	55.16	46075763	96.75	155283.21	37.03	46327683	97.07	245390	39.77
NRIs	154622	0.50	1398	1.39	971430	2.04	22821.28	5.44	943482	1.98	27429	4.45
FIIs	1123	0.00	306	0.30	146	0.00	4983.82	1.19	216	0.00	6335	1.03
Corporates/ Institutions	450132	1.46	43403	43.15	575938	1.21	236233.35	56.34	452330	0.95	337813	54.75
Total	30843942	100	100594	100	47623277	100	419321.66	100	47723711	100	616967	100

The investors hold account with the mutual fund companies, as they invest in the schemes offered by them. The account holding pattern has been skewed in favour of individuals, as 97 percent of the accounts are held by them. This ratio remained, more or less, same overtime. Two percent accounts are held by NRIs and one percent belongs to corporates/institutions. However, the contribution of FIIs is negligible.

However, net assets held by categories show very different picture. The corporates holding accounts ranging from one to one and half percent are holding more than 50 percent of the share in net assets. Whereas, individuals holding 97 percent of accounts are holding 40 percent share of net assets. Around 5 percent share is held by NRIs with 2 percent shares in accounts. Hence, it can be concluded from the foregoing discussion that accounts holding is tilted wholesomely in favour of individuals and asset holding is in favour of corporates. Such result is a matter of concern and suggest for more net assets in favour of individuals for percolating benefits of mutual funds.

Liquid/Money Market Schemes

Mutual fund companies have investments of 18 percent of their total investment in this category. The categories of investors interested in the liquid/money market schemes are presented in table-4.5.

Table-4.5: Liquid/Money Market Schemes

Investor	2009				2015			
	AUM (Rs. Crores)	%age of total	No. of Folios	% of total	AUM (Rs. Crores)	%age of total	No. of Folios	% of total
Corporates	66324.70	73.65	14540	8.47	201036.57	86.29	28234	8.04
Banks/FIs	14541.66	16.15	204	0.12	9319.93	4.00	763	0.22
FIIs	1438.03	1.60	35	0.02	432.26	0.19	37	0.01
HNIs	7081.80	7.86	23758	13.85	18294.62	7.85	59369	16.91
Retail	672.85	0.75	133028	77.53	3886.67	1.67	262690	74.82
Total	90059.04	100	171565	100	232970.05	100	351093	100

The table depicts that 86 percent of assets are held by corporates followed by high net worth individuals with 8 percent share in total assets. The corporates' share has improved overtimes whereas it remained same in HNIs category. However, Banks/FIs share had come down to 4 percent in 2015 compared to 16 percent in 2009. Besides, though individuals are holding majority of folios their share in liquid/money market assets is miniscule (less than 2 percent). What is the implication of such distribution in liquid/money market schemes? Banks/FIs do not have short term surplus funds to park in liquid/money market funds. However, corporates have short term surplus funds and they put such funds in liquid/money market funds. Above all retail investors are not much interested in this variety of funds.

Debt Oriented Schemes

Variety and convenience are two factors that stand out in favour of debt oriented mutual funds. In terms of variety, debt funds are available across horizons and risk appetites. Accordingly, they can be broadly classified into short term and long term debt funds. For short term investment horizons one may choose between liquid funds (3-6 months), ultra short term debt funds (less than one year) and short term debt funds (less than 3 years). One may choose income and gilt funds if investment horizon is more than 3 years.

Such schemes are, generally, considered as risk free; however, they have tax implications for the investors. Therefore, different categories have different reactions to such schemes. Investors' distribution in debt oriented funds is presented in table-4.6.

Table-4.6: Debt Oriented Funds

Investor	2009				2015			
	AUM (Rs. Crores)	%age of total	No. of Folios	% of total	AUM (Rs. Crores)	%age of total	No. of Folios	% of total
Corporates	127845.36	64.75	73072	2.60	318212.3	57.14	112557	1.49
Banks/FIs	2668.60	1.35	5135	0.18	9777.14	1.76	1498	0.02
FIIs	2456.94	1.24	24	0	8374.04	1.5	63	0.00
HNIs	56411.14	28.57	177596	6.32	174886.34	31.41	665640	8.84
Retail	8070.63	4.09	255270	90.90	45613.7	8.19	6752804	89.65
Total	197452.68	100	2811097	100	556863.52	100	7532562	100

Investments in debt oriented schemes are dominated by corporates with 65 percent share in 2009; however, it declined to 57 percent in 2015. The high net worth individuals also has considerable interest in debt oriented instruments of mutual funds. They hold 31 percent of assets under management in these schemes and increased overtimes from 29 percent in 2009. Retail investors have shown considerable interest in such schemes. The share of retail investors was 4 percent in 2009 which increased to 8 percent in 2015. Banks/FIs do not have much interest in such instruments, given the nature of such institutions. As expected, majority of folios are held by individuals. Major conclusion from this table is that about 90 percents of investments in debt oriented schemes are cornered by corporates and HNIs.

Equity Oriented Schemes

"Mutual funds are subject to market risks" is most relevant for equity oriented schemes. Investors who have risk appetite are, generally, interested in this category of schemes. Obviously, the different results are expected in investment patterns of equity oriented schemes. Results are presented in table-4.7.

Table-4.7: Equity Oriented Funds

Investor	2009				2015			
	AUM (Rs. Crores)	%age of total	No. of Folios	% of total	AUM (Rs. Crores)	%age of total	No. of Folios	% of total
Corporates	13213.20	12.07	440280	1.06	61656.36	15.2	256683	0.74
Banks/FIs	1863.21	1.70	2727	0.01	1550.74	0.38	833	0.0
FIIs	834.41	0.76	74	0.00	4164.14	1.03	98	0.0
HNIs	22589.06	20.63	355243	0.85	130338.41	32.13	856137	2.47
Retail	71012.71	64.84	40906104	98.09	207952.64	51.26	33599662	96.79
Total	109512.59	100	41704428	100	405662.28	100	34713413	100

Interestingly, individuals and high net worth individuals are more interested in taking risk compared to other categories of investors. Table-4.7 reveals that more than 80 percent of funds are held by individuals and HNIs. This share has increased from 75 percent in 2009. Along with, corporates have considerable interest in equity oriented schemes. And they have improved their share overtime from 12 percent in 2009 to 15 percent in 2015. This has been established in the literature of investments that more risks are related to more returns. The major inference from the foregoing discussion is that HNIs are supposed to be risk takers and individuals are also trending towards such appetite.

Balanced Funds Schemes

Since balanced fund schemes are designed in such way that some returns are assured through combination of debt and equity instruments. The distribution of investments in balanced funds among investors is presented in table-4.8.

Table-4.8: Balanced Funds

Investor	2009				2015			
	AUM (Rs. Crores)	%age of total	No. of Folios	% of total	AUM (Rs. Crores)	%age of total	No. of Folios	% of total
Corporates	1059.42	9.09	12776	0.53	7476.69	17.72	25003	1.07
Banks/FIs	52.77	0.45	112	0.00	43.88	0.1	67	0
FIIs	1.07	0.01	2	0.00	35.65	0.08	3	0
HNIs	2589.74	22.23	32003	1.32	20310.57	48.14	112607	4.8
Retail	7946.83	68.21	2373594	94.14	14325.89	33.95	2207712	94.13
Total	11649.82	100	2418487	100	42192.67	100	2345392	100

Most interested in balanced fund schemes were retailers accounting for 68.21 percent in 2009. However, this share has declined to 34 percent in 2015. We can say that the retail investors' interest has declined in balanced fund schemes overtime. However, most interested in such schemes are HNIs who cornered 48 percent share of AUM increased from 22 percent in 2009. Besides, corporates have also improved from 9 percent in 2009 to 18 percent in 2015.

Other categories of fund schemes, so far AUM of these schemes are concerned, are insignificant and do not deserved to be discussed here in detail. From the risk perspectives, credit risk and interest rate risk need to be observed. The interest rate risk can be measured by average period of holding assets. Longer period bears higher risk and this risk is relatively less in short tenure. Therefore, liquid funds bear the minimum interest rate risk and gilt funds, due to long duration, carry the highest interest rate risk. So far credit risk is concerned; gilt funds are highly secure as they hold sovereign bonds. Credit risk includes default or delay in payment of principal and interest.

Bank deposits still dominate the deposits; for, about 90 trillion is deployed in bank deposits. This amount is 10 times the money in debt mutual funds. The investors lack awareness regarding benefits of debt funds. There is lot of potential in debt funds and need to be harnessed.

4.5 Portfolio Selection by Asset Management Company

It is very important question for the asset management company to decide that in which of the available options the collected /mobilized funds should be invested to provide the investors with higher returns. It affects not only the investment pattern as a whole but also the profitability of the products.

The different asset class definitions are widely debated, but four common divisions are stocks, bonds, real estate and commodities. The exercising of allocating funds among these assets (and among individual securities within each asset class) is what investment management firms are paid for. Asset classes exhibit different dynamics, and different interaction effects; thus, the allocation of money among asset classes will have a significant effect on the performance of the fund. Existing research suggests that allocation among asset classes has more predictive power than the choice of individual holdings in determining portfolio returns. Arguably, the skill of a successful investment manager resides in constructing the asset allocation, and separately the individual holdings, so as to outperform certain benchmark (such as, the peer group of competing funds, bond and stock indices).

It is important to look at the evidence on the long-term returns to different assets, and to holding period returns (the returns that accrue on average over different lengths of investment). For example, over very long holding periods (10+ years, for example) in most countries, equities have generated higher returns than bonds, and bonds have generated higher returns than cash. According to financial theory, equities are more risky (more volatile) than bonds which are more risky than cash.

Against the background of the asset allocation, fund managers consider the degree of diversification that makes sense for a given client (given its risk preferences) and construct a list of planned holdings accordingly. The list will indicate what percentage of the fund should be invested in each particular stock or bond. The theory of portfolio diversification was originated by Markowitz (and many others). Effective diversification requires management of the correlation between the asset returns and the liability returns, issues internal to the portfolio (individual holdings volatility), and cross-correlations between the returns.

A portfolio manager has to decide on the amount to be invested in the basic categories of Equity, Debt, Balanced and Money market Funds.

4.5.1 *Selecting an Equity Fund*

The equity schemes available are classified in growth, value, equity income, broad based specialty and concentrated. There are two important strategies in fashion (1) selecting mainstream growth or value fund, providing broad based diversification, (2) selecting either a differentiated growth or value fund, or a specialty whose risk return will vary from the overall market or a specialty fund whose risk return will vary from the overall market. Besides, past returns of the available funds are required to be assessed for better fund selection. In addition, various important features of the fund schemes are reviewed such as fund size (smaller funds means higher expenses), fund age - the older the performing fund the better compared a new unproven fund, portfolio manager's experience, cost of investing and so on.

4.5.2 *Portfolio characteristics*

Cash position – equity funds normally hold little cash; say 5 percent, more cash would mean less money is invested. A fund manager might sit on higher cash if he predicts a bull or bear run. *Portfolio concentration* – if the funds' 10 largest holdings account for over 50 percent of the net assets, it is a concentrated portfolio.

Market capitalization of funds – large caps funds are deemed safer to invest in comparison to small cap funds.

Portfolio turnover – A steady holding of investments means long term orientation. Higher turnover could mean higher capital gain but it would also mean higher transaction cost.

Portfolio statistic – compare its performance with others.

4.5.3 Selecting an Debt/ Income/ Bond Fund

Narrow down on choices- debt funds have a larger variety to choose from; short term - long term, government - corporate, high investment grade or low, domestic - global bonds.

Know your investment objective- younger investor need retirement planning, hence long term bonds are appropriate, retired investors need money income schemes.

4.5.4 Selecting a Money Market or Liquid Fund

While selecting a liquid fund the advisor has to keep in mind following points; costs, quality, yields.

4.6 Developing a Model Portfolio

While investing and developing a portfolio for oneself, there are many important points which one should remember. Jacob described these steps of investing in this manner:

Jacob's four step program:

- a) Work with the investors to develop long term goals
- b) Determine the asset allocation of the investment portfolio
- c) Determine the sectoral distribution
- d) Select specific fund managers & their schemes

Jacob's four different portfolios

1) Young unmarried professional: 50 percent in aggressive equity funds, 25 percent in high yield bonds & growth & income funds, 25 percent in conservative money market funds.
2) Young couple with 2 kids: 10 percent in money market funds, 30 percent in aggressive equity funds, 25 percent in high yield bonds & long term growth funds & 35 percent in municipal bond funds.

3) Older couple – single income: 30 percent in short municipal bond funds, 35 percent long term municipal bond funds, 25 percent moderately aggressive equity & 10 percent emerging growth equity.

4) Recently retired couple: 35 percent in conservative equity funds for capital preservation/ income, 25 percent moderately aggressive equity & 40 percent in money market funds.

4.7 Risks-Return Matrix

It has been established in the literature of investment theory that risk and return are two most important attributes of an investment. The two are linked in the capital markets and that generally higher returns can only be achieved by taking on greater risk. Risk is not just the potential loss of return; it is the potential loss of entire investment itself (loss of both principal and interest). Consequently, taking on additional risk in search of higher returns is a decision that should not be taken lightly. In investments, the term risk is often expressed as volatility or variation in returns.

The concept of volatility is the measurement of fluctuations in the market value of various asset classes as they rises and falls overtime. The reward for accepting higher volatility is the likelihood of higher investment returns over mid to longer term.

A flow chart from Least Risky to Highest Risky

Asset classes along with their risk and returns relationship are presented in the following figure. This figure is self explanatory that is higher risk asset category is associated with higher returns and vice-versa.

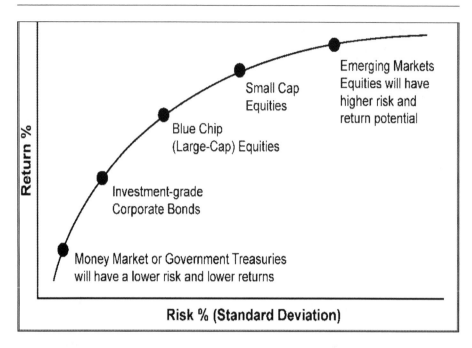

The following inferences can be derived from the foregoing discussion

1. Each asset class has a persistent level of risk and return relative to others over the long-run.
2. There is no free lunch, higher return require greater risk.
3. The higher the percentage of equities in a portfolio, the higher the return and risk.
4. Every investor should make an honest assessment of how much risk they can take on balancing their financial goals vs. their tolerance for losses.

4.8 Efficient Portfolio Frontier through a Diagram

The efficient frontier is the set of optimal portfolios that offers the highest expected return for a defined level of risk or the lowest risk for a given level of expected return. Portfolios that lie below the efficient frontier are sub-optimal, because they do not provide enough return for the level of risk. Portfolios that cluster to the right of the efficient frontier are also sub-optimal, because they have a higher level of risk for the defined rate of return.

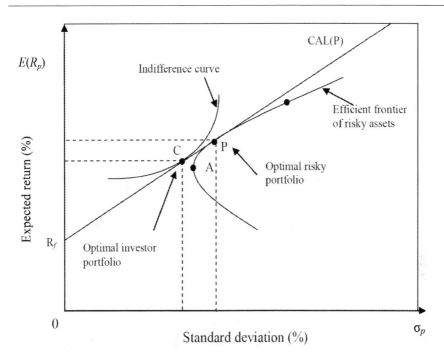

In this figure, CAL (P) is capital allocation line, which measures the relationship between the risks and returns. This also represents the capital allocation between risky and non risky assets. The optimal investor portfolio point is C in the figure, where an indifference curve is tangent to the capital allocation line, CAL (P). Indifference curves with higher utility than this one lie above the capital allocation line, so their portfolios are not achievable. Indifference curves that lie below this one are not preferred because they have lower utility. Thus, the optimal portfolio for the investor with this indifference curve is portfolio C on CAL (P), which is tangent to the indifference curve.

4.9 Concluding Remarks

This chapter discusses the market penetration and investment pattern of asset management companies (AMCs) in India. Investment pattern has its ramifications on the various sectors of the economy. In a country like India, where this industry is growing rapidly, investment pattern may affect the sectoral composition and structure of the economy to large extent. Indian mutual fund industry grew at tremendous rate in recent decade and the assets under management are more than 13 trillion rupees and about 45 fund houses are in operation. The population served by such firms is meager and concentrated. The T-15 cities contribute to 87% of the entire AUM in the country. Even within the T-15 cities, the top five cities (Mumbai, Delhi, Chennai, Kolkata and Bangalore) contribute 85% of the entire AUM at the T- 15 level i.e. 74% of the entire AUM in the country. Besides, large share is cornered by corporates and high net worth individuals. Hence, there is very large scope for the penetration of mutual funds both geographically and investors' classes. This combination of ignorance, risk-aversion and mutual fund complexity are huge hurdles that AMCs in India will have to overcome if there is to be any increase in retail participation in mutual funds. Investors need to be made to look beyond the traditional avenues of investment through sensitization and education.

Contrary to the established belief that equity investments increase overtime could not be proved in India. Aggressiveness in investments did not increase over time and mutual fund companies are also risk averse instead of being risk taking firms.

This has been established that the scope of mutual fund industry in India has expanded overtime and better space has been provided to investors. So far the distribution of such schemes in various categories is concerned large chunk of increase in schemes is cornered by income category funds and followed by equity oriented funds. More than 80 percent of schemes fall in these two categories (income and equity). Indian mutual fund companies invest in three main categories namely - income, equity and liquid/money market. The efforts to popularize the other categories could not be succeeded.

The accounts holding are tilted wholesomely in favour of individuals and asset holding is in favour of corporates. Banks/FIs do not have short term surplus funds to park in liquid/money market funds. However, corporates have short term surplus funds and they put such funds in liquid/money market funds. Above all, retail investors are not much interested in this variety of funds. Investments in debt oriented schemes are dominated by corporates. The high net worth individuals also has considerable interest in debt oriented instruments of mutual funds. And about 90 percents of investments in debt oriented schemes are cornered by corporates and

HNIs. HNIs are supposed to be risk takers and proved true for India and individuals are also trending towards such appetite.

But we still have a long way to go as RBI data indicates that about Rs 90 trillion is parked in bank deposits, 10 times the money in debt mutual funds and over 35 times the retail debt AUM. This is mainly due to lack of awareness about the benefits offered by debt funds besides the 'assured returns' psyche of retail investors. This is bound to change as overall interest rates are likely to fall as India grows.

In addition, each asset class has a persistent level of risk and return relative to others over the long -run. Moreover, higher return requires greater risk and there are no free lunches and higher the percentage of equities in a portfolio, the higher the return and risk. Therefore, every investor should make an honest assessment of how much risk they can take on balancing their financial goals vs. their tolerance for losses.

References

- Adajania K. E. (2013), "MF Industry Needs to Look at Standardization in a New Light", *HT Mint*, September 04.
- Armstrong G. & Kotler P. (2009), *"Marketing. An Introduction"*, 9th ed. Prentice Hall.
- Halan M. (2013), "Why do Indians Buy so much Gold Jewelry?" *HT Mint*, June 11.
- Kotler P. (2000), *"Marketing Management Analysis, Planning Implementation and Control"*, Englowood Cliffs, New Jersey Prentice Hall, Inc.
- Kotler P., Keller K. L. (2008), *"Marketing Management"*, 12th ed., Prentice-Hall.
- Markowitz H.M. (1952), "Portfolio Selection", *The Journal of Finance*, 7 (1), 77–91.
- PWC (2013), "Indian Mutual Fund Industry: Unearthing the Growth Potential in Untapped Markets", CII, available at: *www.pwc.com*.
- World Bank Report (2015)
- www.amfiindia.com
- www.sebi.gov.in

Chapter-5
Concentration and Competition

5.1 Introduction

The policy of liberalization has been put in place, in most of the developing countries, during last two decades of previous century (Ferreira and Ramos, 2009). Financial sector reforms[1] turned out to be integral part of this policy regime. This sector was afflicted with awful structural deficiencies; hence, the performance of financial markets and institutions involved has been proved to be less than optimum levels. Therefore, major objectives of financial sector reforms were to remove such structural flaws and consequently, improve the allocative efficiency of available resources. Besides, financial sector reforms looked for creation of efficient and reliable financial markets and institutions. The Indian financial sector has experienced drastic transformation in the post-liberalization era. As a result, its organizational structure, ownership pattern and domain of operations of institutions have observed changes and the element of competition was infused in the financial sector.

The business of mutual funds was opened to embrace private and foreign sectors in 1992. Subsequently, this industry has recorded major transformations in terms of structure, competition, size, and products. It is considered as untapped business arena[2]; therefore, almost all major players in banks, insurance and manufacturing have entered into the business of mutual funds either individually or in the form of joint ventures (amfi website). About 45 mutual funds firms are now operating in Indian mutual fund industry. Thus, competition, size and new products are obvious consequences.

Therefore, it is of paramount importance to study the competition and concentration in mutual fund industry due to some reasons. Firstly, similar to other industries, the degree of competition is central for quality, variety and costs of products and lack of competition can create inefficiencies. For instance, due to lack of competition, economies of scale are not passed to the investors and performance of the fund may be poor as compared to fee charged for managing the investors' funds (Gruber, 1996; Korkeamaki & Smythe, 2004). Secondly, investors have to be careful; for, competition in the mutual fund industry can intensify conflicts of interest between investors and fund families. Since mutual funds inflows are sensible to past performance, portfolio managers have incentives to manipulate their position in the category ranking by changing the fund volatility (Gaspar, Massa & Matos, 2006). Thirdly, fee disclosure is considered crucial for investor driven competition among the mutual fund firms.

So far Indian mutual industry is concerned; its size in terms of assets under management has now reached to the level of about Rs.13 billion, which is managed by the multiplicity of fund families. Hence, competition among the fund families is obvious and they may be trying hard to compete for market share. Mutual funds in India offer a variety of options to investors such as income funds, balanced funds, liquid funds, gilt funds, index funds, exchange traded funds and sectoral funds. This diversification of funds[3] and schemes may be attributed to the increasing competition among players. Therefore, it is vital to study the competition and concentration in the mutual fund industry in India. It will, thus, help the investors to select the funds in their portfolios. Besides, it may prove useful for the policy makers to frame it in such a manner that adequate competition is maintained.

5.2 Theoretical Underpinning

Mutual funds, generally, fall within the category of financial institutions. Therefore, to study the concentration and competition in mutual funds, it is important to know how it can be, theoretically, treated as an industry. Industrial organisation is, essentially, studied in the structure-conduct performance (SCP) paradigm. SCP was initiated by Bain (1956) and further developed by Needham (1979) and Scherer (1980). The underlying idea is that the industrial structure determines the conduct of firms in the industry and that may, in turn, influence their performance. Variations in structure, conduct, and performance across industries have been recognized due to their varied nature (Scherer, 1980). Later, it was recognized that SCP paradigm can be employed to assess the within industry competition that may ascertain the firm's choice of strategy (Caves, 1980; Porter, 1981).

The structure of an industry is described as number and size distribution of firms in the industry, number and size distribution of buyers of the products of the industry under consideration, product differentiation (homogeneous or heterogeneous), barriers to entry for new firms and exit of existing firms. The structural change in industry may lead to subsequent changes in its behaviour, industrial performance and the ownership pattern (concentration). These changes can also be initiated by governmental interventions[4]. Industrial structure may also change with the creation and adoption of technological innovations[5]. The adopting firm may be able to reduce cost of production and produce better quality products. Hence, improved firm performance may lead to higher market shares and likely to eliminate competitors. The entry of new and better performing firms may, in a similar way, change the industrial structure. The industrial structure assumes to influence conduct (strategy) and performance, but changes in conduct and performance may influence industry structure as well in subsequent rounds of production.

Baumol et.al. (1989) provided a framework in which mutual funds can be treated as industry. The number of firms (funds) operating in the mutual funds are considered as 'sellers' and the investors are labeled as 'buyers'. The schemes offered by mutual funds are their products which can be homogeneous or heterogeneous in nature. The fee charged by the mutual funds is regarded as price of the products (schemes). Size of the existing firms, popularity of incumbent firms among investors, past performance of existing firms, scale economies enjoyed by already established firms and regulatory measures are considered as barriers to

128

entry. Such barriers hamper the flow of funds into industry. Indian mutual fund industry has witnessed remarkable increase in the number of firms, overtime, due to ease of regulatory measures and the big business houses with substantial capacity to invest have entered. Besides, the merger and takeover have happened frequently; hence, the market share must have seen remarkable changes overtime. Consequently, the changes in conduct and performance of firms are, expectedly, obvious outcomes.

The economic theory highlights that strong competition among firms improves efficiency and ensure better performance. In particular, there are two forms of market structure-perfect competition and perfect contestability[6] that constitutes the theoretical ideals of highly effective competition (Baumol, Panzar and Willig, 1988). Baumol et.al. (1989) clearly showed that the changes in the industry concentration would lead to the variation in prices, output and product quality. This chapter strives to address the issue of how does the structure matter for the competition.

5.3 Learning from Previous Studies

Though not much research has been carried out concerning concentration and competition in Indian mutual funds; but comprehensive research is available on various facets of this aspect in other parts of the world. It has been established in due course that mutual funds' business is organised in the form of industrial organisation. The traditional wisdom regarding industrial organisation has, largely, considered the industry as a homogeneous unit. That is, the firms in the same industry are quite similar. However, emerging literature on the industrial organisation established that firms in a typical industry are not alike. Firms, within the same industry, develop very different competitive strategies and create a 'niche' for themselves in the industry (Porter, 1981).

Market share is an essential element of market concentration. Divergent studies have highlighted the factors behind the increase and decrease in the share of a particular firm. Performance is expected to attract more capital and therefore, increase the fund family's market share (Berk and Green, 2004). The positive abnormal performance attracts more assets in subsequent years, while poor performers do not experience outflows of the same magnitude (Ippolito, 1992; Sirri & Tufano, 1998). This asymmetric response suggests that families can experience an increase in their market share, even if they are average performers as a whole, as long as they have one or more top performers in their portfolio of product offerings. Baumol, Goldfeld, Gordon, and Koehn (1990) indicate that there are economies of scale and scope in the US mutual fund industry. This implies that family size has an important effect on profitability. However, Chen, Hong, Huang and Kubik (2004) contend that larger mutual fund companies suffer from a form of diseconomies of scale, hierarchy costs[7] that erode performance.

Massa (2003) adds that fund proliferation[8] becomes an additional tool that can be used to limit competition and increase market coverage. On the empirical side, Khorana and Servaes (1999) studying mutual funds stated that large families and families that have more experience in opening funds in the past are more likely to open new funds. Massa (1998) advocated that fund and category proliferation phenomena can be seen as marketing strategies used by the managing companies to exploit investors' heterogeneity. Investors have different profiles and investment needs that can be explored by fund complexes. Cristoffersen and Musto (2002) advocate that one reason why funds charge different prices to their investors are that they face different demand curves.

Given the nature of the mutual fund industry, there is little scope for product differentiation; however, fund families are able to differentiate their products sufficiently and ease price competition (Wahal & Wang, 2011). Massa (2003) studied the relation between the performance of the fund family and the degree of differentiation of the objectives in which the fund family operates. The schemes offered by fund families are considered as products of different nature.

Gaspar, Massa, and Matos (2006) document that fund families strategically transfer superior performance to their more valuable funds by demonstrating favoritism in IPO allocations. From an investor's perspective, Elton, Gruber, and Green (2007) find that mutual fund returns within a family tend to be highly correlated, which limits the benefit of portfolio diversification for investors with exposure to a single fund family. Mamaysky and Spiegel (2002) develop a theory of mutual fund design, which suggests that fund families should diversify across investment styles to enhance investors' welfare.

There is little relationship between market share and fee charged (Sirri & Tufano, 1993). Moreover, asset inflows to firm in the industry are free from expense ratio (Barber, Odean, and Zheng, 2005). However, Coates and Hubbard (2007) established that fund assets are negatively related to fee and argue that this alone is sufficient to demonstrate that there is price competition in the fund industry. Wilcox (2003) provides experimental evidence, which indicates that consumer pay close attention to fees when selecting mutual funds. In contrast, Capon, Fitzsimons, and Prince (1996) present survey evidence to suggest that only about one quarter of mutual fund investors consider management fees to be important in selecting funds. Evidence presented by Sirri and Tufano (1993), Freeman and Brown (2001), and Barber, Odean, and Zheng (2005) also suggests that price competition is not important in the industry, and Elton, Gruber, and Busse (2004) report that investors in S&P 500 index funds do not necessarily choose the fund with the lowest expenses.

Severe market competition forces firms to engage in riskier decisions compensated by higher returns. Hence, degree of market concentration can be considered as a proxy for the risk factor, such that firms with higher risks in competitive industries may carry higher returns to make up such risks (Hou and Robinson, 2006).

5.4 Competition and Concentration: Hypothesizing

- The financial sector reforms were introduced in the Indian setup after 1991. Mutual fund industry was integral part of it. Private sector and foreign sector allowed in this business. Hence, this industry is expected to have witnessed growth over time in terms of its size and firms operating therein.
- The period under study here (2006-15) includes boom, recession in the world economy. Moreover, the capital market in India also witnessed such moves. Therefore, it seems that merger, acquisition and takeover must be the obvious consequences.

- Though industry grew in terms of number of firms; however, it is expected that firms with experience in financial background could survive. Past performance is an important factor in the funds inflow. So, the concentration in industry is expected to increase overtime.
- This form of business is prevalent only after the new economic policy introduced. Indian private firms did not have adequate skill in this field. Therefore, joint venture with foreign established firms might have dominated the scene.
- Indian investors are, basically, risk averse instead of risk taker. Hence, it is expected that debt/income schemes must have recorded more inflows as compared to equity schemes.

5.5 Measuring Concentration

This study belongs to concentration and competition of mutual fund industry; hence, we require data on the size of the industry and the size of individual firms in the industry overtime. Besides, the data on merger, acquisition and takeover are required to identify the growth of firms by growing organically or through eating the market share of other firms in the industry. Since products of this industry are offered in the forms of schemes; the data on various schemes and their relative position in relation to other schemes are considered necessary to fathom out the competition among the schemes operating in this business.

The study pertains to the period between 2006 and 2015. The relevant data has been culled from the official website of Association of Mutual Funds in India (AMFI). The size of the industry and the firms operating therein has been captured by the assets under management (AUM). Such data is available with AMFI. Hence, data regarding AUMs, various schemes, merger and takeover has been taken from the AMFI. To generate further insight regarding the intra-firm relationship within the industry, the firms operating in the industry are categorized as bank/institution sponsored, private Indian, private foreign, joint ventures predominantly Indian and joint venture predominantly foreign. Though the period of study is dictated by the availability of data; however, this period provides divergent phases of Indian growth story, movements in capital market, boom and slowdown in the global economy. Hence, the selection of this period contains various phases of growth; therefore, may give better insights regarding the changing contours of the market structure of Indian mutual fund industry.

The measures used to estimate the market concentration and competition are discussed below:

a) Market share of a firm in industry has been calculated by the following relationship:

$$MS_{it} = \frac{AUMit}{AUM\,of\,Industry} \times 100 \qquad (1)$$

Here, MS_{it} is a market share of firm i in period t, AUMit is the assets under management of firm i in period t.

b) Concentration Ratio is the market share held by the largest n firms in an industry.

$$CR_n = \sum_{i=0}^{n} S_i \quad n = 2, 4, 8, ---- \qquad (2)$$

Here, CR_n is the Concentration Ratio for n largest firms. Si is the market share of ith firm in the industry. This ratio is generally calculated for the 4, 8 and 20 firms depending upon the number of firms operating in the industry.

c) Herfindhal-Harishman Index (HHI) is a measure of concentration that takes into account all the firms in the industry in the following way:

$$HHI = \sum_{i=1}^{n} Si^2 \times 100 \qquad (3)$$

Here, Si is the market share of ith firm in the industry. HHI may vary from close to 0 to 10,000. Larger value of HHI indicates the higher level of market concentration and vice-versa.

d) The rank correlation coefficient of ranks of firms in the industry over two different period of time has been calculated to identify the change in importance of the firms in the industry over time.

e) To identify the dependence of the ranks in any terminal period is dependent on some initial period, following linear regression has been estimated:

$$Yt = \alpha + \beta Xt + \varepsilon \qquad (4)$$

Here, Yt is the share of firms in the industry in some terminal year and Xt is the share of the firms in the industry in some initial period. Here α and β are constants and to be estimated. Positive significant value of β can be interpreted as present position of the firms are highly dependent on the position in the initial period.

f) However, the value of regression coefficient 'β' alone will not help to understand the movement of the shares across size classes. To capture such relationship, Grossack (1965) decomposition formulae to decompose the regression coefficient is expressed as a product of the correlation coefficient and the concentration ratio. This is an integration of the static and dynamic measure of concentration.

Regression coefficient can be represented as:

$$\beta = r(\sigma_y / \sigma_x) \qquad (5)$$

Here, r is the correlation coefficient of the market shares in two periods and σ_x and σ_y are the standard deviation of the shares in the respective periods.

There are two conditions in respect to this dynamic model:

If β >1 and the value of r close to unity, then it implies increase in concentration.

If β <1, three situations can be identified depending on the value of r and concentration ratio;

a. If r is low and concentration ratio equal to 1 implying large firms lost market to each other.
b. If r is high and concentration ratio is low implying large firms lost market to small firms.
c. If both are low, implying large firms as a group lost market to each other and to small firms.

5.6   AMCs Operating in India

This study pertains to the period between 2006 and 2015 dictated by the company wise availability of data on assets under management. UTI was the sole public sector organisation operating in India till 1987. The financial sector reforms opened the mutual fund services to private and foreign sector firms. Hence, the number of firms operating in India coming from divergent segments entered. They are chiefly categorized as - institutional sponsored AMCs, private sector, foreign sector, joint ventures between Indian and foreign companies. Overtime, the number of firms operating in India registered remarkable increase. And its number increased to the level of 34 by 2006 (Table-5.1). Besides, like goods producing firms, such firms also witnessed entry and exit of firms from the industry; therefore, potential drivers of change in the market structure. Besides, this industry also observed merger and takeover; thus, can be inferred here that mutual fund industry in India was also showing some conduct, may be due to market concentration and performance. For instance, 34 firms were operating during 2006, during this year Birla Sunlife acquired Alliance, Canara Robeco acquired GIC, USA based firm Templeton took over the operations of Kothari Pioneer, and private sector bank HDFC operated mutual funds acquired Zurich. Tata also in the mood of expanding its asset management business acquired the activities of Ind Bank. Pine Bridge, Mirae and J P Morgan entered in the Indian Mutual Fund Industry in 2007 and number of firms operating increased to 37. Goldman Sachs a very reputed company of USA started its operations in India in 2008 and Fortis also entered by acquiring ABN AMRO. Two more firms appeared on the scene namely-BOI AXA, edelweiss. Consequently, the size of industry in terms of firms operating increased to 40 in 2008. Axis, Oswal, Peerless and Shinsei entered in 2009. Goldman Sachs acquired the reputed Benchmark in 2011 and L & T took over Fidelity in 2012. HDFC further expanded its business activities through acquiring Morgan Stanley in 2014. Pine Bridge that entered with fanfare in 2007 surrendered to Kotak in 2015. So, the foregoing discussion highlights that major companies tried their luck in this business. Some were able to survive and others give in to other competitors. It has also been recognized that stock market blood bath during 2008-9 was also responsible for quick changes in the ownership pattern of the industry. Right now, about 45 companies are operating in this business. It can be considered that there is adequate competition in this industry. Therefore, it is interesting to discuss the concentration and competition in this industry. Such competition may be able to provide the good quality schemes (products) to the investors (buyers) at reasonable price (fee).

Table-5.1: Asset Management Companies (AMCs) in Operation

Year	No. of AMCs	Name of AMCs
2006	34	ABN AMRO, Baroda Pioneer, Benchmark, Birla Sun Life (Acquired Alliance), BNP Paribas, Canara Robeco (Acquired GIC), DBS Chola, Deutsche, DSP Blackrock, Escorts, Fidelity, Franklin Templeton (Acquired Kothari Pioneer), HDFC (Acquired Zurich), HSBC, ICICI Prudential, IDFC, ING, JM Financial, Kotak Mahindra, L & T, LIC Nomura, Morgan Stanley, Principal (Acquired Sun F & C), Quantum, Reliance, Religare Invesco, Sahara, SBI, Shriram, Standard Chartered, Sundaram, Tata (Acquired Ind Bank), Tauras, UTI

2007	37	Pine Bridge, Mirae, JP Morgan entered as AMCs
2008	40	BOI AXA, Edelweiss, Fortis (Acquired ABN AMRO), Goldman Sachs entered.
2009	44	Axis, Motilal Oswal, Peerless, Shinsei entered
2010	44	
2011	46	Daiwa (Acquired Shinsei), IIFL, Indiabulls, Union KBC entered Goldman Sachs (Acquired Benchmark)
2012	47	PPFAS, IIFCL entered L &T (Acquired Fidelity)
2013	48	IL & FS, SREI, SBI (Acquired Daiwa),
2014	46	Birla Sunlife (Acquired ING), HDFC (Morgan Stanley)
2015	45	Kotak (Acquired Pinebridge)

5.7   Empirical Results and Discussion

The competition among firms, in an industry, has potential to improve the efficiency of the firms. The firms strive to improve their performance to stay in business for long period. They try hard to corner the share of other firms in the market. The mutual fund industry is not exceptional, and firms in their pursuant to grow, use various strategies to improve their clientele and enjoy the economies of scale and scope. To measure the competition among various firms, the shares of various firms in the total assets under management have been calculated and results are presented in table-5.2.

Table-5.2: Asset Share and Rank of Different Mutual Funds

Fund Name	2006	2008	2010	2012	2015
HDFC Mutual Fund	9.04 (4)	11.81(2)	12.31(2)	12.46 (1)	13.30 (1)
ICICI Prudential	12.37 (2)	10.48 (3)	10.48 (3)	10.75 (3)	12.84 (2)
Reliance	13.48 (1)	16.49 (1)	14.49 (1)	11.58 (2)	11.71 (3)
Birla Sunlife	6.23 (6)	9.59 (5)	9.09 (5)	9.43 (4)	10.19 (4)
UTI	10.64 (3)	9.93 (4)	9.59 (4)	8.51 (5)	7.91 (5)
SBI	5.37 (7)	5.38 (6)	5.95 (6)	6.72 (6)	7.46 (6)
Franklin Templeton	6.32 (5)	3.89 (8)	5.40 (7)	5.09 (7)	5.28 (7)
Kotak Mahindra	3.09 (11)	3.71(9)	4.59 (8)	4.33 (8)	4.09 (8)
IDFC		2.92 (12)	3.03 (11)	4.02 (9)	4.08 (9)
DSP Blackrock	3.63 (9)	2.93 (10)	4.36 (9)	3.96 (10)	2.84 (10)
Axis			1.18 (15)	1.48 (16)	2.57 (11)
Tata	4.09 (8)	3.47 (11)	3.24 (10)	2.44 (11)	2.35 (12)
L & T			0.57 (22)	1.37 (17)	1.87 (13)
Deutsche	1.28 (15)	1.85 (14)	1.17 (16)	2.22 (12)	1.86 (14)
Sundaram	1.84 (14)	1.45 (15)	2.06 (12)	1.82 (14)	1.63 (15)
Religare Invesco	0.41 (18)	1.23 (17)	1.64 (13)	1.74 (15)	1.48 (16)
J M Financial	0.99 (16)		0.84 (18)	0.91 (19)	1.18 (17)
LIC Nomura	3.06 (13)	4.70 (7)	1.60 (14)	0.88 (21)	0.92 (18)
Baroda Pioneer	0.03 (20)	0.23 (20)	0.37 (25)	0.89 (20)	0.69 (19)
HSBC	3.61 (10)	1.95 (13)	0.64 (21)	0.64 (24)	0.57 (20)
IDBI			0.50 (23)	0.77 (22)	0.56 (21)
J P Morgan		0.5 (19)	0.49 (24)	1.94 (13)	0.55 (22)
Canara Robeco	0.61 (17)	0.96 (18)	1.12 (17)	1.08 (18)	0.55 (23)
Goldman Sachs				0.59 (25)	0.51 (24)
Principal	3.07 (12)	1.38 (16)	0.75 (19)	0.68 (23)	0.43 (25)
BNP Paribas			0.67 (20)	0.46 (27)	0.37 (26)
India Bulls				0.32 (28)	0.36 (27)
Motilal Oswal			0.04 (28)	0.06 (30)	0.34 (28)
Taurus	0.07 (19)	0.04 (21)	0.36 (26)	0.58 (26)	0.26 (29)
Mirae		0.03 (22)	0.05 (27)	0.07 (29)	0.21 (30)

Note: Figures in parentheses are ranks of the firms according to size

Table-5.2 highlights that large firms operating in the mutual fund business have more or less retained their ranks with little changes over time. For, Reliance enjoyed first rank in 2006 and was able to retain it till 2010; subsequently, this position topples to second in 2012 and third in 2015. ICICI was at number 2 in 2006 and retained it even in 2015; however, it shifted to number three in intervening periods. HDFC enjoys the top position now had improved from position 4 in 2006 and 2 in 2008 and 2010. UTI registered shrink in its position to 5 from 3 in 2006. Overall, the top five positions were shared by the HDFC, ICICI, Reliance, Birla Sunlife, and UTI with little changes in shares and ranks overtime. SBI though improved in terms of share in 2015; however, its ranking did not improve overtime. Birla Sunlife and HDFC had recorded significant improvement in shares overtime. Two more firms that deserved to be discussed here are Kotak and IDFC. For, both improved their share and ranking overtime. It can be inferred from the table-5.2 that large and small firms are coexisting in this business and major share is cornered by 5-6 firms. Since, the business of mutual funds survive on the distribution network, hence the small firms can also concentrate and survive in the competitive environment. Therefore, there is a scope of niche market for the smaller firms.

Level of concentration in the mutual fund industry has been estimated here by using the techniques of concentration ratio and Herfindhal-Harishman Index (HHI). The level of concentration and its change overtime determine the behaviour of firms in the market that ultimately decide the performance of the firms. Four, eight and twenty firm concentration ratio has been calculated and results are presented in table-5.3.

Table-5.3: Concentration Ratio in Indian Mutual Funds

Year	4-Firm	8-Firm	20-Firm
2006	45.53	67.54	89.23
2008	48.71	72.27	95.85
2010	46.87	71.9	93.56
2012	44.22	68.87	92.74
2015	48.04	72.78	94.82

The table-5.3 reveals that 45.53 percent of market share was cornered by four largest firms in 2006; which has increased to 48.71 percent in 2008. That is, the industry has witnessed increase in concentration and decrease in competition during this period. However, this concentration has started decreasing in 2010 and 2012 (46.87% and 44.04%), but in 2015 four firm concentration again reached to the level of 2008. Similar trends are also visible for eight and twenty firm concentration ratio. Therefore, it can be concluded that despite the entry of new firms in the industry, they stayed at margin and industry witnessed increase in concentration overtime. Though, initially the increase in new firms in the industry had small dent on the concentration, but new firms could not sustain in long period and yielded to larger firms. Decrease in competition is not a good signal for the investors; for, it gives larger space to firms to charge higher fee. Moreover, the pressure of performance eases on the firms.

Since the concentration ratio method does not take into consideration all the firms present in the market; hence, to overcome this drawback HHI has been calculated.

Table-5.4: HHI for Indian Mutual Funds

Year	HHI
2006	739.202
2008	838.781
2010	789.752
2012	719.874
2015	799.296

The resulted depicted by the concentration ratio are vindicated by the HHI method (table-5.4). The value of HHI was 739.202 in 2006 and increased to

828.781 in 2008. It followed a decreasing trend till 2012 and again jumped in 2015.

The results observed in the foregoing discussion have further been corroborated by the figure-1, where the results are plotted on X-Y scale.

Figure-1: Trends in HHI in Mutual Fund Industry

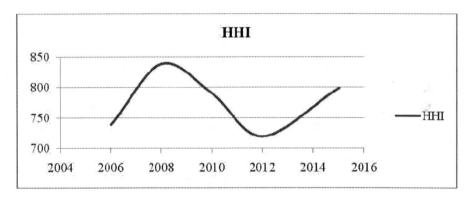

The ranks of firms in terms of shares are reflection of the competition among the firms vying for the larger share in the market. Therefore, rank correlation coefficients have been calculated for two different periods (2010-2012, 2010-2015 and 2012-2015) to understand such phenomenon. The table-5.5 depicts these coefficient values.

Table-5.5: Rank Correlation Coefficient of Market Share

Year	HHI
2010-2012	0.9199
2010-2015	0.9203
2012-2015	0.9537

The rank correlation values in table-5.5 shows that ranking positions have not changed much overtime; for, the coefficient value is very high.

Therefore, it has been established that dominating firms have consolidated their position in the industry overtime.

The HHI has also its own limitations that it gives only the idea of whether the concentration has increased or decreased. However, it does not take care for the nature of competition. The nature has been captured by the Grossack (1965) methodology which incorporates static and dynamic measures. The model would be able to explain whether large firms of some initial years have been able to maintain their market shares up to some terminal year and whether large forms have lost their share to small firms, new entrants or to other large firms. The Grossack model of regression coefficients is obtained by estimating the regression of market share in terminal year to all firms on the initial year. Here, the initial year and terminal years are 2010-2015, 2010-2012 and 2012-2015. The results are presented in table-5.6.

Table-5.6: Regression Results

Dependent Series	Independent Series	Const.	Slope	R^2	F	D.W.
2015	2012	-0.2061 (-1.4127)	1.0751 (36.077)	0.9789	1301.57 (P=0.00)	2.5052
2015	2010	0.0177 (0.0716)	0.9607 (20.225)	0.9359	409.084 (P=0.00)	2.2112
2012	2010	0.3556 (2.2103)	0.9021 (28.705)	0.9671	824.030 (P=0.00)	2.6044

The significant values of F-Statistic defend the regression specifications. The Durbin Watson coefficients elucidate that series are serially correlated. It has been established through the table that firms dominating in the initial years are able to maintain their position in the terminal years. This position is more pronounced from 2012 to 2015; for, the value of the coefficient is more than one, that is dominating firms in 2012 has consolidated their position in 2015. The retaining of dominating position is also established in other regressions. The constant coefficient is significant for the regression 2010-2012 indicates that position in 2012 along with the position in 2010 was also supported by other economic environment. However, this aspect is missing in the regressions of 2010-2015 and 2012-2015. And the position in initial year has determined the position in the terminal year. Hence, the overall concentration has increased from 2012 to 2015; however, it declined by small amount from 2010 to 2012.

Grossack has highlighted that the regression coefficient alone may not help to understand the movement of the shares across size classes. To capture this, he formulated an ingenious decomposition exercise wherein the regression coefficient is expressed as a product of the correlation coefficient and the concentration ratio. This is an integration of the static and dynamic measure of concentration.

Table-5.7: Decomposition of Regression Co-efficient

Year	Correlation	Concentration Ratio	Regression Co-efficient
2010-2012	0.984	0.9170	0.9023
2010-2015	0.967	0.996	0.9631
2012-2015	0.989	1.0867	1.0747

The table-5.7 shows the results of decomposition of the regression in concentration ratio and correlation. The value of regression coefficient is more than one in 2012-2015 and the correlation coefficient is very close to one, therefore, as already stated, the concentration has increased from 2012 to 2015. However, in other cases, though the regression coefficient turned out to be less than one, but the concentration ratio and correlation are high. Therefore, it can be concluded that large firms are retaining their position.

The foregoing discussion provided information regarding the state of competition regarding overall mutual funds in India. It is interesting to know about the nature of competition happening among the sectors and within the sectors. For this purpose, the sector-wise competition and competition within the sectors and schemes wise competition by using standard measures of concentration are estimated.

The table-5.8 lists the major sectors and their constituents. The Indian mutual fund industry segment wise is categorized in five major categories namely-public sector, private sector Indian, private sector foreign, joint ventures predominantly Indian and joint sector predominantly foreign.

Table-5.8: Different Segments of Asset Management Companies

Segment	Name of Fund
Public Sector	BOI AXXA (joint), Canara Robeco (Joint), SBI (Joint), Union KBC (Joint), Baroda Pioneer (Joint), IDBI, UTI, IIFCL, LIC Noumra
Private Sector Indian	Benchmark, Chola, Edelweiss, Escorts, IL&FS, Indiabulls, J M Financial, Kotak Mahindra, L & T, Motilal Oswal, Peerless, PPFAS, Quantum, Reliance, Sahara, Shriram, Sundaram, Tata, Tauras
Private Sector Foreign	BNP Paribas, Franklin Templeton, Goldman Sachs, Mirae, Deutsche
Joint Ventures Predominantly Indian	Axis, Birla Sunlife, DSP Blackrock, HDFC, ICICI Prudential, IDFC, Religare Invesco
Joint Ventures Predominantly Foreign	HSBC, J P Morgan, Principal PNB, DHFL Pramarica

The segment wise concentration of mutual funds highlights the role of public, private and foreign sector in Indian mutual fund industry.

It has been decided by policy parameters to give way to private and foreign sector firms. Knowledge regarding this phenomenon helps us to understand the type of business models are going to be opted. For, the Indian business and financial firms did not have exposure as asset management companies before 1990s. Therefore, integration with foreign firms may prove to be useful. The shares of different segments in mutual fund business have been presented in table-5.9.

The dominating segment in Indian mutual fund industry is joint ventures with Indian domination followed by private sector Indian and public sector. The joint sector with Indian domination has improved its share overtime. For, its share was 34.71 percent in 2006 that increased to 47.31 percent in 2015. That is, almost half the business is controlled by joint venture with Indian domination. Though, private sector Indian proved to be considerable segment of Indian mutual fund business; however, it sheds its share from 28.03 percent in 2006 to 24.21 percent in 2015. Similar trend has also been depicted by public sector. Private foreign sector started with 8 percent share in this business and more or less retained overtime. The joint venture with foreign domination gradually reduced to margin starting with 7.33 percent in 2006-07. We can say that joint venture with Indian domination is leading the scene.

Table-5.9: Share of Different Segments in the Mutual Fund Business

Year	Segments				
	Public Sector	Private Sector Indian	Private Sector Foreign	Joint Venture Indian Domination	Joint Venture Foreign Domination
2006-07	21.59	28.03	8.34	34.71	7.33
2007-08	19.54	32.78	8.35	33.12	6.22
2008-09	22.24	26.88	6.05	40.80	4.00
2009-10	23.85	27.07	6.06	40.70	2.31
2010-11	19.54	27.94	7.44	42.94	2.14
2011-12	19.28	24.42	8.56	45.09	2.64
2012-13	19.49	24.29	8.47	44.13	3.60
2013-14	19.52	23.33	8.00	45.77	3.38
2014-15	17.31	23.26	8.97	47.72	2.73
2015-16	18.52	24.21	8.22	47.31	1.73

So far the concentration within the segments is concerned; two firms and four firms' concentration are calculated for each segment. The glance at the table-5.10 reveals that even segments are highly concentrated. In the public sector, two firms UTI and SBI have cornered little more than 80 percent of the share and in four firm concentration ratio, this ratio was 99 percent in 2006 and gradually reduced to 91.06 percent in 2015. And SBI, UTI, LIC and Canara have dominated the scene; however, Baroda replaced the LIC in 2012 and 2015. Private sector Indian segment has dominated around 65 to 70 percent by two firms. Reliance and Tata were the dominating firms in 2006 and Tata yielded to Kotak in the subsequent years. The concentration ratio reached to the level of between 83 and 89 percents when four largest firms were taken into consideration. Reliance, Kotak, Tata, and Sundaram dominated between 2006 and 2012. However, Sundaram gave way to L&T in 2015. Private sector foreign was highly concentrated; two firms had cornered almost all the share enjoyed by this segment. Franklin Templeton and Deutsche were dominating the scene. Joint Venture with Indian domination enjoys command in the entire business of mutual funds in India (about 50 percent), was also concentrated in its own segment. HDFC and ICICI cornered 67.59 percent business in 2006; however, it reduced to 55.26 percent in 2015. So far four firms concentration is concerned, this ratio increased to 98.72 percent in 2006 represented by HDFC, ICICI, IDFC and Birla Sunlife. Though, this value gradually reduced to 84.41 percent in 2015. Joint venture with foreign domination is dominated by HSBC and Principal.

Table-5.10: Concentration Ratio in Different Segments of Mutual Funds in India

Year→ Segment↓	2006		2010		2012		2015	
	CR2	CR4	CR2	CR4	CR2	CR4	CR2	CR4
Public Sector	81.24 SBI, UTI	99.07 SBI, UTI, LIC, Canara	81.06 SBI, UTI	95.21 SBI, UTI, LIC, Canara	78.62 SBI, UTI	88.83 SBI, UTI, Baroda Canara	83.04 SBI, UTI	91.06 SBI, UTI, Baroda Canara
Private Sector Indian	68.69 Rel., Tata	87.96 Rel., Kotak Tata, Sndrm	69.66 Rel., Kotak	89.01 Rel., Kotak Tata, Sndrm	65.92 Rel., Kotak	83.55 Rel., Kotak Tata, Sndrm	65.3 Rel., Kotak	82.75 Rel., Kotak Tata, L&T
Private Sector Foreign	100.00 F.Tem, Deutsh		99.42 F.Tem, Deutsh		86.81 F.Tem, Deutsh		86.70 F.Tem, Deutsh	
Joint Venture with Indian Domination	67.59 HDFC, ICICI,	98.72 HDFC, ICICI, IDFC, B Snlfe	57.19 HDFC, ICICI,	89.34 HDFC, ICICI, DSP, B Snlfe	52.92 HDFC, ICICI	83.61 HDFC, ICICI, IDFC, B Snlfe	55.26 HDFC, ICICI	85.41 HDFC, ICICI, IDFC, B Snlfe
Joint Venture with Foreign Domination	100.00 HSBC, Prpal		86.94 HSBC, Prpal		73.25 JP Mgn Prpal		65.57 HSBC, JP Mgn	

The products in the form of schemes which are offered to investors in India are basically categorized as debt/income schemes, growth/equity schemes, balanced schemes and others. Share of these categories in the mutual fund industry hold significance; for, we can understand the risk aptitude of the investors and the business inclinations of the firms involved in this activity. In this context, the shares of various schemes in this industry have been calculated. Besides, the HHI index of concentration has been estimated. The table-5.11 discloses that the debt/income category holds the dominating position in the industry. For, its share in total assets of mutual fund industry was 47.49 percent in 2006. It followed increasing trend year after year and ultimately reached to the level of 66.51 percent in 2015.

Table-5.11: Scheme-Wise Share of Mutual Funds in India

Year	Debt/ Income Schemes	Growth/ Equity Schemes	Balanced Schemes	Others	HHI
2006	47.49	34.52	2.23	15.76	3700.28
2008	57.26	26.71	1.20	14.83	4213.50
2010	61.92	30.62	1.75	5.71	4807.34
2012	67.89	25.41	1.71	4.99	5282.54
2015	66.51	29.75	2.91	0.83	5317.81

However, the growth/equity segment, though keep one third of the business in 2006 (34.52 percent), but followed a decreasing trend with fluctuations. Its share declined to 29.75 percent in 2015. The balanced segment, which is considered as a blend of risk and safe investments, does not hold substance in the business of mutual funds in India. Though it possessed 2.23 percent share, it had declined to 1.71 percent in 2012 only to increase to the level of 2.91 percent. Such trend may continue in future, as the investors in recent years are tilting towards this segment of investment products. This table also exposes one more dramatic feature of Indian mutual fund industry is that the share of other category (includes FoFs, ETFs, Gilts, etc) declined to negligible from 15.76 percent in 2006. Hence, the entire industry investment is confined to debt/income and growth/equity segments. So, it can be concluded that in terms of investment in schemes, this industry is highly concentrated. This result has further been corroborated by the HHI index which has adhered to remarkable increasing trend (table-5.11).

The concentration of business among firms has further been explored for the individual schemes also. As already stated that Indian mutual fund industry is highly concentrated and this is no exception for the schemes. Table-5.12 explores this aspect in terms of four firm, eight firm and HHI index for the debt/income schemes category. These schemes turned out to be highly concentrated and it has followed increasing trend overtime. More than 50 percent of this business belongs to four largest firms and it has reached to the level of 93.02 percent for eight firms. This trend has further been vindicated by the values of HHI.

Table-5.12: Concentration in Debt/Income Oriented Schemes in Indian Mutual Funds

Year	Concentration		
	4-Firm	8-Firm	HHI
2006	45.47	67.48	752.25
2008	52.02	75.80	920.57
2010	47.89	71.04	791.46
2012	44.26	68.07	711.05
2015	56.24	93.02	1259.51

Table-5.13 explores the concentration of growth/equity schemes among the firms in the industry. Four largest firms are holding 50 percent of the business and this value increased to the level of 74.64 percent for eight firm concentration ratios, which is less severe than the debt/income category. The concentration has followed increasing trend up to 2012 and then followed decreasing trend in 2015. This trend has been maintained by the HHI also. It can be concluded here that severity of concentration has declined overtime.

Table-5.13: Concentration in Growth/Equity Oriented Schemes in Indian Mutual Funds

Year	Concentration		
	4-Firm	**8-Firm**	**HHI**
2006	47.04	72.84	820.32
2008	50.28	76.42	898.78
2010	51.51	76.70	913.51
2012	55.53	81.15	995.89
2015	49.11	74.64	857.53

Balanced fund schemes hold miniscule part of the total business in the industry, but the level of concentration has declined overtime both in terms of concentration ratio and HHI (table-5.14). Why did this happen? It seems from the foregoing discussion that leading firms have concentrated on the debt/income and growth/equity schemes and they shed this share in favour of relatively smaller firms.

**Table-5.14: Concentration in Balanced Fund
Schemes in Indian Mutual Funds**

Year	Concentration		
	4-Firm	8-Firm	HHI
2006	79.35	94.93	1911.31
2008	69.13	91.41	1806.09
2010	72.84	91.08	2877.57
2012	72.24	89.38	3185.54
2015	69.75	89.60	1826.75

5.8 Concluding Remarks

This chapter highlights the competition and concentration in Indian mutual fund industry. During the last decade of previous century, the entry for the private and foreign sector firms was eased as a part of the financial sector reforms. Major conglomerates in India and foreign firms in the asset management business have tried their luck in this business. Some of them were able to survive in the market and consolidated their position overtime other were compelled to quit the business. It has been recognized that stock market blood bath during 2008-09 was responsible for quick changes in the ownership pattern of the industry. About 45 firms are operating in this business. Hence, it provides adequate competition in the industry.

In spite of entry of new firms in the industry, it witnessed increase in concentration overtime. Though, initially the entry of new firms had small dent on the concentration, but new firms could not sustain in long period and yielded to large firms. Large firms operating in the mutual fund business have more or less retained their positions with little changes overtime. Though, top five positions were shared by HDFC, ICICI, Reliance, Birla Sunlife, and UTI but large and small firms are coexisting in this industry. Firms dominating in the initial years are able to maintain their position in the terminal years. Decrease in competition is not a good signal for the investors; for, it gives larger space to firms to charge higher fee. Moreover, the pressure of performance eases on the firms.

The Indian mutual fund industry segment wise is categorized in five major categories namely-public sector, private sector Indian, private sector foreign, joint ventures predominantly Indian and joint sector predominantly foreign. The dominating segment in Indian mutual fund industry is joint ventures with Indian domination followed by private sector Indian and public sector. Almost half the business is controlled by joint venture with Indian domination. Even these segments themselves are highly concentrated.

The products in the form of schemes which are offered to investors in India are basically categorized as debt/income schemes, growth/equity schemes, balanced schemes and others. The debt/income category holds the dominating position in the industry. The entire industry investment is confined to debt/income and growth/equity segments. So, in terms of investment in schemes, this industry is highly concentrated.

Notes

1. Restrictions on the operation of financial sector reduced, intends to improve economic and allocative efficiency by using variety of financial instruments and creating more competition through increased role for the private sector.
2. Financial inclusion in India is very low; that is, the users of financial sector services are relatively less. So they are devoid of the benefits of such services. There is a great scope in this form of business in India.
3. When funds are invested in variety of uncorrelated instruments.
4. The government policy has potential to change the existing market structure.
5. Innovations are commercial use of inventions.

6. New firms can enter or exit without restrictions and without incurring any sunk cost.
7. Hierarchy costs refer to more expenses on the multi-layered managers.
8. The fund schemes of the same family intend to gain market share.

References

- Bain J. S. (1956), *"Barriers to New Competition, their Character and Consequences in Manufacturing Industries"*, Cambridge, Mass: Harvard University Press, 1956.
- Barber B. M., Odean T., and Zheng L. (2005), "Out of Sight, Out of Mind: The Effects of Expenses on Mutual Fund Flows", *Journal of Business*, 78 (6), 2095–2120.
- Baumol J. W., Stephen G. F., Lilli M., Gordon A., Michael K. F. (1989), "The Economies of Mutual Fund Markets: Competition versus Regulation", *Journal of Finance*, 23 (2), 551-567.
- Baumol J. William, Panzar J. C. and Willig R. D. (1988), *"Contestable Markets and the Theory of Industry Structure"*, San Diego, Calif: Harcourt Brace Jovanovich.
- Baumol W. J., Goldfeld S. M., Gordon L. A. and Koehn M. F. (1990), *"The Economics of Mutual Fund Markets: Competition versus Regulation"*, Kluwer Academic, Boston, Massachusetts.
- Berk J. B. and Green R.C. (2004), "Mutual Fund Flows and Performance in Rational Markets", *Journal of Political Economy*, 112 (7), 1269–1295.
- Capon N., Fitzsimons G. J., and Prince, R. A. (1996), "An Individual Level Analysis of the Mutual Fund Investment Decision", *Journal of Financial Services Research*, 10 (1), 59-82.
- Caves E. R. (1980), "Industrial Organization, Corporate Strategy and Structure", *Journal of Economic Literature*, 18 (1), 64-92.
- Chen J., Hong H., Huang M., and Kubik J. (2004), "Does Fund Size Erode Performance? Liquidity, Organizational Diseconomies and Active Money Management", *American Economic Review*, 94 (5), 1276-1302.
- Christoffersen S. and Musto D. (2002), "Demand Curves and the Pricing of Money Management", *Review of Financial Studies*, 15 (5), 1499-1524.

- Coates J. C., and Hubbard R. G. (2007), "Competition in the Mutual Fund Industry: Evidence and Implications for Policy", *Harvard Law and Economics Discussion Paper 592*, Harvard Law School.
- Elton E. J., Gruber M. J., and Busse, J.A. (2004), "Are Investors Rational? Choices among Index Funds, *Journal of Finance*, 59 (2), 261–288.
- Elton E. J., Gruber M. J., and Green T. C. (2007), "The Impact of Mutual Fund Family Membership on Investor Risk", *Journal of Financial and Quantitative Analysis*, 42 (2), 257-278.
- Ferreira M. A. and Ramos S. B. (2009), "Mutual Fund Industry Competition and Concentration: International Evidence", SSRN Working Paper.
- Freeman J. P. and Brown S. L. (2001), "Mutual Fund Advisory Fees: The Cost of Conflicts of Interest", *The Journal of Corporation Law*, 26 (3), 609–673.
- Gaspar J., Massa M., and Matos P. (2006), "Favoritism in Mutual Fund Families: Evidence on Strategic Cross-Fund Subsidization", *Journal of Finance*, 61(1), 73–104.
- Grossack I. (1965), "Towards an Integration of Static and Dynamic Measures of Industry Concentration", *The Review of Economics and Statistics*, 47 (3), 301-308.
- Gruber M. (1996), "Another Puzzle: The Growth in Actively Managed Mutual Funds", *Journal of Finance*, 51 (), 783-807.
- Hou K. and Robinson D. T. (2006), "Industry Concentration and Average Stock Returns", *Journal of Finance*, 61, 1927-1956.
- Ippolito R. A. (1992), "Consumer Reaction to Measures of Poor Quality: Evidence from the Mutual Fund Industry", *Journal of Law and Economics*, 35 (1), 45–70.
- Khorana, A. and Servaes H. (1999), "The Determinants of Mutual Fund Starts", *Review of Financial Studies*, 12 (5), 1043-1074.
- Korkeamaki T. P. & Smythe T. I (2004), "Effects of Market Segmentation and Bank Concentration on Mutual Fund Expenses and Returns: Evidence from Finland", *European Financial Management*, 10 (3), 413-438.

- Mamaysky, H. and Spiegel, M. (2002), "A Theory of Mutual Funds: Optimal Fund Objectives and Industry Organization", Working Paper, Yale University.
- Massa M. (2003), "How do Family Strategies Affect Fund Performance? When Performance-Maximization is not the only Game in Town", *Journal of Financial Economics*, 67 (2), 249-304.
- Needham D. (1979), *"The Economics of Industrial Structure, Conduct and Performance"*, London: Holt, Rinehart and Winston.
- Porter E. M. (1981), "The Contributions of Industrial Organization to Strategic Management", *The Academy of Management Review*, 6 (4), 609-620.
- Scherer F. M. (1980), *"Industrial Market Structure and Economic Performance"*, 2nd Ed. Chicago: Rand McNally.
- Sirri E. R. and Tufano P. (1993), "Competition and Change in the Mutual Fund Industry, in: S. L. Hayes III, (ed.), *Financial Services: Perspectives and Challenges*, Harvard Business School Press, Boston, Massachusetts.
- Sirri E.R. and Tufano P. (1998), "Costly Search and Mutual Fund Flows, *Journal of Finance*, 53 (6), 1589–1622.
- Wahal S. and Wang A. (2011), "Competition among Mutual Funds", *Journal of Financial Economics*, 99 (1), 40–59.
- Wilcox R. T. (2003), "Bargain Hunting or Star Gazing? Investors Preferences for Stock Mutual Funds", *Journal of Business*, 76 (3), 645–664.

Chapter-6
Market Timing and Selectivity

[This chapter has been reproduced from author's research paper entitled "Market Timing and Selectivity Performance: A Cross-Sectional Analysis of Indian Mutual Funds", published in ELK Asia Pacific Journal of Finance and Risk Management, (2016) Vol. 7 (1), pp 34-66, with permission from the copy right holder(s)]

6.1 Introduction

A mutual fund is a kind of collective investment scheme, managed professionally, that collects funds from investors to invest in capital market. For, the ordinary people are not capable enough to pick the stocks and other assets efficiently. Hence, investing via mutual funds may help them to gain from the capability of professional investment management. Besides, such funds prepare diversified investment portfolios to hedge the risks, so investors may, apparently, earn higher returns at relatively lower risk (Gruber, 1996). Further, such investments are accessible to small investors; else it might be available to larger investors. However, they have to bear expenses for the management of their funds. Divergent opinions have emerged in the literature of finance regarding the better performing ability of fund managers. Are they capable to generate better returns for their clients who have reposed faith in such asset management firms? Furthermore, comprehending mutual fund performance is a recipe to portfolio management. It allows fund managers to recognize their position and helps investors to understand fund managers' strategies and to select the portfolio which best meets their preferences.

The mutual fund industry in India has grown to a remarkable extent in the recent decade; therefore, performance evaluation is potentially important. Developing economies like India have distinctive characteristics in relation to developed economies in terms of their volatility, inefficiency and regulatory arrangements (Beakaert and Harvey, 2002). Hence, evidences from the developed markets may not be able to give the best explanation of mutual fund performance in the economy like India. For, most of the studies in mutual performance in developing economies are still based on prevailing performance measures – such as the Sharpe, Treynor and Jensen ratios –which are based on one fixed risk factor. This undermines the robustness of their results; since, researchers argue that asset returns can be explained by other factors apart from market risk; and such factors are not time invariant (Fama and French, 1992; 1998; Ferson and Warther, 1996; Rouwenhorst, 1999). Further, these studies are either based on small sample and/or based in the data distant in past. As a result, there is an unclear picture of the performance in emerging markets of mutual funds.

Initially, research in this field concentrated on the overall performance of the fund in terms of excess returns over the risk free returns. These measures are based on the single factor Capital Asset Pricing Models (CAPM), namely 'Jenson's Alpha' (Jenson, 1968), and ratios formats 'returns to total risk ratio' (Sharpe, 1966) and 'returns to systemic risk ratio' (Treynor, 1965). Later, it had been recognized that manager's performance is combination of stock selection and timing ability. It has been modeled by Treynor and Mazuy (1966) and Henriksson and Merton (1981) with small difference in methodology. These methods come under the category of unconditional performance; for, ignoring the time element of the systemic risk. Since of mutual funds of similar nature have different performance, therefore, along with the manager's ability, fund characteristics may be responsible for performance results. The objective, size, turnover, age, expense ratio, size of fund family and other attributes of the fund management companies may influence the performance of mutual funds.

The performance of mutual funds has been enormously researched in both developed and developing countries. However, India is lacking for such comprehensive studies. Moreover, market timing and stock selection performances of mutual funds have been studied extensively in developed countries; there is remarkably little evidence on this aspect in developing countries. Most studies that have been carried out in India have focused the research on evaluating overall or aggregate fund performance. Among the limited studies that investigate market timing and security selection abilities of fund manager in India, none has examined what factors influence two distinct performance component due to market timing and stock selection activities. While fund return is generally observable by investors, the extent to which fund characteristics has an influence on fund return is not obvious to the investing public at large. Since fund's return can be driven by manager's selection or/and market timing abilities, it would certainly be of interest to investors to know the extent to which fund characteristics influence the selectivity and timing performance components of their funds. In addition, given that a fund manager's stock selection and market timing skills are not observable, information on what fund attributes contributes to selectivity and timing performances would allow managers to better manage their stock selection and market timing activities. Hence, this study embarks on two objectives; first, the study evaluates the overall risk-adjusted performance and separates the fund performance into selectivity and market timing components. By breaking down the performance components, this study is able to more accurately measure performance based on manager's expertise and thus determine which of the two managerial activities is more rewarding to investors. Second, this study examines to what extent the measures of fund manager's ability to select undervalued securities and to time market movements are related to fund characteristics, such as fund size, expense ratio, portfolio turnover, fund risk, fund age and so on. The information on what fund attributes contribute to selectivity and market timing components would certainly be of interest to both investors and fund managers.

With the onset of financial sector reforms during 1990s, mutual fund industry has recorded remarkable progress in India. The Indian mutual fund industry, though still small in comparison to the size of the Indian economy, offers Indian, and in some cases global investors, both big and small, an avenue to invest safely and securely, at a reduced cost, in a diverse range of securities, spread across a wide range of industries and sectors. There are around 45 asset management companies operating in India with numerous schemes of different categories (amfi) and Rs. 13,00,000 crore are under management of these asset management companies (money control). Given the foregoing discussion, this is in favour of investors to evaluate the performance of fund schemes, so that they may plan their investments efficiently.

6.2 Performance: Established Literature

Since the mutual funds are related to the investment of individual's funds in the capital market, hence, the question arises that are managers of such funds able to earn better return than the investors can do on their own? Do the fund managers have superior ability to make better investments than other investors? Conflicting views have appeared in literature regarding this concern. Jenson (1968) found that for the sample period 1945-1964, MFs earned an excess net of fee (gross) return over the market of -1.1% (-0.4%). Thus, he concluded that MFs did not do better than the market. Several later researchers confirmed Jensen's conclusion that MFs managers do not possess any superior investment skill (Ippolito, 1989; Brown and Goetzmann, 1995; Malkiel, 1995; Gruber, 1996 and Cahart, 1997). More so, Cahart (1997) has also established that poor fund performers persisted on a consistent basis.

However, Deniel, Grinblatt, Titman and Wermers (1997) held that fund returns were attributable to managers stock picking ability and the manager's market timing ability. Deniel et. al. and other papers (Grinblatt and Titman, 1989, 1993; Chen, Jegdeesh and Wermers, 2000) observed evidences of superior ability of fund managers.

Since this study is also intended to discover the impact of fund characteristics on the selectivity and timing ability of fund manager; hence, literature in this context has been explored. Some studies have reported negative relationship between expense ratio and fund performance

(Malkiel, 1995; Cahart, 1997; Otten and Bams, 2002); however, others have proved that fund performance is indifferent to expense ratio. Small equity funds (large assets under management) proved to be better performed (Dahlquist et. al., 2000), on the contrary, other studies have discovered superior performance of the bigger funds (Otten and Bams, 2002; Fortin and Michelson, 2005). Low (2010) found negative effects of uncontrollable growth in fund size. On fund age, Otten and Bams (2002) found that it was negatively related to fund performance; however, Low (2010) did not find any evidence of significant relationships. Dahlquist et. al., (2000) and Fortin and Michelson (2005) expounded that fund turnover is positively related to fund performance; however, other studies did not witness any evidence of such relationship (Ippolito, 1989; Drom and Walker, 1996).

Treynor and Mazuy (1966) and Henriksson-Merton (1981) have decomposed the fund performance into market timing and stock selection capability of fund managers. They have confirmed that the fund managers have the capability to time the market.

Likewise in developed capital markets, the signs of the ability of fund managers to time the market are mixed for the Indian markets. Studies by Gupta (2000), Mishra (2002), Chander (2006), Tripathy (2006), Chopra (2011), and Kumar (2012) found little evidence of market timing skills. However, results of Gupta and Sehgal (2001) observed that Indian fund managers are superior market timers. Further, studies of Sehgal and Jhanwar (2008), Ahmad and Samajpati (2010), Nathani et al. (2011) also confirmed the evidence of market timing. Guha et al. (2007) examined the market timing and stock selection abilities of mutual fund managers using both unconditional and conditional approaches. Using 96 mutual funds schemes during January 2000 to June 2005 the study reported lack of market timing but presence of stock selection abilities of Indian fund managers in both the approaches.

6.3 Performance Measurement and Data Set

This section is devoted to highlight the data set used to analyse the performance of Indian mutual funds. Besides, the methods that have been used to get the final results regarding performance evaluation are discussed in detail. Moreover, for the better understanding of readers variables used are categorically defined and their significance in the mutual fund industry is also discussed.

This study is based on the 51 mutual fund schemes launched by the variety of fund houses. These mutual fund schemes are divided into three categories based on their characteristics namely; Equity Diversified Funds (28), Equity Linked Saving Schemes (ELSS) Funds (15) and Balanced Funds (8). Diversified mutual funds are equity funds which invest across all sectors and categories of the stock market and endeavor to moderate the risk exposure. An Equity Linked Savings Scheme (ELSS) is an equity oriented mutual fund scheme in which the majority corpus (about 80-100 percent) is invested in equities. It qualifies for tax exemption under section 80C of the Indian Income Tax Act, 1961. This type of fund scheme does not just help us to save tax, but also provide an opportunity to grow our money. A fund that combines stock, bond and sometimes money market component in a single portfolio are termed as balanced funds. Generally, 50-75 per cent is equity component and rest is in debt. Such funds are geared towards investors who look for mixture of safety, income and modest capital appreciation.

To study the fund performance, monthly data for the 51 schemes on the fund portfolio return has been used by using the Net Asset Value (NAV) data. Besides, to establish the capacity of fund to beat the benchmark, market data for relevant indices has been used. Since the stock selection and market timing ability of fund managers are influenced by multiplicity of factors. In this context, through the logic generated from economic theory and existing literature some variables are identified namely; Indian Treasury bill returns, expense ratio, fund age, portfolio turnover, fund size and fund's beta value (collectively termed as fund attributes).

This study covers the period from April, 2006 to December 2014. This period incorporates the periods of boom, stagnation and slowdown in the Indian economy in general and stock market in particular. Therefore, this period provides full opportunity to the fund manager to prove his capability in such economic scenarios and the importance of fund characteristics in changing macro-economic environment. The data belongs to this period for the fund schemes that came into existence before April 2006 and those started after this period, data belongs to from year of inception to December 2014

Data Source

Variable	Data Source
Treasury Bill Returns	www.tradingeconomics.com
Assets under Management	www.amfiindia.com
Expense Ratio	www.valueresearchonline.com
Net Asset Value (NAV)	www.amfiindia.com
Stock Market Indices	www.bseindia.com / www.nseindia.com
Date of Inception of Scheme (Age)	www.moneycontrol.com
Fund Beta	Calculated by CAPM
Turnover Ratio	www.morningstar.in

Monthly Returns

Since this study is based on the monthly returns of the fund schemes selected for analysis. The monthly returns for each of the sample scheme have been computed by the following equation;

$$R_t = (NAV_t - NAV_{t-1}) / NAV_{t-1} \qquad (1)$$

Here; R_t is the monthly return of a fund scheme in month 't'. Since the selected fund schemes are in growth option, hence the question to adjust the dividends in calculating the monthly returns does not arise.

Similarly, returns for the various market indices (R_m) used as benchmark have been estimated;

$$R_{mt} = (\text{Market Index}_t - \text{Market Index}_{t-1}) / \text{Market Index}_{t-1} \qquad (2)$$

Here; R_{mt} is the market return in period 't', Market Index$_t$ and Market Index$_{t-1}$ are levels of market index levels in periods 't' and 't-1' respectively.

Table-6.1: Descriptive Statistics of Monthly Returns for the Sampled Mutual Funds

The table reports the descriptive statistics of the monthly returns for 51 mutual funds schemes categorized as equity diversified fund schemes, equity linked saving schemes (ELSS) and balanced fund schemes for the data ranging from April 2006 to December 2014. S D refers to standard deviation. Jerque-Bera test gauge the normality of the distribution of monthly returns. N is the number of observations included to find the descriptive statistics in relevant category of mutual fund.

Statistic	All	Equity Diversified	ELSS	Balanced
Mean	1.3358	1.3570	1.4458	1.1192
Median	1.7325	1.6422	1.9165	1.6812
Maximum	94.2907	94.2907	72.5889	22.1456
Minimum	-71.0340	-47.0413	-45.2993	-71.0340
S D	6.8222	7.1992	6.7663	5.4789
Skewness	1.0504	1.5675	0.9630	-2.8353
Kurtosis	28.3625	28.0293	21.6236	40.3415
Jerque Bera (Prob.)	124654.8 (0.0000)	71981.03 (0.0000)	15847.73 (0.0000)	48562.15 (0.0000)
N	4617	2715	1085	817

Table-6.1 and Table-6.2 reveal that average performance of the schemes at aggregate level and at different groups' level is better than the market return performances. However, volatility in the performance is more or less same evident from the values of standard deviations. Fund scheme return data and market return data follow the normal distribution as the Jerque-Bera test statistic is significant in each category of fund schemes and market returns.

Table-6.2: Descriptive Statistics of Monthly Returns for Market Indices used as Benchmarks

The table reports the descriptive statistics of the monthly returns for various market returns from April 2006 to December 2014. S D refers to standard deviation. Jerque-Bera test is gauge the normality of the distribution of monthly returns. N is the number of observations included to find the descriptive statistics in relevant category of mutual fund.

Statistic	Sensex	BSE-500	BSE-200	BSE-100	BSE-Mid-Cap	Nifty	CNX-Mid-Cap	CNX-500
Mean	1.0901	1.1267	1.1402	1.1470	1.2333	1.1298	1.2333	1.0969
Median	2.2153	2.0333	1.9594	1.9961	2.1971	2.0676	2.1971	2.0230
Maximum	26.2066	27.1860	26.8591	26.4664	24.4671	23.2170	24.4671	26.5557
Minimum	-23.3278	-24.5044	-24.2572	-24.0559	-23.4647	-24.4142	-23.7647	-24.7673
Std. Dev.	6.2185	6.8016	6.6775	6.5727	7.4463	6.1651	7.4463	6.6242
Skewness	-0.0367	-0.0913	-0.0754	-0.0766	-0.1384	-0.3324	-0.1384	-0.1674
Kurtosis	6.6164	5.7774	5.8836	5.9649	3.9372	6.2095	3.9372	6.0298
Jerque Bera (Prob.)	56.6976 (0.0000)	33.5722 (0.0000)	36.1327 (0.0000)	38.1964 (0.0000)	4.1386 (0.0000)	46.5528 (0.0000)	4.1384 (0.0000)	40.2670 (0.0000)
N	104	104	104	104	104	104	104	104

In terms of risk measurement, there are two possible choices for measuring risk, namely, 'total risk' and 'systemic risk'. Total risk is overall risk of a portfolio including both systemic and un-systemic risk and is measured by the portfolio's standard deviation. In contrast, systemic risk (market risk) is measured by the portfolio's beta coefficient which is the sensitivity of the portfolio's return to changes in the return on the market portfolio. This study uses two such measures namely-Treynor Ratio and Sharpe

Ratio. Treynor (1965) introduced the 'Reward to Volatility ratio' or so called Treynor Ratio.

$$T = \frac{Rp - Rf}{\beta_p} \qquad (3)$$

Here, T is Treynor Ratio, Rp is portfolio's return, Rf is risk free return, in this study the monthly yield on 91 days treasury bills of Government of India (GOI) is used as a proxy for risk-free return. β_p is portfolio's beta.

Sharpe (1966) proposed 'Reward to Variability Ratio' called the Sharpe ratio.

$$S = \frac{Rp - Rf}{\sigma_p} \qquad (4)$$

Here, S is Sharpe Ratio, Rp is portfolio's return, Rf is risk free return and σ_p is portfolio's standard deviation.

This study makes use of regression analysis in two stages. In the first stage, this study employs the extensively used Jensen's (1968) model to work out the overall fund performance and the Treynor-Mazuy Measure (TMM) (1966) has been used to decompose the performance into market timing and selectivity components. In the first stage, the regression objective is point estimation that is to obtain coefficient estimates of selectivity and timing measures and not to draw inference based on the significance of the estimates. In other words, Jensen's and TMM models are employed to obtain selectivity and timing coefficient estimates for each of the 51 fund schemes. These coefficient estimates are then used as data points (dependent variables) in the second stage cross-sectional regression analysis that aims to examine the extent to which fund characteristics are related to selectivity and timing performance measure. In the second stage analysis, the objectives are point estimation as well as hypotheses testing. Hence, the assumption of white noise term is critical to the valid interpretation of the regression estimates.

However, in the first stage regression analysis that is in the models of Jenson and TMM, the regression objective is merely to obtain selectivity and timing estimates to be used in the second stage analysis and not to draw inferences based on the significance of the coefficient estimates. It is, thus, sufficient that the unbiasedness property of the coefficient estimates remain intact. As highlighted in the econometric theory, to establish the unbiasedness of regression estimates, it is not necessary that the error term be homoscedastic, and similarly the assumption of non auto-correlated errors is also not required to prove that the coefficient estimate is unbiased.

Jenson's single factor regression based approach is used to establish the portfolio beta, that is portfolio returns effected by the systemic risk and alpha, popularly called Jensen's alpha, indicates the manager's performance coefficient. The Jenson's equation is shown in the following regression specification:

$$R_{pt} - R_{ft} = \alpha_j + \beta_p (R_{mt} - R_{ft}) + \varepsilon_{pt} \qquad (5)$$

Where, R_{pt} is the rate of return of the fund at time t, R_{ft} is the contemporaneous rate of return on a risk free asset, R_{mt} is the rate of return of market portfolio at time t. β_p is the estimated coefficient for the systemic risk level of the fund, α_j is the Jensen's performance coefficient, indicating the risk adjusted performance of the fund and ε_{pt} represents the random error term. This regression equation assumes that the systemic risk of a fund is stationary over time and thus ignores the existence of timing activities of the fund managers.

The Jenson's model, thus, calculate the overall fund performance and all the credit goes to the fund manager in terms of its stock selection capability. However, the overall performance, as already stated, is a combination of stock selection and the timing ability of the manager and Jenson's model is unable to decompose the fund's performance in stock selection and timing ability. In this context, Treynor and Mazuy (1966), model separates the performance into market timing and selectivity components. The Treynor and Mazuy (1966) model is specified as follows;

$$R_{pt} - R_{ft} = \alpha_p + \beta_p (R_{mt} - R_{ft}) + \gamma_p (R_{mt} - R_{ft})^2 + \varepsilon_{pt} \qquad (6)$$

In this equation, γ_p is the manager's ability to time the market movement and α_p is the expected return for portfolio p generated from the manager's selectivity skills. If the manager has successfully timed the market, γ_p will be +ve and significant and $\gamma_p = 0$ would be interpreted as no ability to time the market.

Since this study also proposes to identify the factors that affect the performance of fund in terms of stock selection and market timing. This study uses the Treynor and Mazuy (1966) equation to assess the importance and the impact of fund characteristics on the managerial selectivity and market timing returns. Hence, α_p and γ_p generated in the previous equation are regressed on several fund characteristics variables as follows;

$$\alpha_{pi} = b_0 + b_1 \, Risk_j + b_2 \, Turnover_j + b_3 \, Exp_j + b_4 \, Size_j + b_5 Age_j + \varepsilon_j \qquad (7)$$

$$\gamma_{pj} = b_0 + b_1 \, Risk_j + b_2 \, Turnover_j + b_3 \, Exp_j + b_4 \, Size_j + b_5 Age_j + \varepsilon_j \qquad (8)$$

Where, α_{pj} and γ_{pj} are the selectivity and market-timing measures of fund j estimated from the Treynor and Mazuy equation. Since, the *market risk* is an important variable that influences the stock selection and market timing, therefore, introduced as explanatory variable. $Turnover_j$ is the *turnover ratio* of fund j, measured by the average total acquisition and disposal of securities for the year as percentage of the average net asset value of the fund. This ratio captures the aggressiveness of fund in managing funds by indicating whether managers buy and sell securities frequently or take a longer term approach to investing. Exp_j is the jth fund's *expense ratio*, which is the portion of the fund's average net asset paid for management fee, trustee fee, audit and other administrative fee involved in operating the fund. Age_j is the *fund's age* since inception. $Size_j$ is the logarithm of the fund's year-end total net asset value.

Since the objectives of the second-stage analysis are point estimation as well as hypotheses testing, the assumption of white noise error term is critical to the valid interpretation of the regression estimates. That said diagnostic checks are performed on both the cross-sectional models of selectivity and market timing to ensure that the assumptions underlying the regression residuals are not violated.

6.4 Empirical Results

6.4.1 Risk Adjusted Performance

This section deals with the measurement of overall mutual fund performance of sampled fund schemes by using the ratio techniques (Sharpe ratio and Treynor ratio) and the regression technique (Jensen Alpha). The entire risk is a combination of systemic and non-systemic (unique). Systemic risk is generated by the functioning of the economic system and its impact is irrespective of the fund selection and beyond the control of the fund manager. However, unique risk, on the other hand, is specific to the nature of the fund. In the risk adjusted fund performance analysis, excess returns (difference of fund return and risk free return) are standardized with respect to overall risk (measured by portfolio standard deviation) and with fund beta (systemic risk). Former is termed as Sharpe ratio and latter is called Treynor ratio. The results of Treynor ratio, in this context, are presented in table-6.3 and table-6.4. The table-6.3, reveals that risk adjusted performance was positive in all fund categories, notwithstanding with different levels. Overall aggregate Treynor ratio turned out to be 0.8337 and positive. This ratio was highest (1.005) in the case of equity linked saving schemes (ELSS). However, this ratio was recorded minimum in case of balanced funds (0.7197). Equity diversified fund performed higher than the all sampled funds except ELSS. So far the frequency distribution of the fund schemes are concerned, a large segment of schemes (almost 75 percent) in all fund categories falls in the range above 0.50.

Table-6.3: Mutual Fund Performance Measurement--Treynor Measure

The table reports Treynor ratio calculated by the formula stated in equation-3.

*The beta of portfolio used in the formula is derived
from the Jensen's regression equation.*

Fund Type	Treynor Ratio
All Funds in Sample	0.8337
Equity Diversified	0.8770
ELSS	1.005
Balanced	0.7197

Table-6.4: Frequency Distribution of Sampled Fund Schemes according to Treynor Ratio Performance

The table provides the frequency distribution of the individual funds according to the performance as per Treynor ratio. The ratio range is developed with intuition and common sense to assess the tilt of performance. The numbers in the table are the number of mutual fund schemes falling in the ratio range.

Ratio Range	All	Equity Diversified	ELSS	Balanced
0-0.25	2	0	1	1
0.25-0.50	5	4	0	1
0.50-0.75	14	8	5	1
0.75-1.00	13	8	2	3
1.00 & Above	17	8	7	2
Total	51	28	15	8

Now, the question arises, why the ELSS performed better than other segments? Since there is a provision of lock in period in ELSS, hence, the fund managers have better flexibility and can take more risk to play with funds without the fear of demand for redemption. Therefore, better performance may be the obvious consequence. However, such performance could not be recorded in balanced fund schemes. For, 25-30 percent of the money is invested in debt and do not provide enough freedom to the fund manager in stock selection. Moreover, some funds are always earmarked for the purpose of redemption demands.

Table-6.5: Mutual Fund Performance Measurement-Sharpe Measure

Fund Type	Fund Returns	Market Returns
All Funds in Sample	0.1382	0.0743
Equity Diversified	0.1134	0.0720
ELSS	0.2012	0.0694
Balanced	0.1071	0.0704

The Sharpe ratio reported in the Table-6.5 is almost similar to the Treynor ratio except for equity diversified mutual fund schemes. Moreover, it has also highlighted that fund returns beat the market returns in all fund categories under consideration. All fund schemes reported positive risk adjusted returns. Why did this happen different in the equity diversified category? Since, Sharpe ratio standardize the excess returns with overall risk and variety of schemes are selected in various themes, consequently, the standard deviation of the fund portfolio is expected to increase, albeit diversification is done to reduce the risk of investor. Therefore, return reported in this category is least due to reduced risks reflected in lesser returns. So far the frequency distribution of the fund schemes are concerned, a large segment of schemes (more than 90%) in all fund categories falls in the range 0.-0.2.

Table-6.6: Frequency Distribution of Sampled Fund Schemes according to Sharpe Ratio Performance

The table provides the frequency distribution of the individual funds according to the performance as per Sharpe ratio. The ratio range is developed with intuition and common sense to assess the tilt of performance. The numbers in the table are the number of mutual fund schemes falling in the ratio range.

Ratio Range	All	Equity Diversified	ELSS	Balanced
0-0.1	21	13	05	03
0.1-0.2	19	14	04	05
0.2-0.3	01	00	01	00
0.3-0.4	05	01	04	00
0.4 & above	01	00	01	00
Total	51	28	15	8

The measurement of the performance of fund manager has also been estimated by using the Capital Asset Pricing Model (CAPM) developed by Jensen as stated in equation-5. In this equation, value and significance level of a determine the performance of mutual fund schemes. Results of this regression are presented in table-6.7. A glance at the table reveals that Indian mutual fund industry is capable enough to generate earning for their clients. For, a_j is significant and positive for the entire sample of funds and same is true in all the categories (equity diversified, ELSS and balanced) separately. Though the value recorded in case of balanced funds is least and significant at the brink, but its positive significance status cannot be denied. Its value being least may be due to the facts cited in the previous discussion. Moreover, the value of R-squared is satisfactorily large, which indicates the diversification in Indian mutual fund industry is considerably high. Hence, it can be concluded here that mutual funds in India are providing sufficient returns to their investors and the levels of diversification also save them from the exposure of high risk. This has further been vindicated in table-6.8, which gives the number of fund schemes in positive and negative return categories. Out of the sample of 51 assorted mutual fund schemes, 47 fall in the category of positive returns. This figure is 26 out of 28 in equity diversified fund schemes. Same is also true in cases of ELSS and Balanced fund categories. Here, despite the tremendous performance, 4 funds in overall group are falling in the negative category. Therefore, there is a caution for the investor to properly scrutinize the fund houses and fund schemes before selecting them given the fact that 8% funds are in negative return category.

Table-6.7: Risk Adjusted Performance of Indian Mutual Funds- Jenson's Alpha

The following outputs are yielded from the CAPM estimation by running the regression $R_{pt} - R_{ft} = a_j + \beta_p (R_{mt} - R_{ft}) + \varepsilon_{pt}.$ The t-Statistic is a measure of how extreme a statistical estimate is. The alpha (a) is the intercept of the regression. The coefficient of determination represented by R^2 indicates the explanatory power of the estimations, moreover it also represent the extent of diversification of the portfolio. P-Value is the probability of level of significance.

Fund Type	Alpha (aj)	t-Statistic	R-Squared	P-Value
All Funds in Sample	0.3289*	5.3307	0.6278	0.0000
Equity Diversified	0.3498*	4.0151	0.6078	0.0001
ELSS	0.3480*	2.9902	0.6842	0.0029
Balanced	0.2172*	1.9674	0.6742	0.0495

* Indicates the significant value

**Table-6.8: Frequency Distribution of Fund Schemes in Terms
of positive and Negative Jenson's Alpha Performance**

Table presents the number of funds with positive and negative returns. Number presented in the table is number of fund schemes. Positive means the number of funds reported positive alpha and negative means number of funds reported negative alpha.

Fund Type	Positive	Negative	Total
All Funds in Sample	47	4	51
Equity Diversified	26	2	28
ELSS	14	1	15
Balanced	7	1	8

6.4.2 Selectivity and Market Timing Abilities

Fund manager can help the investors to gain by taking the services of asset management companies, if the fund managers concerned are capable in better selection of the stocks and assets and he should be able to understand the behaviour of the market to decide when to enter and quit a particular stock or segment. Therefore, this section is devoted to calculate the selectivity and timing ability of the fund manager based on the Treynor and Mazuy Model. Results are presented in table-6.9 and table-6.10.

So far the stock selection ability is concerned, it seems from the values reported in table-6.9 that coefficients of selectivity are positive and highly significant; hence, vindicate our previous result that Indian mutual fund industry has the stock selection capability. This is true for all the categories of mutual funds. However, this is not valid in case of market timing. Even the timing capability of the fund managers is contributing negatively to returns. This is evident from the fact that coefficient attached to the market timing variable turned out to be negative in all fund categories. Not even this, this value is significant in ELSS and all fund categories. Suggesting that timing of fund is rather putting down the return. Moreover, the fitting of Treynor and Mazuy model did not change the explanatory power of the Jensen model reported earlier. It is generally talked that markets are always unpredictable and that also hold true in Indian scenario. Indian fund managers are lacking market timing ability.

Table-6.9: Timing Ability and Fund Selectivity Performance (TMM Model)

Table presents the results of Treynor and Mazuy model presented in equation-6. Selectivity is the coefficient of intercept term and market timing is a coefficient gamma attached to the square of excess return variable. Figures in parentheses are t-values to adjudge the significance. R^2 is the coefficient of determination.

Group	Selectivity	Market Timing	R^2
All Funds in Sample	0.4042 (5.9891)	-0.0018 (-2.7434)	0.6284
Equity Diversified	0.4147 (4.3284)	-0.0015 (-1.6257)	0.6081
ELSS	0.4701 (3.7429)	-0.0032 (-2.5481)	0.6861
Balanced	0.2726 (2.2563)	-0.0012 (-1.1283)	0.6747

Table-6.10: Frequency Distribution of Fund Schemes as per Positive and Negative Significant Values of Selectivity and Market Timing (TMM)

Table presents the frequency distribution of all fund schemes selected in the sample in terms of their positive significant, negative significant and insignificant values. Sel refers to the stock selection capability and time refers to the market timing ability of the fund manager. These results are based on Treynor and Mazuy Model applied o the individual fund schemes.

Significance	All		Equity Diversified		ELSS		Balanced	
	Sel	Time	Sel	Time	Sel	Time	Sel	Time
Positive Significant	20	02	11	01	06	01	03	00
Negative Significant	00	08	00	05	00	02	00	01
Insignificant	31	41	17	22	09	12	05	07

To explore further the results obtained in the table-6.9, the TMM model also applied on the individual funds and the results are presented in the form of frequency distribution. The table reveals that, so far the selectivity is concerned; none of the fund scheme in any of the category falls in the negative significant category, however majority of the schemes were in the category of insignificant (may be positive). Even then considerable fund schemes are in the positive significant category. Hence, it can be concluded that Indian mutual funds do have the capability of stock selection. However, they are devoid of such capability so far the market timing is concerned. For, majority of the fund schemes either fall in the category of insignificant or in negatively significant.

Table-6.11 reports summary statistics for mutual fund performance measures estimated from models of Jensen (1968) and Treynor and Muzay (1966). In Jensen's model, selectivity has a mean value of 0.3572 and it measures selectivity performance when market timing ability is not taken into consideration. Since market timing is not taken into consideration, Jensen's Alpha attributes the fund's overall performance entirely to selectivity performance.

TMM model provides the separate selectivity and market timing components as shown by the estimates of TMM Alpha and TMM Gamma respectively. Since the market timing average value is recorded as negative;

therefore, the selectivity value improves in the TMM model. Moreover, variability in the fund selection ability captured by standard deviation shows that variability in stock selection ability is much severe in TM model as compared to Jensen Alpha.

Table-6.11: Summary Statistics

Table presents the summary statistics for Jensen's Alpha calculated from equation-5 and Alpha TMM and Gamma TMM are stock selection and market timing ability calculated from equation-6. Jerque-Bera statistic provides the test for the normality of cross-sectional stock selection and market timing.

Statistic	Jensen's Alpha	Alpha TMM	Gamma TMM
Mean	0.3572	0.4422	-0.0030
Median	0.3600	0.3760	-0.0021
Maximum	1.4200	2.1358	0.0133
Minimum	-0.4800	-0.2009	-0.0447
Std. Dev.	0.3203	0.3844	0.0084
Skewness	0.4202	1.7582	-2.3938
Kurtosis	4.4742	8.7025	13.5326
Jerque Bera (Prob.)	6.1195 (0.0468)	98.3815 (0.0000)	284.44 (0.0000)
N	51	51	51

6.4.3 The Correlation between Performance Measures and Fund Characteristics

Table-6.12 presents pair-wise correlation for performance measures and fund characteristics. Selectivity and timing ability have a high negative correlation coefficient suggesting that there is trade-off between a fund manager's stock selection and market timing ability. Such correlation structure is also an evidence of activity specialization among fund managers, implying that no manager can excel in both activities. Selectivity performance is shown to be inversely related to fund risk with a correlation coefficient -0.0219, meaning thereby, risky funds characterized by high exposures to broad market movements have poor selectivity returns albeit with small value of correlation. Further, stock selection is positively correlated with the size of the fund scheme (0.2711). Suggesting that large fund size possess with better experience and reflected positively in better stock selection. High expense ratio is also negatively related to the selectivity.

Table-6.12: Pair-Wise Correlation Coefficient between the Variables

Table presents the pair-wise correlation coefficient between performance and fund characteristics variables. Sel is the stock selection ability, Time refers to Market Timing ability, Age is the age of fund since inception in months, ER symbolizes the expense ratio of the fund scheme, Risk is fund beta, size is the size of assets of the fund scheme, TO is the turnover ratio of the fund scheme.

Variable	Sel	Time	Age	ER	Risk	Size	TO
Sel	1.0000	-0.5989	-0.3822	-0.2065	-0.0.219	0.2711	-0.0904
Time		1.0000	0.2145	-0.0291	0.0341	0.0662	0.0777
Age			1.0000	-0.1616	0.0705	0.2054	0.1328
ER				1.0000	0.0821	-0.4512	0.1255
Risk					1.0000	0.0010	-0.0839
Size						1.0000	-0.0644
TO							1.0000

Market timing ability is positively related to fund risk, that is, fund managers with better ability to bear the risk are more capable to time the market. It is further corroborated by the positive relation between the size and timing ability; for, large funds have more capacity to face risk. Moreover, high turnover increases the expense ratio and negatively related to risk. Larger funds have relatively lesser expense ratio evident from the negative correlation between size and expense ratio (-0.4512). The positive correlation of 0.2054 between size and age suggest that aged funds are bigger in size.

6.4.4 The Relationship between Selectivity Performance and Fund Characteristics

(a) All Sampled fund Schemes:

This section is devoted to identify the fund characteristics that have capacity to explain the variation in performance of fund selectivity. The panel data of all sampled funds has been used to reach the conclusion. The knowledge of these variables helps the investors to select the fund schemes that can give better returns from their investments. Fund selectivity is the capability of the fund manager complemented by these attributes. The table-6.13 reports the cross-sectional results of selectivity performance as represented by equation-7.

Table-6.13: Cross-Section Regression Results of All Sampled Fund Schemes

(Dependent Variable- Selectivity)

This Table presents the regression results of the panel data of 51 mutual fund schemes. The results are based on the format of regression equation-7. P-value provides the smallest level of significance at which the null hypothesis would be rejected. The smaller the p-value, the stronger the evidence is in favor of the alternative hypothesis. T-statistic is the value provided by the data. F-statistic provides the evidence for the jointly significance of the model (Variables included). ARCH test provides the evidence of auto-correlation of residuals after the estimation.

Variable	Co-efficient	t-Statistic	P-Value
Constant	3.4563	2.9960	0.0044
Risk	-0.1595	2.2214	0.0498
Size	0.2894	2.1011	0.0413
TO	0.0005	0.1932	0.8476
ER	-0.2161	0.9290	0.3578
Age	-1.1419	4.0716	0.0002
R-Squared	0.3347	F-Statistic	4.5291(0.0019)
Durbin Watson	1.5807	N=51	

ARCH-Test	
F-Statistic	0.7264 (0.3982)
Obs*R-Squared	0.7453 (0.3879)

Selectivity regression model is justified by the significant value of F-Statistic. Moreover, the included variables are capable to explain the 33.47 percent variation in the selectivity performance. Significant positive coefficient of the size variable suggests that the managers of large fund schemes are better equipped for stock selection ability. However, age of the fund turned out be negative significant, meaning thereby that old funds show complacency and new fund do this work with more vigor. The coefficient attached to risk variable is negatively significant. Fund risk variable captures a fund's exposures to market risk or broad market movement suggesting that risky funds characterized by high exposures to broad market movements seem to show poor selectivity returns. Given that market movements are generally unpredictable, funds with high exposures to market risk make it all the more challenging for managers to correctly select stocks that would maximize funds' returns. Therefore, funds with such feature may be better managed by managers with market timing abilities to correctly select stocks that would maximize funds' returns. The findings show that portfolio turnover, expense ratio, play no significant roles in influencing the variation in selectivity performance.

The variables included in the model are facilitative in nature that influences the stock selection ability of the fund manager. Otherwise, such capability is innate capability of the manager. Consequently, the constant turned out to be highly significant. This result is on expected lines.

(b) Equity Diversified Sampled Fund Schemes:

Equity diversified fund schemes are concerned to diversify the portfolio in such a way that risk exposure of the portfolio can be reduced to some extent. This segment of the study is based on 28 equity diversified fund schemes and the results of panel data cross section are presented in the table-6.14 based on the equation-7 mentioned in the methodology section. The model is justified by the significant value of F-statistics and the estimated model is free from the problem of auto-correlation and heteroscedatsicty. It is generally expected that funds with more experience (aged) are likely to be more efficient in selectivity. However, such hypothesis does not seem true in the equity diversified mutual fund schemes. Rather they affect negatively the stock selection capability of the fund manager. This might be due the complacency of the fund manager, since the past reputation of the fund pay in the current period also. Since, variable age is negatively significant in the table. Size of the fund and turnover ratio does not influence the stock selection ability of the managers of equity diversified funds. The high expense ratio increases the costs of the fund and consequently reduces the returns and hence, expected to bear negative relationship with stock selection ability and this has been proved true in Indian set up. For, the coefficient attached to the ER variable is negatively significant. It is assumed that high market risk may jeopardize the stock selection ability of the manager. Since broader market movements are unpredictable and increases the risk and reduces the capability of the manager so far the stock selection are concerned. Therefore, systemic risk is beyond the control of manager and may bear negative relationship with selectivity. This has been proved true in equity diversified fund schemes, as the coefficient attached to risk is negatively significant. Besides, the constant is positively significant, suggesting that management capability is absolute is important.

Table-6.14: Cross-Section Regression Results of Equity Diversified Sampled Fund Schemes

(Dependent Variable- Selectivity)

This Table presents the regression results of the panel data of 28 equity diversified mutual fund schemes. The results are based on the format of regression equation-7. P-value provides the smallest level of significance at which the null hypothesis would be rejected. The smaller the p-value, the stronger the evidence is in favor of the alternative hypothesis. t-statistic is the value provided by the data. F-statistic provides the evidence for the jointly significance of the model (variables included). ARCH test provides the evidence of auto-correlation of residuals after the estimation.

Variable	Co-efficient	t-Statistic	P-Value
Constant	4.1797	3.5745	0.0017
Risk	-0.1077	1.9847	0.0436
Size	0.0904	0.6404	0.5285
TO	0.0002	0.8631	0.3974
ER	-0.6902	2.9595	0.0072
Age	-0.9771	2.2237	0.0367

R-Squared 0.4883		**F-Statistic** 4.1993 (0.0078)	
Durbin Watson 1.3680		N=28	

ARCH-Test	
F-Statistic	0.5101 (0.4817)
Obs*R-Squared	0.5398 (0.4624)

(c) ELSS and Balanced Fund Schemes

This segment of the study deals with the factors that influence the selectivity in the ELSS and balanced fund schemes. The cross sectional regression results based on equation-7 are based on the panel data of 23 mutual fund schemes (15 ELSS and 8 balanced). The results are presented in table-6.15.

Table-6.15: Cross-Section Regression Results of ELSS & Balanced Sampled Fund Schemes

(Dependent Variable- Selectivity)

This table presents the regression results of the panel data of 23 equity diversified mutual fund schemes. The results are based on the format of regression equation-7. P-value provides the smallest level of significance at which the null hypothesis would be rejected. The smaller the p-value, the stronger the evidence is in favor of the alternative hypothesis. t-statistic is the value provided by the data. F-statistic provides the evidence for the jointly significance of the model (variables included). ARCH test provides the evidence of auto-correlation of residuals after the estimation.

Variable	Co-efficient	t-Statistic	P-Value
Constant	-1.9873	0.7221	0.4800
Risk	0.3624	0.4269	0.6747
Size	0.8006	3.0389	0.0074
TO	-0.0001	0.6639	0.5156
ER	1.0443	2.0543	0.0500
Age	-1.2812	2.3001	0.0344

R-Squared 0.5217	F-Statistic 3.7087 (0.0187)
Durbin Watson 2.1318	N = 23

ARCH-Test	
F-Statistic	0.4717 (0.5000)
Obs*R-Squared	0.5069 (0.4764)

The table reveals that the model used is justified, as F-statistic is significant and the explanatory power of the facilitative variables is more than 50 percent. Besides, the estimated model is independent of heteroscedatsicty and auto-correlation model. Size of the fund is expected to have positive impact on the selectivity and this is proved true here as size of the fund is highly significant variable. This model also gives one odd result, contrary to expectation that higher ER is positively associated selectivity, which is needed to be explored further. However, contrary to the established belief, aged funds are negatively related to the selectivity, as the coefficient attached to the age variable is negatively significant.

6.4.5 The Relationship between Timing Performance and Fund Characteristics

Is it possible to time the market movement by the fund manager, perhaps not, otherwise every person would have been millionaire. Results shown in the previous sections established that Indian mutual fund industry lacks the market timing ability. Rather there is trade-off between the market timing and stock selectivity. Meaning thereby better selectivity is negatively related to market timing ability. In a less developed economy like India, markets are imperfect and capital market is under-developed. It may be beyond the capability of the even efficient fund managers to time the market accurately. Therefore, the estimation of equation did not give any workable result, which can be used for better investment planning. All the variables shown in table-6.16 are insignificant and the model is also not justified. The signs of the coefficients can be interpreted. All the variables are negatively insignificant. Hence, the market predictability is not the forte of Indian fund managers. Included variables do not impact the timing ability of the fund manager.

Table-6.16: Cross-Section Regression Results of All Sampled Fund Schemes

(Dependent Variable- Timing Ability)

This Table presents the regression results of the panel data of 51 mutual fund schemes. The results are based on the format of regression equation-8. P-value provides the smallest level of significance at which the null hypothesis would be rejected. The smaller the p-value, the stronger the evidence is in favor of the alternative hypothesis. T-statistic is the value provided by the data. F-statistic provides the evidence for the jointly significance of the model (Variables included). ARCH test provides the evidence of auto-correlation of residuals after the estimation.

Variable	Co-efficient	t-Statistic	P-Value
Constant	0.9633	2.0055	0.0509
Risk	-0.1310	0.9654	0.3395
Size	-0.0029	0.0503	0.9601
TO	-0.0075	0.1318	0.8957
ER	-0.0705	0.6688	0.5070
Age	-0.2483	1.7005	0.0559
R-Squared 0.0955		**F-Statistic** 0.9507 (0.4579)	
Durbin Watson 1.7692		N=51	
ARCH-Test			
F-Statistic		1.2933 (0.2611)	
Obs*R-Squared		1.3118 (0.2520)	

6.5 Concluding Remarks

This study is based on the monthly data of NAV of 51 mutual fund schemes categorized as equity diversified, ELSS and Balanced funds spread over the period between April 2006 and December 2014. Indian mutual fund industry is capable enough to generate earning for their clients. Mutual fund returns performances are capable to beat the returns performance of the benchmark markets. Moreover, the portfolios are adequately diversified and save them from the high risk exposures. Due to the provision of lock-in period in ELSS category, fund managers have better flexibility, and can take more risk to play with funds without the fear of demand for redemption. Therefore, risk adjusted performance is highest in this category followed by equity diversified and balanced funds. Even then, there is a word of caution for the investors to properly scrutinize the fund houses and fund schemes; for, 8 percent are in the negative return category.

It is generally talked that markets are always unpredictable and that also hold true in Indian scenario. Indian fund managers are lacking market timing ability. So, we can say that Indian mutual funds do have the ability of stock selection. However, they are devoid of market timing ability; as, majority of the fund schemes either fall in the category of insignificant or in negatively significant.

Even, there is trade-off between a fund manager's stock selection and timing ability. The fund managers cannot excel in both the activities so far the Indian mutual fund industry is concerned. Moreover, managers of large fund schemes are better equipped for stock selection ability. Contrary to the established belief that old funds are better in stock selection does not hold true here, rather new funds do with more vigour. Given that market movements are generally unpredictable, funds with high exposures to market risk make it all the more challenging for managers to correctly select the stocks that would maximize the returns.

In a less developed economy like India, markets are imperfect and capital market is relatively under-developed. It is beyond the capability of even efficient fund managers to time the market accurately. Hence, market predictability is not the forte of Indian fund managers.

References

- Ahmad M. and Samajpati U. (2010), "Evaluation of Stock Selection Skills And Market Timing Abilities of Indian Mutual Fund Managers", *Management Insight*, 6 (2), 71-82.
- Becker C., Ferson W.E., Myers D.H. and Schill M. J. (1999), "Conditional Market Timing with Benchmark Investors", *Journal of Empirical Finance*, 52(1), 119-148.
- Bekaert G. & Harvey C. R. (2002), "Research in Emerging Market Finance: Looking to the Future", available at: https://www0.gsb.columbia.edu.
- Brown S. J. and Goetzmann W. N (1995), "Performance Persistence", *Journal of Finance*, 50 (2), 679-698.
- Cahart M. M. (1997), "On Persistence in Mutual Funds Performance", *Journal of Finance*, 52 (1), 57-82.
- Chander R. (2006), "Investment Managers' Market Timing Abilities: Empirical Evidence from the Indian Capital Market", *IIMB Management Review*, 18 (4), 315-326.
- Chen H. L., Jegadeesh N., and Wermers R. (2000), "The Value of Active Mutual Fund Management: An Examination of the Stock Holding and Trades of Fund Managers, *Journal of Financial and Quantitative Analysis*, 35 (3), 343-368.
- Chopra M. P. (2011), "Do Indian Mutual Fund Managers Select the Stock and Time the Market Correctly?", *The IUP Journal of Applied Finance*, 17 (2), 77-86.
- Dahlquist M., Engstrom S. and Soderlind P. (2000), "Performance and Characteristics of Swedish Mutual Funds", *Journal of Financial and Quantitative Analysis*, 35 (3), 409-423.
- Deniel K., Grinblatt M., Titman S. and Wermers R. (1997), "Measuring Mutual Fund Performance with Characteristics-Based Benchmarks", *Journal of Finance*, 57 (3), 1035-1058.
- Droms W. G. and Walker D. A. (1996), "Mutual Fund Investment Performance", *Quarterly Review of Economics and Finance*, 36 (3), 347-363.
- Fama E. F. & French K. R. (1992), "The Cross-Section of Expected Stock Returns", *The Journal of Finance*, 47 (2), 427-465.

- Fama E. F. & French K. R. (1998), "Value verses Growth: The International Evidence", The Journal of Finance, 53 (6), 1975-1999.
- Ferson W.E. and Schadt R.W. (1996), "Measuring Fund Strategy and Performance in Changing Economic Conditions", *The Journal of Finance*, 51 (2), 425-461.
- Ferson W. & Warther V. A. (1996), "Evaluating Fund Performance in a Dynamic Market", *Financial Analysts Journal*, 52 (6), 20-28.
- Fortin R., and Michelson S. (2005), "Active International Mutual Fund Management: Can Managers Beat the Index?" *Managerial Finance*, 31(1), 41-51.
- Grinblatt M. and Titman S. (1989), "Mutual Fund Performance: An Analysis of Quarterly Portfolio Holdings", *Journal of Business*, 62 (3), 393-416.
- Grinblatt M. and Titman S. (1993), "Performance Measurement without Benchmarks: An Examination of Mutual Fund Returns", *Journal of Business*, 66 (1), 47-68.
- Gruber M. J. (1996), "Another Puzzle: The Growth in Actively Managed Mutual Funds", *Journal of Finance*, 51 (3), 783-801.
- Guha D.S., Banerjee A. and Chakrabarti B. B. (2007), "Market Timing and Stock Selection Ability of Mutual Funds in India: An Empirical Investigation", *Vikalpa*, 32 (2), 39-51.
- Gupta A. (2000), "Market Timing Abilities of Indian Mutual Fund Manager: An Empirical Study", *Applied Finance*, 6 (2), 47-61.
- Gupta O.P. and Sehgal S. (2001), "Investment Performance of Mutual Funds: The Indian Experience". In U. Shashikant and S. Arumugam (Eds.), *Indian Capital Markets: Trends and Dimensions. New Delhi*, Tata McGraw-Hill.
- Henriksson R. D. and Merton R. C. (1981), "On Market Timing and Investment Performance-Statistical procedures for Evaluating Forecasting Skills", *Journal of Business*, 54 (4), 513-533.
- Ippolito R. A. (1989), "Efficiency with Costly Information: A Study of Mutual Fund Performance, 1965-1984", *Quarterly Journal of Economics*, 23 (2), 389-416.
- Jenson C. M. (1968), "The Performance of Mutual Funds in the period 1945-1964", *Journal of Finance*, 104 (1), 1-23.

- Kumar R. (2012), "Market Timing, Selectivity and Mutual Fund Performance: An Empirical Investigation of Selective Equity Diversified Schemes in India", *IUP Journal of Financial Economics*, 10(1), 62-84.
- Low S.W. (2010), "Relationship between Fund Performance and Characteristics of the Malaysia Unit Trust Fund", *Singapore Management Review*, 32 (1), 29-43.
- Malkiel B. G. (1995), "Returns from Investing in Equity mutual funds, 1971-1991, Journal of Finance, 50 (2), 549-572.
- Mishra B. (2002), "Selectivity and Timing Skills of Mutual Funds in India: An Empirical Analysis", *ICFAI Journal of Applied Finance*, 8 (1), 5-16.
- Nathani N., Chakraborty A., Rawat B. and Holani U. (2011), "Timing Skills of Fund Managers: A Study of Equity Mutual Fund Schemes", *Business Spectrum*, 1 (1), 9-18.
- Otten R. & Bams D. (2002), "European Mutual Fund Performance", *European Financial Management*, 8 (1), 75-101.
- Rouwenhorst K. G. (1999), "Local Return Factors and Turnover in Emerging Stock Markets", The Journal of Finance, 54 (4), 1439-1463.
- Saez J.C. (2008), "The Dynamics of Mutual Funds and Market Timing Measurement" *Studies in Nonlinear Dynamics & Econometrics*, 12(4), 1-38.
- Sehgal S. and Jhanwar M. (2008), "On Stock Selection Skills and Market Timing Abilities of Mutual Fund Managers in India", *International Research Journal of Finance & Economics*, 15 (2), 307-317.
- Sharpe W. F. (1966), *"Mutual Fund Performance", Journal of Business*, 39 (1), 119-138.
- Treynor J. L. (1965), "How to Rate Management of Investment Funds", *Harvard Business Review*, 43 (1), 63-75.
- Treynor J. and Mazuy M. (1966) "Can Mutual Funds Outguess the Market?" *Harvard Business Review*, 44(4), 131-36.
- Tripathy N.P. (2006), "Market Timing Abilities and Mutual Fund Performance- An Empirical Investigation into Equity Linked Saving Schemes", *Vilakshan, XIMB Journal of Management*, 127-138.

Chapter-7
Performance Evaluation: Conditional Models

[This chapter has been reproduced from author's research paper entitled "Conditional Models in Performance Evaluation of Mutual Funds in India", published in International Journal of Technical Research and Applications, (2016) Vol. 4 (1), pp 94-101, with permission from the copy right holder(s)]

7.1 Introduction

Indian mutual fund industry has registered remarkable progress in recent decade (amfiindia).[1] In spite of tremendous growth of this delegated asset management industry, the concerns of fund managers' ability to augment value to their portfolios remain vital in investment process. Traditional measures of risk adjusted performance[2], as discussed in the previous chapter, compare the fund returns with a benchmark. These measures are designated as unconditional; as, these measures do not take into account the changes in the conditions of financial markets or the broader economic set up. Besides, they are based on the assumption that fund risks and expected returns are stable overtime. Since system is dynamic, consequently fund risks and risk premiums change over time; therefore, the traditional performance measures confuse time variation with abnormal performance

Unconditional techniques are, thus, incapable to capture the time varying element of expected returns. These measures assume that the systemic risk of a fund is stationary over time, so ignore the existence of timing activities of the fund managers. Due to time variation in actively managed funds, beta (systemic risk) is not time invariant. It may change due to time related factors, weights change in the portfolio due to change in market values and fund may experience large change in fund inflows and outflows which is beyond the control of the fund manager. Moreover, new information on the economy in general or/and on a particular company may change the relative risk of companies and in turn their expected returns. It is acknowledged in the financial literature that investor's expectations and variance of financial securities vary over time (Coggins et. al., 2004).

In the conditional performance evaluation approach, the fund manager's risk exposures and the related market premiums are allowed to vary over time with the state of the economy. Hence, the time varying nature of investment risk should be incorporated into the funds' performance evaluation process (Merton, 1971). This belief gave rise to a new class of conditional performance evaluation models (Ferson and Schadt 1996; Ferson and Warther 1996; Christopherson et al. 1998) that allow both funds' expected returns and risk to vary through time. The state of the economy is measured by using predetermined, public information variables. The conditional performance measure, the conditional alpha, is the difference between a fund's excess returns and that of a strategy that attempts to match the fund's risk dynamics over time based on the predetermined information variables.

Conditional Performance Evaluation, to large extent, is in harmony with a semi-strong form[3] of market efficiency (Fama, 1970). If the market is efficient, a fund manager cannot add value to stocks by using mechanical trading strategy. In order to add value and generate a positive conditional alpha, a manager should offer a higher return than the mechanical-trading strategy. Ferson and Schadt (1996) advocate using performance measures that are conditioned on public information variables in order to avoid the bias induced by using historical average returns to estimate expected performance. A profitable investment strategy relying on public information should not be seen as superior performance by managers. Therefore, traditional performance measures that assume constant risk may assign abnormal performance to a strategy based solely on public information. They propose performance measures in which the mutual fund beta is a linear function of public information as defined by a one-period lag of macroeconomic variables that have predictive power for future stock returns.

In this background, the present study is devoted to evaluate the performance of Indian mutual funds by using the conditional models. The existing performance evaluation models are conditioned by the public information comprising financial and macro variables. Technically, alphas and betas are conditioned with public information. Such results may be more useful for the investors to identify the selectivity and timing ability of the fund managers.

7.2 Use of Conditional Models in Literature

Some theoretical and empirical literature has come to light, over time, on conditional performance of mutual funds. The unconditional fund performance measurement assumes that investment risk is time invariant. Putting in other words, the portfolio's betas are fixed for the whole observation period. This could make the performance unreliable because many empirical studies show that risks and returns are predictable overtime using economic variables such as dividends, interest rate etc. Moreover, it has been established in the literature that investment risk has time varying nature (Merton, 1970). Hence, the literature on conditional performance of mutual funds has emerged. Therefore, it has been realized that such phenomenon should also be considered while evaluating the performance. Conditional models are developed on three assumptions. First, many studies have rejected the CAPM (Capital Asset Pricing Models) due to unconditional nature and evidences suggested that risks and returns of stocks and bonds are predictable, using dividend yields, interest rates and other economic variables. Second, the conventional measures assume that investors have unconditional expectations and any information used by fund managers can be considered as abnormal performance. However, if the market is semi-strong form efficient, as defined by Fama (1970), meaning that market prices fully reflect the public information; hence, a manager who adjusts a portfolio dynamically according to the readily available information should not be viewed as having superior performance. Finally, betas are a functional form due to time varying factor, which may be owing to three sources- the changing betas of underlying assets, the portfolio's re-weighting by active managers and the major fund flows in and out of a portfolio which can change the weight of a passive portfolio.

This conditional beta can be used to replace any of the betas in the unconditional model to capture a dynamic strategy on the part of a fund manager. Many studies incorporate the conditional beta and alpha for the portfolio performance evaluation and suggest that using a conditional model economically and statistically improves portfolio performance and makes performance more neutral (see Ferson and Schadt, 1996; Ferson and Warther, 1996; Sawicki, 2001; Roy and Deb, 2003). Ferson and Schadt argued that all the single and multi-factor measures are biased, since portfolio risk and returns are fixed through time (known as the unconditional measure). For this reason, they propose in their model a conditional measure which allows time-variation. They use both measures to investigate the performance of 67 mutual funds in the U.S. market during the period 1968-1990. They employ five predetermined variables for their conditional measure, namely- one month Treasury bills, dividend yield, slope of term structure, quality of spread in the bond market and a dummy variable for the January effect – and incorporate it with Jensen's single factor measure. Their results show that negative Jensen's alphas (unconditional) shifts and become positive when predetermined variables are included. They also apply their conditional method to Treynor and Mazuy's (1966) and Henriksson and Merton's (1981) market timing measures and use 3 self constructed buy-and-hold portfolios to test the market timing models, as well as data from 67 mutual funds. They conclude that the unconditional market timing models are misspecified, since the results show negative market timing performance even if they are in the buy-and-hold strategy portfolios. When the conditional market timing measures are used, the negative timing coefficients disappeared. Therefore, they confirm that using their conditional model brings both statistical and economic significance and makes the performance of the funds look better.

In a similar way, Sawicki and Ong (2000), apply both unconditional and conditional Jensen's measures, as well as Treynor and Mazuy's market timing model to investigate Australian funds between 1983 and 1995, they found weak evidence of positive performance and negative market timing performance. In consistent to Ferson and Schadt (1996), they confirm the statistical significance of incorporating lagged information variables in the model, in particular with regard to dividend yield. They also confirm that the conditional model shifts the alphas to the right and makes funds look better. Dahlquist et al (2000) explores Swedish fund performance in broad fund classifications from 1993 to 1997, using a conditional measure. He revealed superior performance only for funds in the equity class.

Otten and Bams (2004) examined statistical and economic importance of adding more factors to the unconditional models by using 2436 US mutual funds (1962-2000) with Jensen and Cahart models with unconditional and conditional in alpha and betas. They revealed that conditional models add statistical and economic relevance to performance measurement. The Cahart model is the best in explaining mutual fund returns. At the aggregated level, alphas do not change much between unconditional and conditional models. At style level, moving to the richer models have large impacts on the alphas in income funds. In overall, US mutual funds generate insignificant negative performance. Size and B/M (book to market) factors have explanatory power for all style portfolios. Momentum factor has explanatory power for only three style portfolios. The growth/income portfolio is not statistically exposed to the momentum factor. Conditional model improves performance of funds and makes funds, in overall, look better except income/growth and income portfolios which conditional model decrease performance.

Luis Ferruz et al. (2006) evaluated mutual fund performance of Spanish mutual funds for 225 Spanish equity funds (1994-2002). He used conditional Jensen measure which incorporated seven predetermined variables, namely, dividend yields, T-bills, bond yield, variable that represent inverse wealth, term structure, quality spread, and dummy variable of January effect. Funds display negative alphas but performance improves when using measure. The conditional measure also improves explanatory power of the model.

However, studies of Becker et al. (1999), Holmes and Faff (2004) and Saez (2008) showed little evidence of market timing even in a conditional framework.

Guha Deb et al. (2007) examined the market timing and stock selection abilities of mutual fund managers using both unconditional and conditional approaches. Using 96 mutual funds schemes during January 2000 to June 2005 the study reported lack of market timing but presence of stock selection abilities of Indian fund managers in both the approaches.

Roy, et.al (2003) conducted an empirical study on conditional performance of Indian mutual funds. This paper uses a technique called conditional performance evaluation on a sample of eighty-nine Indian mutual fund schemes. This paper measures the performance of various mutual funds with both unconditional and conditional form of CAPM, Treynor-Mazuy model and Henriksson-Merton model. The effect of incorporating lagged information variables into the evaluation of mutual fund managers' performance is examined in the Indian context. The results suggest that the use of conditioning lagged information variables improves the performance of mutual fund schemes, causing alphas to shift towards right and reducing the number of negative timing coefficients.

7.3   Unconditional and Conditional Models

This section highlights the data set used to evaluate performance of Indian mutual funds. Besides, the techniques that have been used to get the final results regarding performance evaluation are discussed in detail. Moreover, for the better understanding of readers, variables used are categorically defined and their significance in the mutual fund industry is also discussed.

This study is based on the 51 mutual fund schemes launched by the variety of fund houses. These mutual fund schemes are divided into three categories based on their characteristics namely; Equity Diversified Funds (28), Equity Linked Saving Schemes (ELSS) Funds (15) and Balanced Funds (8). Diversified mutual funds are equity funds which invest across divergent sectors and categories of the stock market and endeavor to moderate the risk exposures. An Equity Linked Savings Scheme (ELSS) is an equity oriented mutual fund scheme in which the majority corpus (about 80-100 percent) is invested in equities. It qualifies for tax exemption under section 80C of the Indian Income Tax Act, 1961. This type of fund scheme does not just help us to save tax, but also provide an opportunity to grow our money. A fund that combines stock, bond and sometimes money market component in a single portfolio are termed as balanced funds. Generally, 50-75 per cent is equity component and rest is in debt. Such funds are geared towards investors who look for mixture of safety, income and modest capital appreciation.

To study the fund performance, monthly data for the 51 schemes on the fund portfolio return has been used by using the Net Asset Value Data (NAV). Besides, to establish the capacity of fund to beat the benchmark, market data for relevant indices has been used.

This study covers the period from April, 2006 to December 2014. This period incorporates the periods of boom, stagnation and slowdown in the Indian economy in general and stock market in particular. Therefore, this period provides full opportunity to the fund manager to prove his capability in such economic scenarios and the importance of fund characteristics in changing macro-economic environment. The data belongs to this period for the fund schemes that came into existence before April 2006 and for those started after this period; data belongs from the year of inception to December 2014.

Data Source

Variable	Data Source
Treasury Bill Returns	www.tradingeconomics.com
FII Net Investment	www.fpi.nsdl.co.in
Inflation Rate	www.inflation.edu.com
Net Asset Value (NAV)	www.amfiindia.com
Stock Market Indices	www.bseindia.com / www.nseindia.com
Index of Industrial production	www.mospi.nic.in
Dividend Yield Value	www.bseindia.com / www.nseindia.com

Jenson's single factor regression based approach is used to establish the portfolio beta, that is portfolio returns effected by the systemic risk and alpha, popularly called Jensen's alpha, indicates the manager's performance coefficient. The Jenson's equation is shown in the following regression specification:

$$R_{pt} - R_{ft} = \alpha_j + \beta_p (R_{mt} - R_{ft}) + \varepsilon_{pt} \quad (1)$$

Where, R_{pt} is the rate of return of the fund at time t, R_{ft} is the contemporaneous rate of return on a risk free asset, R_{mt} is the rate of return of market portfolio at time t. β_p is the estimated coefficient for the systemic risk level of the fund, α_j is the Jensen's performance coefficient, indicating the risk adjusted performance of the fund and ε_{pt} represents the random error term. This regression equation assumes that the systemic risk of a fund is stationary over time and thus ignores the existence of timing activities of the fund managers.

The Jenson's model, thus, calculate the overall fund performance and all the credit goes to the fund manager in terms of its stock selection capability. However, the overall performance is a combination of stock selection and the timing ability of the manager and Jenson's model is unable to decompose the fund's performance in stock selection and timing ability. In this context, Treynor and Mazuy (1966), model separates the performance into market timing and selectivity components. The Treynor and Mazuy (1966) model is specified as follows;

$$R_{pt} - R_{ft} = \alpha_p + \beta_p (R_{mt} - R_{ft}) + \gamma_p (R_{mt} - R_{ft})^2 + \varepsilon_{pt} \text{ (2)}$$

In this equation, γ_p is the manager's ability to time the market movement and α_p is the expected return for portfolio p generated from the manager's selectivity skills. If the manager has successfully timed the market, γ_p will be +ve and significant and $\gamma_p = 0$ would be interpreted as no ability to time the market.

The single-index 'alpha model' has been the predominant approach to performance evaluation until recently when researchers began employing a multi-index model to improve the accuracy performance measurement. Both single- and multi index models, however, may suffer from another problem: time-variation in risks and expected returns that may be misinterpreted as superior selectivity or timing skills. If the market risk premium changes and the performance metric does not control for this, time variation in the market risk premium will be reflected in the estimate of abnormal performance and mistaken for manager under or over-performance.

Ferson and Schadt (1996) argue that evidence of return predictability using predetermined variables represents changing required returns. They propose a modification to the Jensen alpha and market timing models to incorporate conditioning information that allows for the estimation of time-varying conditional betas. Ferson and Schadt (1996) modify the traditional Jensen alpha model by adding a vector of lagged public information variables.

Ferson and Schadt (1996) point out that a profitable investment strategy relying on public information should not be seen as superior performance by managers. Therefore, traditional performance measures that assume constant risk may assign abnormal performance to strategy based solely on public information. They propose performance measures in which the mutual fund beta is a linear function of monthly public information as defined by a one period lag of macroeconomic variables that have predictive power for future stock returns. Hence, the conditional performance measures of Treynor and Mazuy (1966) and Henriksson and Merton (1981) are presented in the format which incorporates public information, that is the alphas and the betas are conditioned with the public information. This study proposed to use five return predictive variables for conditioning the alphas and betas. Among these, market dividend yield (DP) and short-term Treasury bill yield (TB) are used as important public information variables. It is further stated that influence market returns are those that change discount factors and expected cash flows, inflation rate (IF) is used as information variable. Further, changes in the level of real production affect the current value of cash flows and thereby market returns. So, growth rate of index of industrial production (IIP) is considered as another explanatory variable. Finally, monthly growth in net foreign institutional (FII) flows is taken as another macroeconomic variable. These variables are used in one period time lag format.

The Conditional Jenson's Model

$$R_{pt} - R_{ft} = a_p + \beta_p (R_{mt} - R_{ft}) + C_p'[Z_{t-1}(R_{mt} - R_{ft})] \quad (3)$$

The Conditional Treynor-Mazuy Model

$$R_{pt} - R_{ft} = a_p + \beta_p (R_{mt} - R_{ft}) + C_p'[Z_{t-1}(R_{mt} - R_{ft})] + \gamma_p (R_{mt} - R_{ft})^2 + \boxtimes_{pt} \quad (4)$$

Where, coefficient vector C_p' captures the response of manager's beta to the entire public information Z_{t-1} (represented by four variables in this study). The coefficient γ_p measures the sensitivity of the manager's beta to the private timing signal. The bias due to readily available information is controlled by the term $C_p[Z_{t-1}((R_{mt} - R_{ft})]$. Rest of the terms in these equations is same as in the unconditional models.

Variables

Monthly returns: Since this study is based on the monthly returns of the fund schemes selected for analysis. The monthly returns for each of the sample scheme have been computed by the following equation;

$$R_{t=} (NAV_t - NAV_{t-1})/ NAV_{t-1}$$

Here; R_t is the monthly return of a fund scheme in month 't'. Since the selected fund schemes are in growth option, hence the question to adjust the dividends in calculating the monthly returns does not arise.

Market Monthly Returns: Returns for the various market indices (R_m) used as benchmark, so market returns have been estimated;

$$R_{mt=} (Market\ Index_t - Market\ Index_{t-1})/ Market\ Index_{t-1}$$

Here; R_{mt} is the market return in period 't', Market Index$_t$ and Market Index$_{t-1}$ are levels of market index levels in periods 't' and 't-1' respectively.

Treasury Bill Returns: T-bills are like promissory notes issued by central government as a primary instrument for regulating money supply and raising funds via open market operations. T-bills are sold at discount and their returns being the difference between the purchase price and the par value (redemption value), as t- bills are sold on discount and devoid of explicit interest rate. Such bills are, generally, used risk free investments as being backed by the government's full faith and credit. Therefore, Treasury bill returns are used to as risk free returns to calculate the excess returns generated by the fund managers.

FII Investment: FIIs are those institutional investors which invest in the assets that belong to different country other than those where these organizations are based. Foreign institutional investors play a very important role in any economy. These are the big companies such as investment banks, mutual funds etc, who invest considerable amount of money in the Indian markets. With the buying of securities by these big players, markets trend to move upward and vice-versa. They exert strong influence on the total inflows coming into the economy. Hence, considerably influence the market returns and other parameters of the economy.

Inflation Rate: The inflation rate is the percentage rate of change of a price index over time. This study relies on consumer price index (CPI) to calculate inflation rate in Indian economy. Inflation rate in the economy is an important macroeconomic variable that influence the returns and a source of public information regarding the fragility of the economy.

Index of Industrial Production (IIP): An index of the total output from manufacturing, mining and utility companies. It is seen as an indicator of macroeconomic trends. A high IIP indicates economic growth. This variable is an important public information variable, hence exclusively introduced as a conditional variable in the mutual fund performance models.

Dividend Yield Value: Dividend yield equals the weighted average across the market index of each individual public firm's dividend paid divided by share price.

7.4 Empirical Findings and Discussion

7.4.1 Selectivity in Jensen's Conditional Model

This section is concerned with the performance of mutual funds overtime. In the previous chapter, performance evaluation was based on the unconditional measures. In this chapter, an attempt has been made to see the fund performance after introducing the public information variables in the basic unconditional models of performance evaluation. Table-7.1 reveals the performance measured by Jensen's Alpha taking into consideration both conditional (equation-3) and unconditional measures (equation-1).

Table-7.1: Jenson Performance Measure (Panel Data)

Fund Category	Unconditional		Conditional	
	Alpha	**R^2**	**Alpha**	**R^2**
All Sample Funds	0.3289 (5.33)	0.6278	0.4205 (44.41)	0.6305
Equity Diversified	0.3498 (4.01)	0.6078	0.4315 (23.85)	0.6128
ELSS	0.3480 (2.99)	0.6842	0.4597 (14.11)	0.6867
Balanced	0.2172 (1.97)	0.6742	0.2862 (6.69)	0.6766

Individual Levels (Number of Positive and Negative [ ] Funds		
Fund Category	Unconditional	Conditional
All Sample Funds	47 [4]	46 [5]
Equity Diversified	26 [2]	25 [3]
ELSS	14 [1]	14 [1]
Balanced	7 [1]	7 [1]

Values in Parentheses are t-values

Unconditional Jensen's alpha captures the stock selection capability of the fund manager that is whether he can add value to the portfolio by selecting appropriate stocks. Since it is not conditioned by any other information; hence, termed as unconditional alpha. Table-7.1 reveals that fund managers of Indian mutual fund industry have stock selection capability; for, the alpha in all fund categories and in aggregate turned out to be positively significant. Highest performance is registered by the equity diversified category (0.3498 value of alpha coefficient) followed by the ELSS category (0.3480 value of alpha coefficient), all sampled funds (0.3289) and the least performing segment proved to be balanced funds (0.2172). When the funds' portfolio is diversified, then it has scope to perform better than other funds due to opportunity of hedging or spreading of risks across the sectors. Equity linked saving schemes (ELSS) is also diversified funds and are also performing at almost same footing. In this category of funds, the fund manager has better flexibility to use the funds; as, the redemption pressure is very less given the lock in period provision. The investors are permitted to withdraw the money only after a few years. However, explanatory power of unconditional Jensen's model is highest in the ELSS model followed by the balanced funds. This power is least in the case of equity diversified funds. What is the explanation of such phenomenon? In case of equity diversified funds, role of market movement is highest, and markets are unpredictable. However, markets are more predictable in other categories of mutual funds as the relatively higher level of explanatory power.

The situation has changed to some extent, when the fund returns are conditioned by the public information variables (equation-3). The Jensen's alpha has improved to some extent in all categories of mutual funds along with the improvement in the explanatory power of the Jensen's model. Therefore, it can be concluded here that use of public information which has direct bearing on the stock market, fund managers' can improve the stock picking ability. ELSS and diversified funds proved to be best funds so far the selectivity capability of fund managers is concerned. So far the performance of individual fund schemes is concerned, positive and negative performing fund schemes remained same except for one shifting from positive performance in the equity diversified categories. Therefore, fund managers should be capable to process the public information that is available to all, to adjust the portfolio for better returns.

A study by Ferson and Schadt (1996) suggests that the unconditional performance measure leads to negative performance because the betas of mutual funds are negatively related to the expected market return, which moves together with its volatility. Therefore, when time variation in beta is controlled, mutual fund performance improves and shifts the alphas to the right. Studies by Ferson and Warther (1996), Sawicki and Ong (2000) and Roy and Deb (2003) also confirm these findings. The results of this study are also in the same line.

7.4.2 Selectivity and Market Timing Ability

Timing ability is the ability of a fund manager to adjust his portfolio's risk according to the expected change in economic situation. The timing ability model separates timing ability from selectivity ability and if the manager has timing ability the square term of the market return should be positive and significant (Equation 2 & 4).

Table-7.2: Panel Data Results for Selectivity and Market Timing

(Conditional TMM Model)

Fund Category	Unconditional		Conditional	
	Selectivity	Market Timing	Selectivity	Market Timing
ALL	0.4042 (5.9847)	-0.0018 (2.7734)	0.4205 (44.4083)	-0.0034 (30.2101)
Equity Diversified	0.4147 (4.3284)	-0.0015 (1.6287)	0.4315 (23.8540)	-0.0038 (17.903)
ELSS	0.4701 (3.7429)	-0.0032 (2.5481)	0.4597 (14.1119)	-0.0032 (7.5441)
Balanced	0.2726 (2.2563)	-0.0012 (1.1283)	0.2862 (6.6963)	-0.0004 (0.9278)

Note: Figures in parentheses are t-values

The table-7.2 reveals the results of the Treynor and Mazuy model (TMM) of selectivity and market timing. The results of market timing ability in both conditional and unconditional models are negative, meaning thereby Indian mutual fund industry is devoid of market timing ability. Rather, it plays perverse in the market returns. That is any effort by the fund managers to improve the returns by timing the market could not succeed. This is true in both the conditional as well as the unconditional models. The public information did not fructify in market timing ability.

Moreover, so far as the stock picking ability is concerned, it has been proved in the Jensen's model and this model that Indian mutual fund industry has stock picking ability. This ability has improved to some extent when the model is conditioned with public information except the ELSS category. It can be concluded in this section that Indian mutual fund industry has stock selection ability but lacking market timing irrespective of the public information.

7.4.3 Relationship between Selectivity and Market Timing

Can a fund manager behave holistically, that is, he shows all capabilities simultaneously? If any fund manager is highly capable then he may show prowess picking the performing stocks and can time the market accurately, then his performance will turn out to be marvelous. It can be other way round, that there is trade-off between the market timing and stock selection. To answer this question in Indian mutual fund industry, correlation between the market timing coefficient and stock picking coefficient has been estimated in the 51 sampled fund schemes. Moreover, same has been calculated in the categories chosen namely-equity diversified, ELSS and balanced funds. Results are presented in the table-7.3.

Table-7.3: Correlation between the Selectivity and the Market Timing

(TMM Model)

Fund Category	Correlation (ρ)	Funds with Opposite Sign (%)
ALL	-0.4382	60.78
Equity Diversified	-0.2222	67.85
ELSS	-0.5222	53.33
Balanced	-0.0385	50.00

The table exhibit negative correlation in the stock selection and market timing ability. Meaning thereby, when the fund manager is able to show his strength in one type of capability he is lacking the same in the other. He is unable to prove his strength simultaneously. For, the correlation coefficient is -0.4382 and the 60.78% fund schemes have shown opposite sign. So far the categories of funds in this context are concerned, correlation value (-0.0385) is observed least in balanced funds and 50% of the sampled balanced funds observed opposite sign. Negative correlation coefficient (-0.5222) is highest in ELSS category. This value is relatively smaller in equity diversified funds category (-0.2222). It can be concluded in this section that fund managers in Indian mutual fund industry are unable to show prowess in both the capabilities simultaneously.

7.4.4 Fund Factor Sensitivities

This section of the discussion is devoted to sensitivities of the fund returns to market in unconditional model and market and other factors in the conditional model. As we are aware with the fact that funds with high and significant value of beta, returns are prone to change with the change in market conditions. In this context, panel data has been estimated and the sensitivities are presented in the table-7.4.

Table-7.4: Fund Factor Sensitivities (Panel Data)

Fund Category	Unconditional	Conditional				
	$Beta_m$	$Beta_m$	$Beta_{if}$	$Beta_{dp}$	$Beta_{iip}$	$Betaf_{ii}$
All Sample Funds	0.8318 (88.24)	0.9872 (73.91)	-0.0102 (17.51)	0.1163 (26.52)	-0.0015 (17.74)	0.0001 (6.37)
Equity Diversified	0.8521 (64.84)	1.2473 (50.15)	-0.0143 (10.74)	0.1441 (19.43)	-0.0032 (18.88)	0.0001 (5.06)
ELSS	0.9058 (48.44)	0.9033 (17.89)	-0.0041 (2.77)	-0.0369 (1.81)	0.0005 (1.75)	0.0001 (2.95)
Balanced	0.6799 (41.07)	0.7864 (12.48)	0.0109 (3.31)	-0.0088 (0.34)	-0.0012 (2.81)	0.0001 (3.33)
Individual Levels (Number of Positive and Negative [ ] Funds						

	Unconditional	Conditional				
All Sample Funds	51 [0]	46 [5]	16 [35]	22 [29]	22 [29]	27 [24]
Equity Diversified	28 [0]	26 [2]	9 [19]	12 [16]	9 [19]	15 [13]
ELSS	15 [0]	12 [3]	6 [9]	7 [8]	9 [6]	10 [5]
Balanced	08 [0]	8 [0]	7 [1]	3 [5]	4 [4]	2 [6]

Values in Parentheses are t-values

In the aggregate fund category, fund returns sensitivity to the market is very high in the unconditional model. The coefficient of beta$_m$ (0.8318) turned out to be positively highly significant. It can be termed as high beta funds and this is true for all the fund schemes in the sample. Same result is also true in the fund categories. All fund categories have witnessed high fund return sensitiveness to market movements. This value is highest in the case of ELSS (0.9058) followed by equity diversified (0.8521) and turned out least in the case of balanced funds (0.6799). The less value of coefficient is obvious, given the nature of the fund category.

What happened to fund returns sensitiveness when the models are conditioned with public information. Interestingly, the value of market coefficient has improved in aggregate and fund categories. Even, this value has increased to more than one in equity diversified fund category. In spite of high sensitivities to market, 5 fund schemes (2 in equity diversified category and 3 in ELSS category) shifted to negative sensitiveness.

What about the fund returns sensitivities to inflation ratio? Its value is negative in all categories except for balanced funds. Given the nature of the balanced funds, the returns are positively affected by the inflation. In spite of these results 9 fund schemes in equity diversified, 6 in ELSS and 1 in balanced have shown positive relationship. In nut shell, it can be inferred that inflation has negative relationship with the fund returns except the balanced fund category.

Dividend yields, generally, has the potential to boost the market. But this variable turned out to be insignificant in ELSS and balanced fund categories. Whereas, this coefficient is positively significant in case of equity diversified fund category. Even then fund schemes in negative segment are dominating. It can be concluded here that dividend yields effect is not even to all fund schemes and categories.

Industrial production is an indicator of positive growth in the economy. It is a signal to the market to perform better. This has been measured by index of industrial production (IIP). Its coefficients are either negatively significant or insignificant. Contrary to the established belief, index of industrial production is negatively impacting the fund returns. Why did this happen? This is a matter of further investigation and can be addressed in a separate research.

It is an established fact that Indian stock market is driven by the inflow of foreign institutional investments. More flows are positively reflected in fund returns. This has been proved true in Indian mutual fund industry as all coefficients, albeit small, turned out to be significant in all fund categories. However, at individual levels more than 40% have reported this value negative.

7.5 Concluding Remarks

This study evaluates the performance of mutual funds based on the 51 mutual fund schemes between 2006 and 2014. This study uses conditional models to evaluate performance, meaning thereby it is based on the semi-strong form market efficiency model of Fama. The study reveals that Indian mutual fund managers have strong stock picking ability. Moreover, use of public information which has direct bearing on the stock market, fund managers can improve their selectivity ability. Fund manager should be able to process the public information to adjust its portfolio for better returns. Indian fund managers are devoid of market timing ability and even public information did not fructify to improve the market timing capability. Besides, there is a trade-off between the selectivity and market timing ability, that is he is unable show his prowess in both the categories simultaneously.

Fund returns are very much sensitive to market movements. Inflation rate is negatively related to fund returns except the balanced fund category. Contrary to established belief that industrial production is positively related to returns do not hold true in mutual fund returns in India. Since Indian stock market is driven by the FII flows and this variable has positively reflected in fund returns.

Notes

1. More than 13 billion rupees are involved in Indian mutual fund industry now.
2. Such as Treynor Ratio, Sharpe Ratio and Jensen' alpha etc.
3. This class of Efficient Market Hypothesis suggests that only information that is not publicly available can benefit investors seeking to earn abnormal returns on investments. All other information is accounted for in the stocks' price and, regardless of the amount of fundamental and technical analysis one performs, above normal returns will not be had.

References

- Becker C, Ferson W, Myers E.H., Schill M.J. (1999), "Conditional Market Timing with Benchmark Investors", Journal of Financial Economics, 52 (1), 119-148.
- Christopherson J.A., Ferson W.E., and Glassman D.A. (1998), "Conditioning Manager Alphas on Economic Information: Another look at the Persistence of Performance", *Review of Financial Studies*, 11(1), 111-142.
- Coggins F, Beaulieu M.C., & Gendron M. (2004), "Mutual Fund Daily Conditional Performance", available at: www.usherbrooke.ca.
- Dahlquist M., Engstrom S. & Soderlind P. (2000), "Performance and Characteristics of Swedish Mutual Funds", Journal of Financial and Quantitative Analysis, 35 (3), 409-423.
- Fama E. F. (1970), "Efficient Capital Markets: A Review of Theory and Empirical Work", *Journal of Finance*, 25 (2), 383-417.
- Ferson W. E. and Schadt R. W. (1996), "Measuring Fund Strategy and Performance in Changing Economic Conditions", *Journal of Finance*, 51 (2), 425-461.

- Ferson W. E. and Warther V. A. (1996), "Evaluating Fund Performance in a Dynamic Market", *Financial Analysts Journal*, 52 (6), 20-28.
- Guha Deb S., Banerjee A. & Chakrabarti B.B, (2007), "Market Timing And Stock Selection Ability Of Mutual Funds In India: An Empirical Investigation", *Vikalpa*, 32(2), 39-51.
- Henriksson R. D. & Merton R. C. (1981), "On Market Timing and Investment Performance, *Journal of Business*, 54 (4), 513-533.
- Holmes K. A. & Faff W R. (2004), "Stability, Asymmetry And Seasonality Of Fund Performance: An Analysis Of Australian Multi-Sector Managed Funds", *Journal of Business Finance and Accounting*, 31(3&4), 539- 578.
- Luis Ferruz A., María Vargas M. & José L. S. (2006), "Evaluation of Performance and Conditional Information: The Case of Spanish Mutual Funds", *Applied Financial Economics*, 16 (11 803-823.
- Merton R. C. (1971), "Optimum Consumption and Portfolio Rules in a Continuous Time Model", *Journal of Economic Theory*, 3 (2), 373-413.
- Otten R. & Bams D. (2004), "How to Measure Mutual Fund Performance: Economic versus Statistical Relevance", *Journal of Accounting and Finance*, 44(2), 203-222.
- Roy B. & Deb S. S. (2004), "Conditional Alpha and Performance Persistence for Indian Mutual Funds: Empirical Evidence", *The ICFAI Journal of Applied Finance*, 10(1), 30-48.
- Roy B. and Deb S. S (2003), "The Conditional Performance of Indian Mutual Funds: An Empirical Study", Working paper, http://papers. ssrn.com.
- Saez J.C. (2008), "The Dynamics of Mutual Funds and Market Timing Measurement", *Studies in Nonlinear Dynamics & Econometrics*, 12(1), 1-38
- Sawicki J. & Ong F. (2000), "Evaluating Managed Fund Performance using Conditional Measures: Australian Evidence", *Pacific-Basin Finance Journal*, 8 (4), 505-528.
- Sawicki J. (2001), "Investors' Differential Response to Managed Fund Performance", *Journal of Financial Research*, 24 (3), 367-384.
- Treynor J. L. & Mazuy K. K. (1966), "Can Mutual Funds Outguess the Market?" *Harvard Business Review*, 44 (4), 131-136.

Appendix

Mutual Fund Schemes used in Analysis

1. Birla Sunlife Advantage Fund (Growth)
2. Birla Sunlife Frontline Equity (Growth)
3. BNP Paribas Equity Fund (Growth)
4. Canara Robeco Equity Diversified (Growth)
5. DSP-Black Rock Opportunities Fund (Growth)
6. DSP- Black Rock Top-100 Equity (Growth)
7. Franklin India Blue Chip (Growth)
8. HDFC Equity Fund (Growth)
9. HDFC Mid-Cap Opportunity Fund (Growth)
10. HDFC Top 200 Equity (Growth)
11. HSBC Equity Fund (Growth)
12. ICICI Prudential Dynamic Fund (Growth) A
13. ICICI Focused Blue Chip Equity Fund (Growth)
14. ICICI Prudential Top 100 Fund (Growth)
15. IDFC Premium Equity (Growth)
16. Kotak Mid Cap Fund (Growth)
17. L & T Mid Cap Fund (Growth)
18. Principal Emerging Blue Chip Fund (Growth)
19. Principal Large Cap Fund (Growth)
20. Quantum Long Term Equity Fund (Growth)
21. Reliance Growth Fund (Growth)

22. Reliance Regular Saving Fund-Equity (Growth)
23. SBI Blue Chip Fund (Growth)
24. SBI Magnum Mid Cap Fund (Growth)
25. SBI Magnum Multi Cap Fund (Growth)
26. Tata Equity Opportunity Fund (Growth)
27. Tata Mid Cap Growth Fund (Growth)
28. UTI Equity Fund (Growth)
29. Axis Long Term Equity Fund (G-ELSS)
30. Birla Sunlife Tax Relief 96 (G-ELSS)
31. BNP Paribas Long Term Equity Fund (G-ELSS)
32. Canara Robeco Equity Tax Savers (G-ELSS)
33. DSP-BR Tax Saver Fund (G-ELSS)
34. Franklin India Tax Shield (G-ELSS)
35. HDFC Tax Saver (G-ELSS)
36. HSBC Tax Saver Equity Fund (G-ELSS)
37. ICICI Prudential Tax Plan (G-ELSS)
38. IDFC Tax Advantage (G-ELSS)
39. L & T Tax Advantage (G-ELSS)
40. Principal Tax Saving (G-ELSS)
41. Reliance Tax Savers (G-ELSS)
42. SBI Magnum Tax Gainer (G-ELSS)
43. UTI Equity Tax Saving (G-ELSS)
44. Birla Sunlife 95 Fund (G-Balanced)
45. Canara Robeco Balanced (G-Balanced)
46. HDFC Balanced Fund (G-Balanced)
47. HDFC Prudence Fund (G-Balanced)
48. ICICI Prudential Balanced Fund (G-Balanced)
49. SBI Magnum Balanced Fund (G-Balanced)
50. Tata Balanced Fund (G-Balanced)
51. UTI Balanced Fund (G-Balanced)

Bibliography

- Adajania K. E. (2013), "MF Industry Needs to Look at Standardization in a New Light", *HT Mint*, Sept. 04.
- Ahmad M. & Samajpati U. (2010), "Evaluation of Stock Selection Skills and Market Timing Abilities of Indian Mutual Fund Managers", *Management Insight*, 6 (2), 71-82.
- Allen F. and Gorton G. (1993), "Churning Bubbles", *Review of Economic Studies*, 60 (4), 813-836.
- Ang J. and Lin W. (2001), "A Fundamental Approach to Estimating Economies of Scale and Scope of Financial Products: The Case of Mutual Funds", *Review of Quantitative Finance and Accounting*, 16 (3), 205-222.
- Armstrong G. & Kotler P. (2009), *"Marketing. An Introduction"*, 9th ed. Prentice Hall.
- Ashraf S.H., Sharma D. (2014), "Performance Evaluation of Indian Equity Mutual Funds against Established Benchmarks Index", *International Journal of Accounts*, 2(1), 1-7.
- Bain J. S. (1956), *"Barriers to New Competition, their Character and Consequences in Manufacturing Industries"*, Cambridge, Mass: Harvard University Press, 1956.
- Barber B. M., Odean T., and Zheng L. (2005), "Out of Sight, Out of Mind: The Effects of Expenses on Mutual Fund Flows", *Journal of Business*, 78 (6), 2095–2120.
- Barber B.M., Odean T., Zheng L. (2000), "The Behaviour of Mutual Fund Investors", Graduate School of Management, University of California-Davis, Working Paper.

- Baumol J. W., Stephen G. F., Lilli M., Gordon A., Michael K. F. (1989), "The Economies of Mutual Fund Markets: Competition versus Regulation", *Journal of Finance*, 23 (2), 551-567.
- Baumol J. William, Panzar J. C. and Willig R. D. (1988), *"Contestable Markets and the Theory of Industry Structure"*, San Diego, Calif: Harcourt Brace Jovanovich.
- Baumol W. J., Goldfeld S. M., Gordon L. A. and Koehn M. F. (1990), *"The Economics of Mutual Fund Markets: Competition versus Regulation"*, Kluwer Academic, Boston, Massachusetts.
- Becker C, Ferson W, Myers E.H., Schill M.J. (1999), "Conditional Market Timing with Benchmark Investors", Journal of Financial Economics, 52 (1), 119-148.
- Bekaert G. & Harvey C. R. (2002), "Research in Emerging Market Finance: Looking to the Future", available at: https://www0.gsb.columbia.edu.
- Berk J. & Green R. (2004), "Mutual Fund Flows and Performance in Rational Markets", *Journal of Political Economy*, 112 (7), 1269–1295.
- Brown K. C., Harlow W. V., and Starks L. T. (1996), "Of Tournaments and Temptations: An Analysis of Managerial Incentives in the Mutual Fund Industry", *Journal of Finance*, 51 (1), 85–110.
- Brown S. J. and Goetzmann W. N (1995), "Performance Persistence", *Journal of Finance*, 50 (2), 679-698.
- Bryant L.L. and Chen Liu H. (2009), "Management Structure and the Risk of Mutual Fund Managers, *Journal of Finance and Accountancy*, 1 (1), 1-17.
- Cahart M. M. (1997), "On Persistence in Mutual Funds Performance", *Journal of Finance*, 52 (1), 57-82.
- Capon N., Fitzsimons G. J., and Prince, R. A. (1996), "An Individual Level Analysis of the Mutual Fund Investment Decision", *Journal of Financial Services Research*, 10 (1), 59-82.
- Caves E. R. (1980), "Industrial Organization, Corporate Strategy and Structure", *Journal of Economic Literature*, 18 (1), 64-92.
- Chan L. K. C., Chen H. L. and Josef L (2002), "On Mutual Funds Investments Styles", *The Review of Financial Studies*, 15 (5), 1407-1437.

- Chander R. (2006), "Investment Managers' Market Timing Abilities: Empirical Evidence from the Indian Capital Market", *IIMB Management Review*, 18 (4), 315-326.
- Chen H. L., Jegadeesh N., and Wermers R. (2000), "The Value of Active Mutual Fund Management: An Examination of the Stock Holding and Trades of Fund Managers", *Journal of Financial and Quantitative Analysis*, 35 (3), 343-368.
- Chen J., Hong H, Huang M., Kubik J. D. (2004), "Does Fund Size Erode Mutual Fund Performance? The Role of Liquidity and Organization", *The American Economic Review*, 94 (5), 1276-1302.
- Chevalier J. and Ellison G. (1997), "Risk Taking by Mutual Funds as a Response to Incentives", *Journal of Political Economy*, 105 (6), 1167–1200.
- Chevalier J. and Ellison G. (1999), "Career Concerns of Mutual Fund Managers", *Quarterly Journal of Economics*, 114 (2), 389-432.
- Chopra M. P. (2011), "Do Indian Mutual Fund Managers Select the Stock and Time the Market Correctly?",*The IUP Journal of Applied Finance*, 17 (2), 77-86.
- Christoffersen S. & Musto D. (2002), "Demand Curves and the Pricing of Money Management", *Review of Financial Studies*, 15 (5), 1499-1524.
- Christoffersen S., Evans R. and Musto D. (2012), "What do Consumers' Fund Flows Maximize? Evidence from their Brokers' Incentives", *Journal of Finance*, 59 (6), 1979-2012.
- Christopherson J.A., Ferson W.E., and Glassman D.A. (1998), "Conditioning Manager Alphas on Economic Information: Another look at the Persistence of Performance", *Review of Financial Studies*, 11(1), 111-142.
- CII & PWC (2010), "Indian Mutual Fund Industry-Towards 2015, Sustaining Inclusive Growth-Evolving Business Models", available at: www.pwc.in.
- Coates J. C., and Hubbard R. G. (2007), "Competition in the Mutual Fund Industry: Evidence and Implications for Policy", *Harvard Law and Economics Discussion Paper 592*, Harvard Law School.
- Coggins F, Beaulieu M.C., & Gendron M. (2004), "Mutual Fund Daily Conditional Performance", available at: www.usherbrooke.ca.

- Cremer M. and Petajisto A. (2009), "How Active is your Fund Manager? A New Measure that Predicts Performance", *Review of Financial Studies*, 22 (9), 3329-3365.
- Cremers M. and Petajisto A. (2009), "How Active is your Fund Manager? A New Measure that Predicts Performance", *Review of Financial Studies*, 22 (9), 3329–3365.
- Dahlquist M., Engstrom S. & Soderlind P. (2000), "Performance and Characteristics of Swedish Mutual Funds", Journal of Financial and Quantitative Analysis, 35 (3), 409-423.
- Das S.R. and Sundaram S. R. (2000), "Fee Speech: Signaling, Risk-Sharing, and the Impact of Fee Structures on Investor Welfare", *Working Paper*. AEI Brookings Joint Center for Regulatory Studies.
- Dave S. A. (1992), "Mutual Funds: Growth and Development", *The Journal of the Indian Institute of Bankers*, 63 (1), 41-53.
- De Long, Bradford J., Summers L. and Waldmann (1990), "Noise Traders Risk in Financial Markets", *The Journal of Political Economy*, 98 (2), 703-738.
- Deniel K., Grinblatt M., Titman S. and Wermers R. (1997), "Measuring Mutual Fund Performance with Characteristics-Based Benchmarks", *Journal of Finance*, 57 (3), 1035-1058.
- Dow J. and Gorton G. (1997), "Noise Trading, Delegated Portfolio Management, and Economic Welfare", *Journal of Political Economy*, 105, 1024-1050.
- Droms W. G. & Walker D. A. (1996), "Mutual Fund Investment Performance", *Quarterly Review of Economics and Finance*, 36 (3), 347-363.
- Duca, J. V. (2001), "The Democratization of America's Capital Markets", *Economic and Financial Review*, (second quarter), 10–19. Federal Reserve Bank of Dallas.
- Edwards F. R. & Zhang X. (1998), "Mutual Funds and Stock and Bond Market Stability", *Journal of Financial Service Research*, 13 (3), 257-282.
- Elton E. J., Gruber M. J., and Busse, J.A. (2004), "Are Investors Rational? Choices among Index Funds, *Journal of Finance*, 59 (2), 261–288.

- Elton E. J., Gruber M. J., and Green T. C. (2007), "The Impact of Mutual Fund Family Membership on Investor Risk", *Journal of Financial and Quantitative Analysis*, 42 (2), 257-278.
- Fama E. F. (1970), "Efficient Capital Markets: A Review of Theory and Empirical Work", *Journal of Finance*, 25 (2), 383-417.
- Fama E. F. & French K. R. (1992), "The Cross-Section of Expected Stock Returns", *The Journal of Finance*, 47 (2), 427-465.
- Fama E. F. & French K. R. (1998), "Value verses Growth: The International Evidence", The Journal of Finance, 53 (6), 1975-1999.
- Fama E.F. (1980), "Agency Problems and the Theory of the Firm", *Journal of Political Economy*, 88 (2), 288-307.
- Ferreira M. A. and Ramos S. B. (2009), "Mutual Fund Industry Competition and Concentration: International Evidence", Social Science Research Network, Working paper.
- Ferson W. & Warther V. A. (1996), "Evaluating Fund Performance in a Dynamic Market", *Financial Analysts Journal*, 52 (6), 20-28.
- Ferson W. E. & Schadt R. W. (1996), "Measuring Fund Strategy and Performance in Changing Economic Conditions", *Journal of Finance*, 51 (2), 425-461.
- Ferson W. E. & Warther V. A. (1996), "Evaluating Fund Performance in a Dynamic Market", *Financial Analysts Journal*, 52 (6), 20-28.
- Ferson W.E. & Schadt R.W. (1996), "Measuring Fund Strategy and Performance in Changing Economic Conditions", *The Journal of Finance*, 51 (2), 425-461.
- Fortin R. & Michelson S. (2005), "Active International Mutual Fund Management: Can Managers Beat the Index?" *Managerial Finance*, 31(1), 41-51.
- Freeman J. P. & Brown S. L. (2001), "Mutual Fund Advisory Fees: The Cost of Conflicts of Interest", *The Journal of Corporation Law*, 26 (3), 609–673.
- Gaspar J., Massa M., and Matos P. (2006), "Favoritism in Mutual Fund Families: Evidence on Strategic Cross-Fund Subsidization", *Journal of Finance*, 61(1), 73–104.
- Ghosh P., Kale J. R. & Panchapagesan V. (2014), "Do Indian Business Group Owned Mutual Funds Maximize Value for their Investors?" *IIM Bangalore Research Paper*, (463).

- Goetzmann W. N. & Peles N. (1997), "Cognitive Dissonance and Mutual Fund Investors", *The Journal of Financial Research*, 20 (2), 145-158.
- Grinblatt M. & Keloharju M. (2000), "What Makes Investors Trade", *Journal of Finance*, 56 (2), 589-616.
- Grinblatt M. & Titman S. (1989), "Mutual Fund Performance: An Analysis of Quarterly Portfolio Holdings", *Journal of Business*, 62 (3), 393-416.
- Grinblatt M. & Titman S. (1993), "Performance Measurement without Benchmarks: An Examination of Mutual Fund Returns", *Journal of Business*, 66 (1), 47-68.
- Grossack I. (1965), "Towards an Integration of Static and Dynamic Measures of Industry Concentration", *The Review of Economics and Statistics*, 47 (3), 301-308.
- Grossman S. (1976), "On the Efficiency of Competitive Stock Markets Where Trades have Diverse Information", *Journal of Finance*, 31(2), 573-585.
- Gruber M. (1996), "Another puzzle: The Growth in Actively Managed Mutual Funds", *Journal of Finance*, 51 (3), 783–810.
- Guercio D.D., and Reuter J. (2013), "Mutual Fund Performance and the Incentive to Generate Alpha", *Journal of Finance*, 69 (4), 1673-1704.
- Guha D.S., Banerjee A. and Chakrabarti B. B. (2007), "Market Timing and Stock Selection Ability of Mutual Funds in India: An Empirical Investigation", *Vikalpa*, 32 (2), 39-51.
- Gupta A. (2000), "Market Timing Abilities of Indian Mutual Fund Manager: An Empirical Study", *Applied Finance*, 6 (2), 47-61.
- Gupta O.P. and Sehgal S. (2001), "Investment Performance of Mutual Funds: The Indian Experience". In U. Shashikant and S. Arumugam (Eds.), *Indian Capital Markets: Trends and Dimensions. New Delhi*, Tata McGraw-Hill.
- Gustavsson M. & Riben J. (2012), "Risk Shifting and Mutual Fund Performance: A Swedish Perspective", Bachelor's Thesis, Department of Finance, Stockholm School of Economics.
- Halan M. (2013), "Why do Indians Buy so much Gold Jewelry?" *HT Mint*, June 11.

- Henriksson R. D. and Merton R. C. (1981), "On Market Timing and Investment Performance-Statistical Procedures for Evaluating Forecasting Skills", *Journal of Business*, 54 (4), 513-533.
- Holmes K. A. & Faff W R. (2004), "Stability, Asymmetry And Seasonality Of Fund Performance: An Analysis Of Australian Multi-Sector Managed Funds", *Journal of Business Finance and Accounting*, 31 (3&4), 539- 578.
- Holmstrom B. (2000), "Managerial Incentive Problems-A Dynamic Perspective," *Essays in Economics and Management*, in Honor of Lars Wahlbeck, (Helsinki: Swedish School of Economics, 1982), available at: www.investopedia.com.
- Hortacsu, A. & Syverson C. (2004), "Product Differentiation, Search Costs and Competition in the Mutual Fund Industry: A Case Study of S&P 500 Index Funds, *The Quarterly Journal of Economics*, 119 (3), 403– 456.
- Hou K. and Robinson D. T. (2006), "Industry Concentration and Average Stock Returns", *Journal of Finance*, 61, 1927-1956.
- Huij J. & Post J. (2011), "On the Performance of Emerging Market Equity Mutual Funds", *Emerging Markets Review*, 12 (3), 238-249.
- Huij J. and Verbeek M. (2007), "Spillover Effects of Marketing in Mutual Fund Families" available at: ssrn.com/abstract.
- Ippolito R. A. (1989), "Efficiency with Costly Information: A Study of Mutual Fund Performance, 1965-1984", *Quarterly Journal of Economics*, 23 (2), 389-416.
- Ippolito R. A. (1992), "Consumer Reaction to Measures of Poor Quality: Evidence from the Mutual Fund Industry", *The Journal of Law and Economics*, 35 (1), 45-70.
- Jenson C. M. (1968), "The Performance of Mutual Funds in the period 1945-1964", *Journal of Finance*, 104 (1), 1-23.
- Kacperczyk M., Nieuwerburgh S. V., Veldkamp L. (2014), "A Rational Theory of Mutual Funds' Attention Allocation", NYU Working Paper.
- Kempf A., Ruenzi, S., and Thiele, T. (2009), "Employment Risk, Compensation Incentives, and Managerial Risk Taking: Evidence from the Mutual Fund Industry", *Journal of Financial Economics*, 92 (1), 92–108.

- Khan M. Y. (2001), *"Indian Financial System"*, Tata Mc Graw-Hill, New Delhi.
- Khorana A. (1996), "Top Management Turnover: An Empirical Investigation of Mutual Fund Managers", *Journal of Financial Economics*, 40 (3), 403-427.
- Khorana A. (2001), "Performance Changes following Top Management Turnover: Evidence from Open-End Mutual Funds", *Journal of Financial and Quantitative Analysis*, 36 (3), 371-393.
- Khorana, A. and Servaes H. (1999), "The Determinants of Mutual Fund Starts", *Review of Financial Studies*, 12 (5), 1043-1074.
- Kim M., Shukla R., & Tomas M. (2000), "Mutual Fund Objective Misclassification", *Journal of Economics and Business*, 52(4), 309-323.
- Korkeamaki T. P. & Smythe T. I (2004), "Effects of Market Segmentation and Bank Concentration on Mutual Fund Expenses and Returns: Evidence from Finland", *European Financial Management*, 10 (3), 413-438.
- *Kotak Securities (2014), "Mutual Funds in India", available at:* www. kotaksecurities.com.
- Kotler P. (2000), *"Marketing Management Analysis, Planning Implementation and Control"*, Englowood Cliffs, New Jersey Prentice Hall, Inc.
- Kotler P., Keller K. L. (2008), *"Marketing Management"*, 12th ed., Prentice-Hall.
- KPMG (2014), "Indian Mutual Fund Industry Distribution Continuum: Key to Success", available at: www.kpmg.com.
- *Kumar D. (2013), "Mutual Funds: A Selective Saving Grace", Business Standard, July 9.*
- Kumar R. (2012), "Market Timing, Selectivity and Mutual Fund Performance: An Empirical Investigation of Selective Equity Diversified Schemes in India", *IUP Journal of Financial Economics*, 10(1), 62- 84.
- Kwan S. and Laderman E. (1999), "On the Portfolio Effects of Financial Convergence- A Review of the Literature", *Federal Reserve Bank of San Francisco Economic Review*, No. 2, 18-31.

- Lazear E., and Rosen S. (1981), "Rank-Order Tournaments as Optimum Labor Contracts" *Journal of Political Economy*, 89 (5), 841–864.
- Lemeshko O. & Rejnuš O. (2015), "Modeling the Size of the Mutual Fund Industry in Countries of Central and Eastern Europe", *Financial Assets and Investing*, 6 (1), 7-34.
- Low S.W. (2010), "Relationship between Fund Performance and Characteristics of the Malaysia Unit Trust Fund", *Singapore Management Review*, 32 (1), 29-43.
- Luis Ferruz A., María Vargas M. & José L. S. (2006), "Evaluation of Performance and Conditional Information: The Case of Spanish Mutual Funds", *Applied Financial Economics*, 16 (11), 803-823.
- Machiraju H. R. (2009), *"Indian Financial System"*, Vikas Publishing House Pvt. Ltd.
- Malkiel B. G. (1995), "Returns from Investing in Equity mutual funds, 1971-1991, Journal of Finance, 50 (2), 549-572.
- Mamaysky H., and Spiegel M. (2002), "A Theory of Mutual Funds: Optimal Fund Objectives and Industry Organization", Working Paper, Yale University.
- Markowitz H. M. (1952), "Portfolio Selection", *The Journal of Finance*, **7** (1), 77–91.
- Massa M. (1998), "Are there too many Mutual Funds? Mutual Fund Families, Market Segmentation and Financial Performance", Working Paper, INSEAD.
- Massa M. (2003), "How do Family Strategies affect Fund Performance? When Performance Maximization is not the only Game in Town", Journal of Financial Economics, 67 (2), 249-304.
- *Matthew P. F. (2011), "The Rise of Mutual Funds: Insider's View", (2nd ed.), Oxford University Press.*
- McGough R. (1997), "Money Pours into Mutual Funds at Frantic Pace so far in January", *The Wall Street Journal*, PC1.
- Merton R. C. (1971), "Optimum Consumption and Portfolio Rules in a Continuous Time Model", *Journal of Economic Theory*, 3 (2), 373-413.

- Mishra B. (2002), "Selectivity and Timing Skills of Mutual Funds in India: An Empirical Analysis", *ICFAI Journal of Applied Finance*, 8 (1), 5-16.
- Modigliani F. & Modigliani L. (1997), "Risk-Adjusted Performance", *The Journal of Portfolio Management*, 23 (2), 45-54.
- Nanda V., Wang Z. J. and Zheng L. (2004), "Family Values and the Star Phenomenon", Review of Financial Studies, 17 (3), 667-698.
- Nanigian D. (2012), "Why does Mutual Fund Expenses Matter?" *Financial Services Review*, 21(2), 239-257.
- Nathani N., Chakraborty A., Rawat B. and Holani U. (2011), "Timing Skills of Fund Managers: A Study of Equity Mutual Fund Schemes", *Business Spectrum*, 1 (1), 9-18.
- Needham D. (1979), *"The Economics of Industrial Structure, Conduct and Performance"*, London: Holt, Rinehart and Winston.
- Nishith Desai Associates (2003), "Mutual Funds in India: An Overview" A Report, available at: www.nishithdesai.com.
- Odean T. (1998), "Are Investors Reluctant to Realize their Losses?" *Journal of Finance*, 53 (5), 1775-1798.
- Otten R. & Bams D. (2002), "European Mutual Fund Performance", *European Financial Management*, 8 (1), 75-101.
- Otten R. & Bams D. (2004), "How to Measure Mutual Fund Performance: Economic versus Statistical Relevance", *Journal of Accounting and Finance*, 44(2), 203-222.
- Pandian P. (2008), "Security Analysis and Portfolio Management", Vikas Publication, New Delhi.
- Patil R.H. (2010), "Financial Sector Reforms: Realities and Myths", *Economic and Political Weekly*, 45 (1), 48-61.
- Petajisto A. (2010), "Active Share and Mutual Fund Performance", Working Paper, New York University.
- Porter E. M. (1981), "The Contributions of Industrial Organization to Strategic Management", *The Academy of Management Review*, 6 (4), 609-620.
- Pozen R. & Hamacher T. (2014), *"The Fund Industry: How Your Money is Managed (Second Edition)"*, John Wiley & Sons.
- *Pozen R. & Hamacher T. (2015), "The Fund Industry: How your Money is Managed", Hoboken, NJ: Wiley Finance.*

- Prendergast C. and Stole L. (1996), "Impetuous Youngsters and Jaded Old-Timers: Acquiring a Reputation for Learning", *Journal of Political Economy*, 104 (6), 1105-1134.
- PWC (2013), "Indian Mutual Fund Industry, Unearthing the Growth Potential in Untapped Markets", available at: www.pwc.in/assets.
- Raja R. (2003), "Determinants of Portfolio Choice of Individual Investors", *The Indian Economic Journal*, 50(1), 81-84.
- Rouwenhorst K. G. (1999), "Local Return Factors and Turnover in Emerging Stock Markets", The Journal of Finance, 54 (4), 1439-1463.
- Roy B. & Deb S. S. (2004), "Conditional Alpha and Performance Persistence for Indian Mutual Funds: Empirical Evidence", *The ICFAI Journal of Applied Finance*, 10 (1), 30-48.
- Roy B. and Deb S. S (2003), "The Conditional Performance of Indian Mutual Funds: An Empirical Study", Working paper, http://papers.ssrn.com.
- Saez J.C. (2008), "The Dynamics of Mutual Funds and Market Timing Measurement", *Studies in Nonlinear Dynamics & Econometrics*, 12(1), 1-38.
- Salam A. & Kulsum U. (2003), "Savings Behaviour in India: An Empirical Study", *The Indian Economic Journal*, 50 (1), 77-80.
- Sawicki J. & Ong F. (2000), "Evaluating Managed Fund Performance using Conditional Measures: Australian Evidence", *Pacific-Basin Finance Journal*, 8 (4), 505-528.
- Sawicki J. (2001), "Investors' Differential Response to Managed Fund Performance", *Journal of Financial Research*, 24 (3), 367-384.
- Scharfstein D. S. and Stein J. C. (1990), "Herd Behavior and Investment", *American Economic Review*, 80 (3), 465-489.
- Scherer F. M. (1980), "*Industrial Market Structure and Economic Performance*", 2nd Ed. Chicago: Rand McNally.
- Sehgal S. and Jhanwar M. (2008), "On Stock Selection Skills and Market Timing Abilities of Mutual Fund Managers in India", *International Research Journal of Finance & Economics*, 15 (2), 307-317.
- Sharpe W. F. (1966), "*Mutual Fund Performance*", *Journal of Business*, 39 (1), 119-138.

- Shefrin H. & Statman M. (1985), "The Disposition to Sell Winners too Early and Ride Losers too Long: Theory and Evidence", *Journal of Finance*, 40 (4), 777-790.
- Sialm C. & Tham T. M. (2012), "Spillover Effects in Mutual Fund Companies", *Management Science*, available at: http://ssrn.com/abstract.
- Sirri E. R. & Tufano P. (1993), "Competition and Change in the Mutual Fund Industry, in: S. L. Hayes III, (ed.), *Financial Services: Perspectives and Challenges*, Harvard Business School Press, Boston, Massachusetts.
- Sirri E. R. & Tufano P. (1998), "Costly Search and Mutual Fund Flows", *Journal of Finance*, 53 (5) 1589-1622.
- Tirole J, (2004), "*The Theory of Industrial Organisation*", MIT Press, Cambridge M.
- Tobin J. (1958). "Liquidity Preference as Behavior towards Risk". *Review of Economic Studies*, 25 (1), 65-86.
- Treynor J. and Mazuy M. (1966) "Can Mutual Funds Outguess the Market?" *Harvard Business Review*, 44(4), 131-36.
- Treynor J. L. & Mazuy K. K. (1966), "Can Mutual Funds Outguess the Market?" *Harvard Business Review*, 44 (4), 131-136.
- Treynor J. L. (1965), "How to Rate Management of Investment Funds", *Harvard Business Review*, 43 (1), 63-75.
- Tripathy N.P. (2006), "Market Timing Abilities and Mutual Fund Performance- An Empirical Investigation into Equity Linked Saving Schemes", *Vilakshan, XIMB Journal of Management*, 127-138.
- US Securities and Exchange Commission (2010): "*A Guide for Investors*", available at: www.sec.gov.
- Wahal S. and Wang A. (2011), "Competition among Mutual Funds", *Journal of Financial Economics*, 99 (1), 40–59.
- Walter A. and Weber F. M. (2006), "Herding in the German Mutual Fund Industry", *European Financial Management*, 12 (3), 375-406.
- Wermers R. (2000), "Mutual Fund Performance: An Empirical Decomposition into Stock-Picking Talent, Style, Transaction Costs, and Expenses", *Journal of Finance*, 55 (4), 1655–1695.

- Wilcox R. T. (2003), "Bargain Hunting or Star Gazing? Investors Preferences for Stock Mutual Funds", *Journal of Business*, 76 (3), 645–664.
- World Bank Report (2015)
- www.amfiindia.com
- www.camsonlime.com
- www.cic.com
- *www.economictimes.indiatimes.com/mutual funds*
- www.icraindia.com
- www.indiainfoline.com
- www.moneycontrol.com
- www.mutualfundindia.com
- www.prudentialchannel.com
- www.rbi.com
- www.sebi.com
- Wyatt E. (1996), "Some Worries about the Rush into Mutual Funds", *New York Times*, PA1.
- Zwiebel L. (1995), "Corporate Conservatism and Relative Compensation", *Journal of Political Economy*, 103 (1), 1-25.